*Devoted to the Goddess*

*SUNY Series in Hindu Studies*
*Wendy Doniger, Editor*

# *Devoted to the Goddess*

The
Life and Work of Ramprasad

*Malcolm McLean*

State University of New York Press

Published by
State University of New York Press, Albany



Printed in the United States of America



For information, address State University of New York
Press, State University Plaza, Albany, NY, 12246

Production by E. Moore
Marketing by Fran Keneston

Library of Congress Cataloging-in-Publication Data

McLean, Malcolm, 1939–
Devoted to the Goddess : the life and work of Ramprasad / Malcolm McLean.
p. cm. — (SUNY series in Hindu studies)
Includes bibliographical references and index.
ISBN 0-7914-3689-6 (hc : alk. paper). — ISBN 0-7914-3690-X (pbk. : alk. paper)
1. Rāmaprasāda Sena, 1718–1775—Criticism and interpretation.
I. Title. II. Series.
PK1718.R2514Z78 1998
891.4'413—dc21 97-19307
CIP

10 9 8 7 6 5 4 3 2 1

এ সব ক্ষেপা মায়ের খেলা ।
যার মায়ায় ত্রিভুবন বিভোলা ।।
মাগীর আপ্তবাক্যে গুপ্ত লীলা -
সে যে আপনি ক্ষেপা, কর্ত্তা ক্ষেপা, ক্ষেপা দুটা চেলা ।।
কি রূপ, কি গুণ-ভঙ্গী, কি ভাব, কিছুই যায় না বলা ।
যার নাম জপিয়ে কপাল পোড়ে, কণ্ঠে বিষের জ্বালা ।।
সগুণে নির্গুণে বাঁধিয়ে বিবাদ, ঢ্যালা দিয়ে ভাঙ্গছে ঢ্যালা ।।
মাগী সকল বিষয়ে সমান রাজী, নারাজ কেবল কাজের বেলা ।।
প্রসাদ বলে, থাকো বসে ভবার্ণবে ভাসিয়ে ভেলা ।
যখন আসবে জোয়ার উজিয়ে যাবে, ভাঁটিয়ে যাবে ভাঁটার বেলা ।।

All this is the mad Mother's game,
The three worlds are deluded by her māyā.
The bitch's true nature is hidden by her līlā—
She herself is mad, her husband and his two attendants too.
Which is her true form and which her disguise, what is her true nature, no-one at all can say,
Those who repeat her name are down on their luck, and poison burns their throats.
She makes a fight between saguṇa and nirguṇa, and breaks a clod with a stone.
The bitch promises to be impartial to all, but changes her mind when the crunch comes.
Prasad says, Stay on that raft floating on the world ocean,
Float up with the flood tide and down on the ebb.

Those who are sincere Tantrikas or who have deep intuitions in the matter will gain real appreciation of these immortal songs which those without will not have. This is a difficult matter, especially as there are so many deep meanings in Ramprasad's songs.

—Isvarachandra Gupta

*for*
*Jane Bodkin*

# Contents

# Preface

This study sums up a long period of research and reflection on the life and work of Ramprasad. During this time I have become indebted to a large number of Bengali scholars and friends. The reader will see that I have drawn heavily on the considerable scholarship in Bengali, without which it would be impossible to write a book such as this, and I hope that by making the work of these scholars known to a wider audience I have been able to discharge some of the debt that I owe them.

My research has been greatly assisted over the years by a number of friends who have pointed me in the direction of certain sources, or spent hours discussing my work with me. Chief among these are Lakshmi Subramanian, Rajat Ray, Manashi Das Gupta, Gautam Bhadra, and Ashin Das Gupta. Without their help, and the insights they have shared with me, this book would hardly have been possible. I offer them my grateful thanks.

My research carried me into many libraries, and I wish also to thank the staff who assisted me in them. Among these is the library at Visvabharati University at Santiniketan; the National Library, the Ramakrishna Mission Institute of Culture library and the Bangiya Sahitya Pasishad, all of Calcutta; the Cambridge University Library and that of St. Edmund's College and the Oriental Faculty, all in Cambridge; the India Office Library and the School of Oriental and African Studies in London; and most of all my own "home" library at the University of Otago.

During this time I received assistance also from the American Institute of Indian Studies in Calcutta, from St. Edmund's College in Cambridge, and considerable assistance from my University which regularly funds my research leave in India and the United Kingdom. To them I render my gratitude.

Many have read drafts of or listened to versions of different portions of this work. I would like to thank Julius Lipner in Cambridge and Adrienne Wyatt in Auckland; those who attended seminars I gave in the History Department at Calcutta University, the Divinity Faculty at Cambridge, and at the School of Oriental and African Studies in London; and Jeff Kripal and Rachel McDermott in the United States. Jeff and Rachel read the whole of the initial manuscript of the book and subjected it to sustained and insightful criticism, which forced me to further justify my argument and made this a much better book. The readers to whom the Press sent the original manuscript, among whom were Thomas Coburn and David Kinsley, also made many helpful suggestions which aided me considerably in preparing the final version of the book, and to them also I offer my thanks.

Two chapters of this book were originally published as articles in journals, chapter 1 in *South Asia* (IX/2, December 1986) as "Tradition and History in Isvaracandra Gupta's Biography of Ramprasad Sen," and chapter 2 in the *Scottish Journal of Religious Studies* (XI/2 1990) as "Ramprasad Sen and the Deconstruction of a Literary Tradition." I am grateful to the editors of these journals for permission to reproduce this material.

## *Note on Transliteration*

The transliteration of Bengali words is fraught with difficulty. There is no system which does not present some anomalies. There is not even agreement about whether transliteration should primarily reflect the Sanskrit backround of Bengali or its quite different pronunciation, and these two are irreconcilable.

I have decided that the best way to proceed through these difficulties is to follow as closely as possible the system proposed by E.C. Dimock and R. Inden in "Problems of Transliteration in Bengal Studies" in *Bengal East and West,* A. Lipski (ed), East Lansing, Michigan, Asian Studies Centre Michigan State University, n.d. I have not, however, applied this system to all Indian words. I believe that words like "Krishna" and "Sakta" should be viewed as loan-words in English, just as much as the originally Indian word "verandah" is. This seems obviously to be the case when we talk about "Krishna's flute" because neither Sanskrit nor Bengali have an "-'s" ending for the genitive case. For these words I have not used diacritical marks.

To distinguish these loan-words from Bengali ones which I have transliterated, I have used italic script for the latter. I should perhaps say at this point that when citing songs by Ramprasad I have done so by giving the first line. This will enable the reader to find the song in any collection of songs, while I myself have preferred to use the collection in S.N. Bhattacharya's *Rāmprasād: jībanī ō racanāsamagra.*

# *Introduction*

## *The Popularity of Ramprasad Sen*

In a book published in 1923 the Bengali scholar E.J. Thompson recalled an incident from a visit to the Bengal countryside:

> Once I asked the top class in a mofussil high school to write out a song of Rabindranath Tagore's; two boys out of forty succeeded, a result which I consider showed the very real diffusion of his songs. But, when I asked for a song of Rāmprasād's, every boy except two responded. Truly, a poet who is known both by work and name to boys between fourteen and eighteen, is a national poet.

He goes on to say that Ramprasad's songs are heard everywhere in the villages of Bengal:

> These have gone to the heart of a people as few poets' work has done. Such songs as the exquisite 'This day will surely pass, Mother, this day will pass,' I have heard from coolies on the road or workers in the paddy fields; I have heard it by broad rivers at sunset, when the parrots were flying to roost and the village folk thronging from marketing to the ferry.

But lest he leave the impression that Ramprasad is popular only among peasants he quotes from a letter from Dr Dineshchandra

Sen, "The peasants and the *paṇḍits* enjoy his songs equally. They draw solace from them in the hour of despair and even at the moment of death. The dying man brought to the banks of the Ganges asks his companions to sing Rāmprasādī songs."[1]

Nor has the breadth or the depth of this appeal declined. I have on a number of occasions heard poor people who were working the trains for a meagre living singing Ramprasadi songs to touch the hearts of their *bhadralōk* audience. And cassette tape recordings of Ramprasadi songs are readily available at all the music shops and stalls in Calcutta, and enjoy wide sales, indicating that his popularity, even if it has not grown, has certainly not waned.

This book is a study of the life and work of Ramprasad. It is the study of the life because of his historical importance. He was a major influence on the perhaps better-known nineteenth century religious figure Ramakrishna Paramahamsa.[2] And as I hope to demonstrate, he was the major figure in the eighteenth century revival of Sakta practice in Bengal. But the life of such a figure cannot be understood without an examination of his work, as it was his work which lead to his becoming well-known throughout Bengal, and thus an important historical figure, and we need to see just what it was about his work that lead to such popularity. As a literary figure, he is discussed at some length in all the histories of Bengali literature,[3] his work is still always in print, and he is still read as a poet in his own right.

## *Who Was Ramprasad?*

When we come to examine Ramprasad's contribution to the religious life of Bengal, however, we face a number of difficulties. On the historical side, we want to know as much as possible about the man and his life, his community, and the way he interacted with his community, in order to assess his impact on the wider populace of his times. But when we examine the evidence, as presented in chapter 1, we find that there is little verifiable historical material on which we can rely. People are always happy to relate stories about Ramprasad which have a wide circulation, but these prove on investigation to be legendary tales which are impossible to relate back to firm facts about the man. This is, of course, not a happy situation for one about whom I have already made the significant claim of being an important historical figure.

When we turn from the man to his work, with emphasis primarily on his songs, the *padābalī,* which are of greatest significance when we consider the religious importance of Ramprasad, and which are also the most popular part of his work, we find ourselves in an equally unenviable position. We find we have an embarrassingly small number of songs from among the large number he is supposed to have written, and we find that there are almost intractable problems determining which songs are authentically by Ramprasad Sen. Yet I additionally claim that he was also a great poet. Will the evidence allow us to sustain this argument?

As if this were not difficult enough, there is also the possibility that there were two Ramprasads, both devotees of the Mother Goddess, both living at about the same time and writing songs in her praise, one living in West Bengal and the other living in East Bengal.

## *Interpreting the Life of Ramprasad*

It is difficult to locate our author in history because he is virtually "dead" in terms of what a traditional historian would call a "life." But his followers treasure a large and very important tradition of biographical material which is widely disseminated among them. This book argues that this biographical "text" is, despite historical scepticism, still a valuable resource for our investigation of the historical importance of Ramprasad, especially as we look into the ways it was, and is still, used by his Sakta followers—for it is they who have written this life. If we read this traditional life correctly, then the dead author comes to life again, in a new and productive way. It is also true that Saktas have rather less difficulty with the problem of establishing a canon of Ramprasadi songs. In fact, as we shall see, there is a general acceptance of about 350 songs said to be by "Ramprasad" which continue to be used in ritual and in devotion. What then becomes of importance to the scholar is not whether all of these songs were actually composed by the historical Ramprasad, but that there is a "text" which functions as an acceptable canon amongst Saktas, and a more profitable line of enquiry is to see how this text is "read" by them.[4]

So the scholar has two texts, the one concerning the life and the other the work of Ramprasad. When we look closely at these texts we find that they in many ways work together, as respectively the biography of the composer of the songs, and the work of the Ramprasad of the biography, with biography functioning as a supplement to the more important text of the songs, but at the same time itself dependent on the songs. In a number of instances (see chapter 3) a particular biographical event is related directly to a particular song, the song thus confirming the event (or perhaps, to the scholar, being the source of the tradition to which it is linked). In other important respects these texts work against each other, to complicate the intertextuality. There is a tension between the texts, but the tension is creative.

The most important of these tensions involves the way in which, this book argues, an important distinction can be made between the form and the content of the whole tradition as it was created from the eighteenth century on. In terms of its form, the tradition created a figure which served a particular purpose (to create a Sakta leader in many ways modeled on, and certainly as important as, the Vaisnava saint Caitanya). The main tool in this process was the biographical tradition. The idea was to provide an acceptable model which could be used to legitimate an otherwise up to that time dubious and underground (*gūhȳa*) cult. In terms of its content, however, the tradition was as different from Caitanya's Vaisnavism as it is possible to be. The content of the tradition, found in the text of the songs thus works against the grain of the biographical text, to establish a tradition of Sakta belief and practice, the nature of which is examined at some length below.

Nonetheless, there certainly was an historical Ramprasad Sen who did live in Bengal at some time in the eighteenth century. There is sufficient evidence to accept him as the author of a poem called *Bidȳāsundar* in which he gives details of his family. These details tally with later family records, and place him in the period of roughly 1720 to 1780. We know the author of this poem was connected with the court of an important local zamindar, Maharaja Krishnachandra of Krishnanagore. And we know that among his other works was a number of songs in which he addresses the Goddess, and which were very popular even in his own day. It is this Ramprasad Sen with whom we begin this study.

## Summary

Chapter 1 examines the historical evidence for Ramprasad and his work, attempting to sort out what is legend from what is history, and determining to what extent we can rely on the evidence. Chapter 2 examines the problems raised by the existence of these uncertainties, and proposes a methodology, based on certain post-modern approaches to history and literature, that I believe will open up a profitable way to understand the problems concerning his life and work.

Chapter 3 applies this methodology to the Life of Ramprasad, based on the earliest published account, that of Isvarachandra Gupta in 1853, and proposes a way of reading this life which takes us to the heart of the historical understanding of Ramprasad. Chapters 4, 5, and 6 apply the methodology to the principal work of Ramprasad. In these chapters I look at the central themes of the songs, especially as they relate to Ramprasad's picture of the Goddess, and then examine in some detail the antecedents of this picture, in the classical Puranic tradition, Bengali folk religion, and otherwise secret Tantric practices. Here I also argue that the Tantric side of Ramprasad has often been overlooked and that he is definitely to be reckoned as a Tantrika. Next, I look at the image of the Goddess as the daughter of Ramprasad, and see how this complements his image of her as mother. This focus in turn underlines the importance of Ramprasad, historically and as a religious figure, and shows why his songs are so popular.

Chapter 7 looks at how Ramprasad might be understood today; how he is perceived as a poet not only with historical importance but one with contemporary relevance. Ramprasad is still popular, and it is striking that this popularity exists among religious and non-religious people alike, among the educated and the non-educated. This is surprising because all of Ramprasad's songs employ religious imagery explicitly throughout. So while one would not be surprised to find his work enjoyed by devotees of the Goddess, one would be less likely to expect him to be appreciated by a secular educated audience. Thus, this book accounts for an appreciation of Ramprasad as a poet in his own right, and shows that a secular reading even of his apparently most religious work is not a misreading. In this way, Ramprasad's work may even be appreciated by a Western reader.

Finally, in the Appendix, I have attached my own translation of Isvarachandra Gupta's ground-breaking biography of Ramprasad, the biography which stands behind all accounts of the life of Ramprasad as discussed at length in chapter 3. This enables the reader to understand the beginning of the growing tradition surrounding the dominant figure of the Saktism of Bengal.

# *Part I*

# *The Life*

# ONE

# *The Search for the Historical Ramprasad*

## *The Scarcity of Historical Detail*

Historians of Indian religion know a great deal about the life of the great sixteenth-century religious reformer and founder of Gauriya Vaisnavism, Sri Caitanya (1486–1533 AD). This is largely due to the amount of biographical material left to us by his contemporaries and followers. S.K. De has said,

> There is no dearth of materials for a study of Caitanya's life and personality. A fairly large number of lives in Sanskrit and Bengali came into existence not many years after his death, and they supply valuable materials . . . regarding the details of his career . . .[1]

On the other hand much less is known of the much later (eighteenth century) and equally important figure Ramprasad, who did for Bengal Saktism what Caitanya had done for Bengal Vaisnavism.

Ramprasad is mentioned only briefly in Thompson and Spencer's *Bengali Religious Lyrics, Sakta,* E.A. Payne's *The Saktas,* R.C. Dutt's *Cultural Heritage of Bengal,* D. Zbavitel's *Bengali Literature,* and J. Sinha's *Rama Prasada's Devotional Songs.*[2] Sinha, while giving a slightly fuller account of his life, is uncritical and gives almost no indication of sources. At best these give the probable date of his birth (1718–1720) and death (1775–1781), refer briefly to his principal works (the *Bidyāsundar, Kālīkīrttan, Kṛiṣṇakīrttan* and his songs, the *padābalī*), and acknowledge his status as an important Sakta poet. Thompson and Spencer and Sinha also recount a few legends associated with his life.

The contrast with the situation in Bengal could hardly be greater. There in the land of his birth Ramprasad is well-known to scholar and simple devotee alike and there are many books of his songs, and about his life and faith—some of a popular and others of a scholarly nature.[3] Stories about his life are almost universally known and readily recounted. These are stories such as his meeting with the Mughal nawab Siraj-ad-daulah who heard Ramprasad singing while passing by on the river and was so spellbound that he ordered his boat to the bank so that he might listen further to the enchanting songs—which were addressed of course to the goddess Kali. What is the reason for this disparity? Is it that the material available in Bengali is so legendary as to be unreliable? Is what seems unlikely on the surface, as in the story just related, true—that a Muslim nawab would interrupt a journey to listen to hymns to Kali. Nathan and Seeley, in a recently published small collection of Ramprasad songs say, "We know almost nothing about his life except that he was born and flourished in the Bengal of the 18th century . . ." and "Direct information about Ramprasad is almost nonexistent or is compromised by doubt."[4]

The other question to be asked is whether Ramprasad warrants more attention in the West, and this I think can be answered unequivocally. Janhabikumar Chakrabarti[5] says that he is the greatest composer of Sakta verse (*padābalī)* and places him among the greatest rishis of India. Satyanarayan Bhattacharya[6] calls him a superior *sādhaka*, foremost creator of Sakta *padābalī* and most beloved of Bengali poets. His contribution to the development of Saktism in Bengal is immense, and he was a major influence on the nineteenth century mystic and religious leader more familiar to the West, Ramakrishna. Unless Bengal Saktism is considered unimportant, Ramprasad warrants more attention.

One of the reasons for the comparative neglect of a poet like Ramprasad, and the skepticism of scholars like Nathan and Seeley, probably lies in the fact that in Ramprasad's case the biographical material we have is scarce and late. There is, however, some biographical material available, such as the short biography published by Isvarachandra Gupta as early as 1853. It is the intention of this chapter to make a critical assessment of this life of Ramprasad.[7]

## *The First Biography of Ramprasad*

Isvarachandra Gupta was a Bengali poet who in 1831 at the age of 20, began to edit and publish his own literary magazine, the *Saṅbādprabhākar*. The magazine was given to preserving literary works of the past as well as disseminating contemporary work, and in 1833 it carried Ramprasad's *Kālīkīrttan* with a brief introduction by the editor. From this introduction we learn that Gupta shared Ramprasad's own Sakta faith at the time and that he seems to have developed a particular passion for the life and work of Ramprasad. As a result he devoted himself, from the age of seventeen, to the collecting and preserving of Ramprasad's work and to researching the facts of his life. He had been raised in a village near Ramprasad's and the material he assembled was based on his own childhood memories and of those of other people who lived there during his childhood. Since he was born thirty years after the death of Ramprasad, according to his own calculations, he would have come into contact with people who were personally acquainted with him.

By the time he published his biography of Ramprasad in the *Saṅbād prabhākar* in 1853 he had already spent twenty-five years diligently collecting and researching Ramprasad's songs:

> Twenty-five years have now passed during which I have been engaged in collecting Ramprasad songs, and until now however hard I have tried I have had little success. Some I have even been able to see only with the greatest difficulty. Some have been eaten by insects, some have been inadvertently copied incorrectly and there is an awful risk in trying to establish the substance of these. Because of this I modestly request those people for whom this is now an important concern not to keep these things to themselves but allow us to have them printed. Then there will be an inexpressible gratitude felt throughout the country and great joy at their being made available in this way. I have been able with great difficulty to secure some songs, and I hope that as more are found I will be able by mutual agreement to remove people's doubts about publishing them.[8]

And he concluded:

> Though this account of the life of Ramprasad has now come to an end the task is not completed for much research remains

> to be done. . . . However, in the spirit of 'do or die' let us see what happens. I will certainly do what I can, whatever the cost and whatever the shortcomings in what I have been able to achieve. This task has taken on the nature of a crusade, so I am appealing to the general public for help in this matter. We will acknowledge a life-long debt of gratitude to any who assist us in this way, and it is not only we who will benefit but the whole country, so we ask you to be generous with such assistance, whether there is any reward in it or not. However that may be, if the task can be completed I will be satisfied.[9]

As a result of this call for assistance from others in his research, Gupta received and published in the following issue of the *Saṅbādprabhākar* a letter from one respondent who claimed to be a native of Ramprasad's village, giving further information about Ramprasad.[10]

## The Problem of Corroboration

The first problem concerning Gupta's biography is the absence of any corroborating mention of Ramprasad in some notable early works on the religious life of eighteenth-century Bengal. This is strange if he was as well-known in his day as he is reputed to have been, especially as he is said to have been associated with the court of Raja Krishnachandra of Krishnanagore, from whom he supposedly received his title "Kabiranjan" (one who delights with his verse):

> At the court of Maharaja Krishnachandra Ray Bahadur there resided many men learned in the scriptures, many poets such as Bharatchandra Ray Gunakar and many men highly qualified in other matters. But even in the company of such eminent men the people were greatly pleased to listen to the work of that descendent of a *boidya* family from Kumarhatt, Ramprasad Sen, the *Kālīkīrttan, Kṛiṣṇakīrttan* and *Bidyāsundar*, and thought him the greatest poet of them all. . . . The Navadvip ruler wanted Ramprasad to remain with him in his service but this was not to be as by this time Ramprasad had no concern at all for worldly desires. What Ramprasad wanted, and what the Maharaja agreed to, was that from time to time he would come to Halisahore and set up his court in Ramprasad's house for a few days in order to listen to his

> songs. Everyone was so delighted by what they heard that the Maharaja gave him the title 'Kabiranjan'. Ramprasad then composed his *Bidyāsundar* in response to the royal favour of the granting of the title. In this matter there is clear proof that the Maharaja, after seeing Ramprasad's *Bidyāsundar*, gave orders to Bharatchandra to compose one too. This he did and became famous everywhere because of the beauty of his work.[11]

Ramprasad is said to have lived in the village of Kumarhatt, also known as Halisahore, on the bank of the Ganges a short distance north of Calcutta, in the heartland of Bengal. It is surprising then to find no mention of him in the first edition of Ward's *A View of the History, Literature & Mythology of the Hindoos*, published at Serampore in 1818.[12] Ward gathered the material for his work with the help of local brahmin pundits and is considered very reliable on social and religious matters. It is noteworthy that he mentions Ramprasad's near contemporary the poet Bharatchandra Ray. In a later edition, published in London in 1822, Ward does refer to Ramprasad (to a "Kalee Keerthunn by Ramprasad a Shoodra"), but the omission from the first edition is remarkable even if Ward's informants were brahmin pundits (Ramprasad's popularity was certainly greatest among the less orthodox Saktas) as Ramprasad was from a high caste, the *boidya* (physician) caste, and we can tell from his work that he was educated in Sanskrit and Persian as well as Bengali.[13]

Then, in 1768–1769 the brother of the dewan of the then Governor of Bengal, Harry Verelst, made a pilgrimage along the Ganges from Calcutta to Gaya, Varanasi, and Allahabad and back, an account of which was published by his companion and physician Vijayram Sen in his *Tirthamaṅala.*[14] Though Vijayram was a Sakta and his patron (Krishnachandra Ghosal) a well-known *bhakta*, and though Kumarhatt and Halisahore are mentioned in the book, there is no mention of Ramprasad. Krishnachandra Ghosal is even said to have tied up his boat at the Kumarhatt ghat and it is quite astonishing that there is no mention of the famour Sakta *sādhaka* and poet who is supposed to have been living there at the time.

Another traveller in the area who wrote of his experiences was Bholanath Chandra whose *The Travels of a Hindu* (1896) shows a particular interest in religious matters both historical and contemporary. His account of the river journey from Calcutta to Krishnanagore mentions neither Kumarhatt nor Halisahore, and there is no reference to Ramprasad.[15]

It is certainly surprising that Ramprasad, who was supposed to have been a well-known and loved religious poet, as well as a court poet of some repute and favor, was so little-known to travellers and researchers in Bengal. A later biographer, Dayalchandra Ghosh, says in his *Prasādprasaṅa,* written in Dacca in 1875, that after three years of time-consuming research all he could discover about the composer of the songs, which had so much interested him when he heard them, was that Ramprasad was a *boidya* and a contemporary of Maharaja Krishnachandra, that he was a prominent Sakta *sādhaka,* and that he lived in Kumarhatt.[16]

However, that Ramprasad Sen did live at about the time Gupta suggests may be confirmed from other sources such as some contemporary land records, from contemporary *boidya* "clan" chronicles (*kulaśāstra)* and from the works of Ramprasad himself. With respect to the latter we should mention that Ramprasad is generally accepted to have composed a *Kālīkīrttan,* a *Kṛiṣṇakīrttan,* a *Bidyāsundar* and many songs collected as the *padābalī,* and here we must give credit to Gupta whose work in collecting, publishing, and preserving the work of Ramprasad is more important than his biography.

At the end of the *Bidyāsundar* [17] Ramprasad refers to his own family and line *(gōtra)* mentioning first his father Ramram and grandfather Ramesvar, his two sisters, Bhabani and Ambika, his brother Visvanath and his stepbrother Nidhiram. From this we can see that his father had married twice, the first marriage producing Ambika, Bhabani, Ramprasad and Visvanath, and the second Nidhiram. Ramprasad also mentions that Bhabani, whom he mentions with great affection, was married to a Calcuttan named Lakshminarayan Das. It is possible that, consistent with the report that when he left Kumarhatt he went to work in Calcutta, he stayed with her at the time.

However that may be, we are fortunate that the facts related here may be checked against the contemporary *boidya* clan chronicles, the *Candraprabhā* and *Ratnaprabhā* by Bharat Mallick. These contain details of the Sen family line which confirm the details given by Ramprasad and trace the line back to Krittibas. From them we also learn that the family had declined into "misfortune and poverty." Recently *kulaśāstras* like the *Candraprabhā* and *Ratnaprabhā* have come under some criticism regarding their reliability as historical sources; R.C. Mazumdar and Sukhamoy Mukhopadhyay[18] have pointed out that the writers of these chronicles included much non-factual information with the factual material in their books, some of it quite supernatural and unbelievable. This was because they had no modern historical outlook and the recording of hearsay evidence was the custom of the times, and because their main concern was, after all, to glorify the clan *(kula)* whose history they were recording. Mazumdar has pointed out that the earlier the period under discussion the more unreliable the material, as most of the *śāstras* were not written till the fifteenth or sixteenth centuries at the earliest.[19] But Mukhopadhyay has argued that the *boidÿa* chronicles, the *Candraprabhā* and *Ratnaprabhā*, are much more reliable than the brahmin *kulaśāstras* with which Mazumdar was chiefly concerned.[20]

It is fortunate for us that the chronicles with which we are concerned are the most reliable, and were written about the period we are interested in.[21] They are therefore likely to be fairly reliable sources for confirming the existence of Ramprasad Sen in the eighteenth century and giving information concerning his family.

In both the *Bidÿāsundar* and the *padābalī*[22] Ramprasad refers to Kumarhatt as his home and mentions its importance as a center for Tantric *sādhana*, and the records confirm that his branch of the family had settled in that area. It is also possible, as the chronicles continue beyond Ramprasad himself, by counting back through his successors, to determine approximately when it was that Ramprasad lived in the eighteenth century.[23] It would seem then that when Ramprasad refers in his work to these facts of his life there is no reason to doubt him.

Gupta says in his biography that in 1759 Maharaja Krishnachandra gave fourteen bighas of tax-free land to Ramprasad, land which was "uncultivated jungle land . . . for the occupation and enjoyment of your sons and grandsons:"

> In the Bengali year 1165 [1759 AD] Maharaja Krishnachandra gave Ramprasad Sen 14 bighas of land tax-free, land described in the deed as 'uncultivated jungle land for your sons and grandsons to occupy and enjoy'. The land is very close to Kumarhatt and the name and seal of the raja are found on the deed.[24]

Dineshchandra Bhattacharya[25] thinks Gupta had not actually seen this deed but reported from hearsay. This is confirmed by the deed itself which does refer to "rent-free uncultivated jungle land" but not in the words cited by Gupta.[26] Nor is the amount of land mentioned in the deed, a total of thirty-one bighas, the same as Gupta says it was.

This deed also confirms the connection of Ramprasad with the court of Raja Krishnachandra because his name is found on the deed. But perhaps more importantly, Ramprasad's title "Kabiranjan" is not used. This makes it very unlikely that it was Krishnachandra who conferred the title on Ramprasad because if he had he would almost certainly have used it, especially as in a similar deed granting land to Bharatchandra Ray at about the same time Krishnachandra does use his title, "Gunakar," which he had conferred on him.[27] There are also other deeds showing that Ramprasad received land from other patrons before the gift by Krishnachandra, and it is more likely that it was one of these patrons who gave him the title "Kabiranjan."[28]

While the deeds throw light in this way on the patronage Ramprasad received from the local zamindars, it also yet again undermines the reliability of Gupta's biography. He has reported the gift of land from hearsay, misrepresented the contents of the deed, and drawn an invalid reference from it with regard to Ramprasad's title (and incidentally to the whole related problem of when Ramprasad composed his *Bidyāsundar*, and for whom).

## *Which Came First, the Songs or the Stories?*

A further problem pertains to the style of Gupta's biography. Time and time again he relates some incident in the life of Ramprasad and then, with words such as "the evidence for it is found in one of his songs" gives one of the songs in full. No other evidence than the song is educed in support:

> There is also a rumour that the Kabiranjan composed 100,000 songs, but there is no proof of this, the only evidence for it is found in one of his songs:
>
> I have heard that Mother Shyama's court is very difficult,
> The clerk calls the plaintiff but none appears. What defense
> can I offer in a court where Siva is petitioner,
> O Mother you have appointed yourself as dewan, how can I
> trust your words?
> I have briefed 100,000 lawyers, what more can I do? I call you
> by your name Tara (the Deliverer), but you don't listen.
> So I abuse you and you become Kali (dark) at the indignity.
> Ramprasad says, You have ruined my life.

It is certainly not impossible that Ramprasad wrote 100,000 songs, and it is in many respects likely, because he never ceased composing them from his youth to the day of his death. Whatever came to his mind he turned into poetry.[29]

Ramprasad Sen started out as a clerk for an accountant in some famous wealthy household in or near Calcutta, but as he was not able to apply his mind closely to such wordly affairs he had no liking for such work. So he would neglect his work, entirely oblivious of the fact of his master's dissatisfaction, and every day he would take up his place at his desk, open his account book and fill whole pages with nothing but the name "Durga, Durga." Finally one day he sat and wrote this song:

Make me your accounts clerk, O Mother,
I will never betray your trust.
Everyone else plunders the treasury of your feet, and I can't bear it.
You have left it in the charge of the forgetful Siva.
He is fickle and gives away your property, yet still you trust him.
He receives half your body as a grant, as well as a good wage,
While I work without any wages, wanting only the dust from your feet.
If you remain with your father, then I am lost,
If you stay with my father Siva then I will receive my due, Mother.
Prasad says, Let me die at those feet of yours which dispel all misfortunes,
In that position I will be safe from all dangers.

When the accounts clerk saw this poem on the last pages of the book he was very angry and said to his master, "Sir, this mad or drunk fellow who at first inspired faith through his work has now ruined everything! See, he has completely spoiled this beautiful new book, there isn't a single figure in it, only this lunacy . . . " On hearing that his master looked at all the pages of the book, and as he read again and again the poem "Make me your accounts clerk, O Mother", a strange mood came over him. He was so moved by it that tears came to his eyes and he said to the cashier, "Who are you accusing

> of being mad or drunk? This fellow hasn't spoiled a good book, you are so drunk with the wine of worldliness that you haven't been able to grasp the true sentiment of this song. Ramprasad is no ordinary man, he is a holy man, an incarnate son of the Goddess." Then he addressed the Kabiranjan with words of devotion and said, "Ramprasad, as long as you remain on the path you have set out on nothing but trouble will befall you. So as long as you wander in the forests of this world I will give you 30 rupees per month stipend, there is no need for you to stay here any longer, go now to your house and keep up your good work."[30]

The question to be settled here is to what extent Ramprasad's poetical work was autobiographical. Did Ramprasad compose songs directly out of the experiences of his own life (as the tradition undoubtedly has it)? Or did he merely use as subject-matter for his songs the everyday experiences of the villagers who were the audience for them, experiences which then became attached to him in legend on the assumption that he must have composed songs directly out of his own experience? Take for example the story of Ramprasad's doodling in his account book and subsequent discovery by his employer. Here the song is taken as support of the story. But does it prove that he worked as an accounts clerk? Is it not at least as likely that Ramprasad thought that the venality of accountants provided a nice conceit with which to begin a song to the Mother which he personalized, putting himself as a devotee into the song in the process?

It is not possible to answer this question conclusively, but the constant repetition in Gupta's biography of the formula, story-proof clause-song, would certainly give pause to anyone familiar with literary form-criticism, and raises further doubts about the reliability of Gupta's evidence. If the legends are based on the songs, then the letter Gupta published (referred to above) shows at least that the process took place before Gupta's time during the fifty years between Ramprasad's death and the commencement of his research, and he accurately reports what was currently believed by his time. Gupta reliably reports the traditions, but are the traditions reliable?

It is also difficult to give much credence to stories like that of the Goddess Annapurna building his fence, or of the Muslim ruler, Siraj-ad-daulah taking time off to listen to Hindu devotional songs:

With regard to his Sakta devotionalism everyone referred to him as Kali's heroic son, they used to say that Annapurna used to come from Kashi every day and inspire his speech and he would compel her to listen to his songs. With respect to this, one astonishing miracle is talked about all over the country—'One day, in order to repair the fence round his house, he gathered together all the materials and went in search of a builder. When he returned with the builder a few moments later, the materials had gone and the fence was all fixed. Immediately there was an uproar among the neighbouring villagers who said, "Annapurna herself has come from Kashi and fixed up Ramprasad Sen's fence".' So many wonderful happenings like this are reported that if they were to be described they could not be contained in a single book. But Ramprasad never made any such claim himself, lest it detract from reference to his compositions.[31]

Once the magnanimous governor of Navadvip, Maharaja Krishnachandra Ray Bahadur, went by boat, accompanied by Sen, to Murshidabad where they stayed for a few days in the boat. Ramprasad spent the whole time singing songs to the glory of God. One day the nawab Siraj-ad-daulah passing in his boat as he enjoyed the evening breeze heard Sen singing, and being captivated by it asked whose boat it was and who the singer was. Later when he had established his identity and summoned Sen over to his boat and commanded him to sing, the Kabiranjan sang a *kheyāl* and *gajal* for the nawab's entertainment. But the nawab was displeased and said, 'I have no desire to hear your *kheyāl* and such', and told him to sing the hymns to Kali which he had previously been singing. At the nawab's command he began to sing one of his own songs filled with devotion to Shyama, and even such a hard-hearted man as Siraj-ad-daulah was powerless to prevent tears coming to his eyes. When the song had ended the nawab applauded him and said, "Ramprasad, you have received divine favour, if you accept my patronage I will give you high rank," but Ramprasad had no desire for worldly wealth as a result of accepting such patronage. Let the reader judge what kind of man Ramprasad was and what a hardhearted atheist Siraj-ad-daulah was.[32]

This kind of legend makes a theological point which may have been of interest to Gupta and to his readers as Sakta devotees, something considered further in chapter 3. Although it is of no use at all to the contemporary historian constructing a biography of Ramprasad, there is an important principle at work here. Dimock points out that in India where ideas of time and hence history are different from our own, those who recorded these traditions were not interested in historical detail but in the kind of meaning that the lives had for devotees, and which only true devotees could comprehend.[33] That this was true in Ramprasad's case is seen in the fact that most of Gupta's biography is concerned with Ramprasad as a devotee of Kali, and illustrates the great depth of faith and devotion he possessed.

## *Isvarachandra Gupta as an Historian*

There are grounds also for calling into question Gupta's methods of research. From what he himself says, and from the tone of the letter he published, it seems certain that Gupta had not himself actually visited Ramprasad's village in order to question the old people who had known him:

> It is a matter of some regret that I have not been able to write more. I had intended to record the biographies of the poets of the past who have become famous in this country, but because of the difficulty of collecting material this has not been an easy task to complete. Today none of their contemporaries are alive, and those old people who are are not especially informed. A few of them know a little but regrettably I have not been able to meet any of them.[34]

And from the letter:

> . . . The Kabiranjan's spirituality and scholarship have never before received the serious attention that you have given them, and we can vouch for the accuracy of your account because Ramprasad was a native of our village and we were well acquainted with him. And when what you had written was read to the wise and knowledgeable old people of the village they unhesitantly agreed, after hearing it, with what was written . . .[35]

Gupta does admit the hearsay nature of his material and on occasions recounts two conflicting traditions he has heard without attempting to resolve which was the correct one, as for example the identity of the person for whom Ramprasad worked as a clerk:

> Here there are two traditions, some say Ramprasad used to work as a clerk for Gokulchandra Ghosal, dewan of Kidderpur, others say he worked in Calcutta for Durgacharan Mitra's family.[36]

As a source of religious history, Gupta's work is very rich. The songs and poems provide a tremendous amount of information about Ramprasad's Sakta faith and the biography shows how Ramprasad had come to be regarded by the early nineteenth century. Because of Ramprasad's dominant place in the revival of Saktism in the eighteenth century this is invaluable.

Gupta's antiquarian interest in recording details of the lives of ancient poets shows that he had the interests of the modern historian at heart. His work coincides with the earlier stages of a change in Indian scholarship away from the traditionally Indian towards Western notions of historiography.[37] This is what motivated his quest. But we can see from the style of his biography and the fact that he himself never undertook to visit Ramprasad's village to collect data, and never actually sighted the land deed from which he "quotes," in short, that he was still very much under the influence of more traditional ideas.

We may be grateful to Gupta for collecting what he has about Ramprasad, but he has also left us with considerable difficulties. His reliance on older methods of historiography has led to his recording much legendary material, while his reputation as a "modern" historian has resulted in much of it being regarded as historical ever since.

But Gupta's biography does make a valuable contribution to our knowledge of Ramprasad; it is the earliest such record and summarizes the received tradition as it stood in 1853. Here the letter also published by Gupta is valuable; it supports what Gupta said in his biography, coming as it does from someone who was a native of Ramprasad's village. But we must always bear in mind that all this took place some time after Ramprasad's death, and that it is based on hearsay and must be constantly checked and evaluated before too much weight is put on it. At times it also can be shown to be probably in error.

What we can take with certainty from all this is a good picture of Ramprasad's Sakta faith, and it is this after all for which he is principally renowned. So altogether a reasonable portrait of this much-loved *sādhaka*-poet emerges, one which I think lends color to an assessment of his contribution to the development of Saktism in Bengal.

Glimpses of the historical Ramprasad Sen are there for the keen observer. He may be seen at the court of Raja Krishnachandra of Krishnanagore, or back at Halisahore on the banks of the Ganges, or farming his block of rent-free land. But these glimpses are almost obscured by the shadows. Where exactly was that piece of land, at Nadia or Halisahore? What was he doing in Krishnanagore, debating the aesthetics of erotic poetry with Bharatchandra, or religion with Aju Goswami? Did he leave Halisahore to work as a clerk in Calcutta, or was it somewhere else? Was he a brahmin or a *boidya*? And was he ever to be seen boating along the rivers and streams of East Bengal?

It is obvious that these glimpses are hidden by the shadows of time, and of other real or mythical Ramprasads. In spite of this it was not long before interest in Ramprasad began to grow; the first biography had been written, his songs were being collected and published in literary journals, and he had been enobled with the epithet *Kabirañjan* because the hearers received such delight from them. Unfortunately it was already too late to distinguish between the various images of these Ramprasads, or biographers no longer had the desire to do so. A great many songs were lost forever. The Ramprasad who emerges into this new light is a figure of legend more than history, but of glorious and compelling legend.

In the process the focus shifted. Those who were interested in him were interested not so much in the literary figure of the Krishnanagore court as in the Sakta *sādhaka*, the devotee of the Goddess. And it is this Ramprasad and this devotion which is the subject of this book.

TWO

# The Deconstruction of the Tradition

The introduction to this book stated that a new approach was taken to examine the problems surrounding the question of the authenticity of Ramprasadi songs. This is because the traditional textual-critical methods cannot solve most of the problems, and do not open up the study of these songs in any fruitful way. Such methods lead to insurmountable problems which force us to look elsewhere for a method of interpretation which will enable us not only to move forward in this study of Ramprasad, but also to better understand his songs. There is, however, an approach called deconstruction theory that is used increasingly for these purposes.

Unfortunately, deconstruction theory has become a fad in many circles, and in my opinion it has been taken to unacceptable extremes. One should be wary of the temptation to leap on-board every time a new bandwagon passes by oneself as the beleaguered scholar, but sometimes a new wave of academic fashion does bring with it new insights which may illuminate otherwise intractable problems. In this case, deconstruction does provide us with a tool for solving one such problem of interpretation in the study of Bengali religious verse.

## Which Songs Are by Ramprasad Sen?

For an eighteenth-century Indian poet like Ramprasad it is not an easy task to establish precisely which songs he himself composed. Authorship at this time was usually indicated in a brief colophon, or *bhaṇitā*, usually the last line or couplet of a verse in which the author used his name (thus at the same time including himself in the context of the verse). For example, the author would be named as the devotee if the verse was devotional, thereby indicating his authorship:

> Prasad says, Let me die at those feet of yours which dispel all misfortunes,
> In that position I will be safe from all dangers.[1]

The first problem we face when attempting to decide the authenticity of such attributions is that for a poet like Ramprasad no autograph manuscripts are available. Manuscripts deteriorate rapidly in a monsoon climate like Bengal's, and anyway it is doubtful if Ramprasad actually wrote down any of his work. He is much more likely to have composed and sung his songs, which were then memorized and handed down orally by his followers before being finally committed to paper, probably not until some time in the nineteenth century.

The problem is compounded by the fact that anyone could compose a verse (or song, as they were usually sung) and use Ramprasad's, or anyone else's name in the *bhaṇitā*. We must remember that such a practice would not at the time been considered unethical. There were no copyright laws, and the then contemporary attitude to plagiarism was not what it is among western scholars today. Anyone composing a Sakta lyric who wished for a wider acceptance of it could attach a *bhaṇitā* with a name that was well-known and had wide acceptance, thus leaving it to the hearers/readers to decide for themselves on its merits, instead of as now seeking out a good publisher with a wide distribution network.

We are also confronted here with the additional problem that a name like Ramprasad was by no means an uncommon one. Further the habit of a person with such a name calling himself only Prasad makes the name even more common. "Ram-prasad" means roughly "blessed of Ram" so that Prasad then means something like "your devotee" or "receiver of your grace" when used on its own in a *bhaṇitā*. Not only was Prasad in that sense used in many names—Guruprasad, Sivaprasad, Hariprasad, and so on, but Prasad could be used by anyone in the sense of "your devotee" without it actually being part of their name.

Finally other descriptive titles were sometimes used with the names Prasad and Ramprasad such as Din (wretchedly poor) Ramprasad, Ramprasad Das (Das means servant, but it is also a low-caste marker), and Dvija Ramprasad (Dvija means twice born but usually indicates a brahmin). With respect to these we have to decide whether Ramprasad Sen was using these adjectives to describe features of his character or state to enhance the force of his poetic conceit, or whether some other Ramprasad (or Prasad) was using them just to distinguish himself from Ramprasad Sen.

The problem is not made any easier by the fact that if any composer wanted to present his work as that of Ramprasad it might be just because it was in the religious or literary style of Ramprasad Sen. This makes it very difficult to decide questions of authorship on stylistic grounds, although we should not rule out stylistic considerations altogether—another poet's stylistic imitation might be a poor one and thus unconvincing.

The first problem is often one of knowing where to start, or deciding which work is definitely by the author one is concerned with so that other contenders may be considered relative to it. For example, in establishing the *oeuvre* of the Buddhist philosopher Nagarjuna (second century AD), we usually mean by Nagarjuna the writer of the *Mūlamadhyamakakārikās* and the *Vigrahavyāvartanī*.[2] Other works attributed to Nagarjuna can then be compared to the ones whose authenticity is generally accepted. Fortunately in this present case we do also have a concrete point of departure; we are concerned with that Rampasad Sen who was a Sakta poet living in Bengal in the eighteenth century, who was known by the title Kabiranjan Ramprasad Sen, and was the subject of an early biography by Isvarachandra Gupta. According to the biography, and to a very strong tradition of the time, this Ramprasad was the author of a long narrative poem called *Bidyāsundar,* the story of two lovers Bidya and Sundar. From this we can get some idea of the kind of verse Ramprasad composed, and by studying the *bhaṇitās* used in that work (e.g., Sri Kabiranjan forty-five times, Prasad twenty-seven times, Sri Ramprasad and Sri Prasad five times each, Ramprasad, Kabiranjan, Kabi Ram, Prasad Kabi and Ram once each) we gain insight into his use of different forms of his name in his verse. In this way we know who we are talking about, and the question becomes how many of the other works traditionally ascribed to him, especially the religious songs known as *padābalī,* were in fact his.

## *Dayalchandra Ghosh and the Problem of a Second Ramprasad*

Some of the facets of this question are difficult, if not impossible, to solve. Let us take for example one of the most discussed issues: whether or not Kabiranjan Ramprasad Sen is the same as the so-called Dvija Ramprasad.

Ramprasad Sen is thought to have lived from around 1718–1720 to 1775–1781 and his first "biographers" (who in fact gave only brief biographical notes), namely Isvarachandra Gupta, writing in 1853, and Dayalchandra Ghosh in 1875,[3] faced some of the same problems which face us here—was Ramprasad a *boidӯa* (physician caste) or a brahmin, and did he live in West Bengal or East Bengal? Or were there two Ramprasads, one a *boidӯa* and the other a brahmin? Isvara Gupta, who began his researches into the life of Ramprasad in 1833, places him in West Bengal and thinks that he worked initially as an accounts clerk for some famous family in Calcutta. Later, when talking about the songs, he says that he has not reproduced in his collection the Ramprasadi songs well-known in East Bengal, songs sung by the boatmen in the Dacca, Serajgunj, and Pabna regions.[4] Yet he gives no reason for this strange omission, strange because he was obviously keen to collect as many Ramprasadi songs as possible. It may be that he already knew of a tradition naming another Ramprasad who lived in the East Bengal area, and that these boatmen's songs were by that Ramprasad.

In any event, Dayalchandra Ghosh, writing his *Prasādprasaṅa* in Dacca in East Bengal, certainly knew of the tradition. This Eastern Ramprasad he says was a native of Mahesvardi, or was born in a village on the Padma, and was a brahmin lawyer.[5] The people of the area were themselves already very vague about this Ramprasad. Ghosh then went to Calcutta where he was told about the *boidӯa* Ramprasad from West Bengal, and gives details of him consistent with those given by Isvara Gupta, and possibly based on Gupta's account, with which he was familiar.[6] A little later he takes up again the question of Ramprasad's caste, saying that at first he thought Ramprasad was a brahmin *(dvija),* as many in East Bengal did, but later changed his mind. This is due most likely to the credence he gave to the tradition circulating in the Eastern regions, especially because he had already found songs with the *bhaṇitā* Dvija Ramprasad. So how was he to square these facts with the stronger tradition that Ramprasad was a *boidӯa,* and lived at Halisahore in West Bengal? He first suggests what many others have seen as a possible way out, that strictly speaking *dvija* applies to the three twice-born classes *(varna)* and in this basic sense could apply to Ramprasad. Also, because when an individual is released *(mukta),* they become *dvija* when united with God.[7] But then he muddies the issue by adding that the songs attributed to Dvija Ramprasad "are all comparatively quite frivolous" and that Ramprasad possibly only used the *bhaṇitā* Dvija in his youth.[8] Finally admitting that he cannot solve the problem, he marks the songs attributed to Dvija Ramprasad in his collection with a cross (+), believing they should be accepted as by Ramprasad until evidence to the contrary comes to hand. He also admits the possibility that other poets might have used the signature Ramprasad in the *bhaṇitās* of their work—suggesting that some verses attributed to Ramprasad may not be genuine.[9]

The whole discussion of the problem of Dvija Ramprasad has continued to revolve around these issues. In attempting to settle the question, the issue of caste is relevant. Would a *boidȳa,* which Kabiranjan Ramprasad Sen was, have used the word Dvija, usually taken to refer to brahmins, to refer to himself? On the one hand, we are reminded that *boidȳas* are from the Sudra class, not of the twice-born at all.[10] On the other hand, it has been suggested that because *boidȳas* are considered a high caste, and were learned and respected members of society at the time, such a usage would be acceptable.[11] In support of this latter suggestion it has been pointed out also that at the time of Ramprasad in West Bengal *boidȳas* and brahmins even "shared the hookah," such close sharing of smoking instruments indicating close caste bonds.[12] It has also been suggested that as a Tantrika, Ramprasad might have regarded himself as a *dvija* before attaining the state of *siddhi* or the perfected state of a *sādhaka,* after which he would have assumed the epithet Prasad only and used it to refer to himself in his songs, though I must say I find this unlikely.[13]

Some who have suggested this latter explanation claim to see supporting evidence in the style and content of the songs—those with the Dvija *bhaṇitā* are held inferior in spiritual content and style, this being consistent with a lower level of spiritual development. The songs attributed to Prasad show by contrast a deeper maturity and spirituality. But others claim that no such difference on stylistic grounds can be detected.[14]

Stylistic arguments are difficult to settle, especially when dealing with an uncertain textual situation like this. For example, many of the songs attributed to Ramprasad have come down to us in different versions. Sometimes the same song will be extant in versions attributed to Dvija Ramprasad and to some other Ramprasad in their *bhaṇitās*. Sometimes a song exists in versions attributing it to some Ramprasad and to some entirely different author.[15] This may be because of a tendency by authors seeking acceptance of their work to attribute it to Ramprasad as an acknowledged authority, or merely because changes often creep unknowingly into texts when passed down orally for periods of time, and then passed from hand to hand for generations even when written in manuscript form. We know that an educated and interested researcher such as Dayalchandra Ghosh himself was not above altering texts which came to him as songs of Ramprasad![16]

Finally all these matters might not seem so problematic if we knew of only one (West Bengal, Kabiranjan) Ramprasad. But we do have the enigmatic references to this East Bengali Ramprasad, also known as Dvija Ramprasad in certain circles. The references are so vague, and historical knowledge of him is so scarce even at an early date, that we are left to wonder if it is not this Ramprasad who is the mythical one. But the hints of his existence are just strong enough and early enough to make the existence of two Ramprasads, both Saktas, tantalizingly possible.

After examining all the evidence, most recent scholarship has concluded that the question is incapable of solution. Satyanarayan Bhattacharya certainly believes all the problems of attribution will never be untangled.[17] Even the unlikely discovery of more textual material, more songs in earlier versions, for example, or perhaps earlier biographies, is unlikely to help to settle the issue. This evidence would be subject to the same doubts as those already in existence.

## *Collecting and Preserving the Songs*

Now let us return to a problem previously referenced: the chance nature of the body of work attributed to Ramprasad. The songs were probably never written down by Ramprasad himself.[18] Once committed to writing from the fallible memories of his followers (after how much time?) they would be circulated on paper which had a very short life due to the nature of the climate of Bengal and the treatment it received from devotees. As Isvarachandra Gupta informs us:[19]

> Other works of his which had been collected together earlier have by now almost disappeared, because in those days people

> used to guard them carefully like some secret mantra, not showing them to anyone even at the cost of their lives, bringing them out only at puja time to decorate them with flowers and sandalwood paste, as some people still do today, and though we would have given all we had we were not able to obtain any of the verses. Hidden in this way they have become completely destroyed. Worms and other insects ate them, moisture decomposed them, fire burned them, they were used by the impotent as charms to secure beautiful women or long life, and so people destroyed Ramprasad's reputation . . . Some (songs) I have been able to see only with the greatest difficulty. Some have been eaten by insects, some have been inadvenently copied incorrectly, and there is an awful risk in trying to establish the substance of these.

So the element of chance in the preservation of these songs is extremely great. Systematic attempts to collect Ramprasad's work proceeded in the face of great difficulty So how can we possibly hope to assess Ramprasad's teaching, even if problems of attribution were settled satisfactorily, on the basis of the collection we have? Were there important songs which have not come down to us? Even if we do not accept the tradition that he composed 100,000 songs,[20] it seems likely that his output was very large. Yet Bhattacharya in his collection of Ramprasad songs lists only 321 (including those by Dvija Ramprasad). This is a very small sample on which to base an analysis of the work of an author.

## *Deconstruction as a Solution to Historical Problems*

Though some scholars still long for some evidence to come to hand which will settle some of these questions, especially those regarding attribution of authorship, I doubt whether this is any longer possible. I now want to raise a different question, whether or not we should even want to settle it. It does seem to me that the question is to a certain extent improper. It is based on a view of authorship which was neither current at the time when Saktism flourished around Ramprasad in the eighteenth century, nor most helpful for a modern understanding of the movement.

It is also based on a particularly Western academic textual-critical understanding of the problem. Those who are anxious to settle the question are usually Western or Western-trained textual and literary critics. Today, even in the West the assumptions underlying this view of authorship, and of an author's output or *oeuvre,* are being called in question. For example in considering T. S. Eliot's work, which *Waste Land* do we regard as Eliot's, the version published in 1932, or the earlier and longer version which he sent to Pound, and which Pound radically revised and cut?[21] Is not this latter the Eliot version, and the published one the Pound-Eliot version? Michel Foucault has posed the problem quite powerfully:[22]

> The problems raised by the (concept of an) *oeuvre* . . . are difficult. Yet, at first sight, what could be more simple? A collection of texts that can be designate by the sign of a proper name. But this designation (even leaving to one side the problems of attribution) is not a homogeneous function: does the name of an author designate in the same way a text that he has published under his name, a text that he has presented under a pseudonym, another found after his death in the form of an unfinished draft, and another text that is merely a collection of jottings, a notebook? The establishment of a complete *oeuvre* presupposes a number of choices that are difficult to justify or even to formulate: is it enough to add to the texts published by an author those that he intended for publication but which remain unfinished by the fact of his death? Should one also include all his sketches and first drafts, with all their corrections and crossings out? Should one add sketches that he himself had abandoned? And what status should be given to letters, notes, reported conversations, transcriptions of what he said made by those present at the time, in short to that vast mass of verbal traces left by an individual at his death, and which speak in an endless confusion so many different languages.

Foucault has called into question traditional ways of viewing, among other things, history and literature, and called for them to be examined in a new way. This new way involves nothing less than a radical questioning of the very roots of our understanding of the structures of these disciplines. What Foucault wants to do is to "deconstruct" the idea of the author or to move away from the idea of the author as the most important center of focus for the interpretation of texts.[23] One reason for this is that the idea of the author as an identifiable person responsible for a self-contained and straightforward body of work, an *oeuvre,* is problematic in a way that has not always been recognised, as he has shown in the passage quoted above. The problem with the *oeuvre* as a subject for analysis is that an *oeuvre* is defined in terms of an author. The name of the author separates off certain works from others, it can "group together a number of texts and thus differentiate them from others. A name also establishes forms of relationships among texts,"[24] it "points to the existence of certain groups of discourse and refers to the status of this discourse within a society and culture."[25] Then, paradoxically, we try to recover the intentionality of the author from the *oeuvre* we have established based on his/her authorship. As Barthes puts it, "The *explanation* of a work is always sought in the man or woman who produced it, as if it were always in the end . . . the voice of a single person, the *author* 'confiding' in us."[26] But says Foucault, "these aspects of (the) individual, which we designate as (the) author (or which comprise an individual as an author), are projections, in terms always more or less psychological, of our way of handling texts."[27] In other words they represent our own subjective interests.

So there is need of a new theory of interpretation. We must "accept the groupings that history suggests only to subject them at once to interrogation; to break them up and then to see whether they can be legitimately reformed . . . "[28] Then "by freeing them of all the groupings that purport to be natural, immediate, universal unities, (such as the *oeuvre* of an author) one is able to describe other unities but this time by means of a group of controlled decisions."[29]

This also enables one to concentrate on the text in a new way, to see "what is the specific existence that emerges from what is said and nowhere else?"[30]

> But if we isolate, in relation to the language and to thought, the occurrence of the statement/event, it is not in order to spread over anything the dust of facts. It is in order to be sure that this occurrence is not linked with synthesizing operations of a purely psychological kind (the intention of the author, the form of his mind, the vigour of his thoughts, the themes that obsess him, the project that traverses his existence and gives it meaning) and to be able to grasp other forms of regularity, other types of relations.[31]

We need then to have a method to decide on what constitutes our chosen field which avoids both the circularity and the subjectivity of the above process, and Foucault does proceed in *The Archaeology of Knowledge* to outline such rules.

Here, however, rather than outlining this method, I want to pursue further the question of the author and his or her work. Though in his article Foucault has pronounced the author "dead" we can profit from further examination of how the idea of the author has functioned in criticism up to now, and thus see what new light has been thrown on the problem by this demise. Foucault says:

> . . . the (authorial) subject should not be entirely abandoned. It should be reconsidered, not to restore the theme of an originating subject, but to seize its functions, its intervention in the discourse, and its system of dependencies. We should suspend the typical questions: how does it accomplish its design by animating the rules of discourse from within? Rather, we should ask: under what conditions and through what forms can an entity like the subject appear in the order of discourse; what position does it occupy; what function does it follow in each type of discourse.[32]

When examining this "author-function" Foucault points out that it has a complex social and institutional function. An author is more than just a person who wrote a book: "a person can be the author of much more than a book—of a theory, for instance, or a tradition or a discipline within which new books and authors can proliferate,"[33] and mentions as examples of this Freud and Marx. Figures like them become "initiators of discursive practice," when their work attains importance of a paradigmatic kind, as founders of traditions to which others contribute by extending the traditions of, in these cases, Freudian psychology and Marxism.

## *A New Light on Old Songs*

All of this is intended to be positive rather than just negative. It should be a liberating process opening up new prospects, new ways of seeing texts, so that the scholar faces no longer the tiresome repetetives:

"Who is the real author?"
"Have we proof of his authenticity and originality?"
"What has he revealed of his most profound self in his language?"
New questions will be heard:
"What are the modes of existence of this discourse?"

"Where does it come from; how is it circulated; who controls it?"
"What placements are determined for possible subjects?"
"Who can fulfil these diverse functions of the subject?"[34]

When we address these new questions we begin to get new insights into the work of Ramprasad. When we address the first question (What are the modes of existence of this discourse?) we are forced to stop looking at the work of Ramprasad in isolation, as a group of songs which may be interpreted this way or that, and to see how they relate to a community of Sakta belief and practice, which they inspired and which in turn preserved them, and gave them an authority as a canonical text which transforms any individual meaning any song might have. This enquiry leads us to the next question, focusing on the community of faith and its role in the transmission of the text, and the possible power relations which developed within the Sakta community and between it and other groups in Bengal (e.g., Gauriya Vaisnavas). The third question—What placements are determined for possible subjects?—focuses attention on the ordinary *sādhakas* and their role within these developments, how they used the songs, and what meaning they had for these people—rather than determining what they mean "in themselves" if that is possible. And the last question forces us to ask who these people were anyway, underlining the social significance of the work of Ramprasad in the religious development of Bengal.

In other words the study of Ramprasad's work becomes contextualized, and the dynamics of interaction between literary work and human context greatly affect what we mean by the meaning of the work. And this is as it should be. Later chapters in this book attempt the uncovering of this kind of meaning.

Returning now to the body of work attributed to Ramprasad, we see that the name Ramprasad, and all its variants used in the *bhaṇitās,* functions in a way similar to that of Marx or Freud in the cases referred to above—it marks out a specific body of discourse, based originally on the spiritual experience of an actual individual, Kabiranjan Ramprasad Sen, about whom we do know something as shown in chapter 1, although not as much as we know about Freud or Marx. But more importantly, it is not necessary to know whether or not a particular verse is actually by that individual. This tradition was a dynamic one which grew and reflected the beliefs and aspirations of its adherents rather than of any single author. So Din Ramprasad in a *bhaṇitā* does not necessarily mean that authorship is to go to some impoverished Ramprasad, Ramprasad Sen, or some other, but may reflect the fact that in the latter part of the eighteenth century many ordinary Bengalis suffered great hardship[35] and the language of the songs is the language of the poor and powerless of society from whom Saktism drew its strength. Similarly the prominent theme of the poverty of the author may be seen as the homologization of the poverty of the people to their spiritual poverty as devotees, or perhaps even as a conceit adopted by a courtly poet (which Kabiranjan Ramprasad at one time was) to deflect any rebellious action on the part of poor subjects. The "I" of the song is the individual Sakta, and the "Prasad" of the *bhaṇitā* is the devotee him or herself. So there is no need to decide which *bhaṇitās* are genuine. They are all genuine. As songs by Dvija Ramprasad were (and are) accepted by most Saktas as by the Ramprasad who marks out this first stage of their tradition, so should they be by us, rendering the historical question irrelevant. Interestingly, this brings scholarship much closer to the tradition of the followers of Ramprasad.

This body of Ramprasad songs (this "discourse" as it is called) then became authoritative. After a while it was no longer acceptable to add to the tradition, and later verses are attributed to other devotees, such as Kamalakantha, who added their own emphases.[36] But the body of Ramprasadi songs functions in a particular way for the tradition, much as the so-called "Fifth Veda" of other traditions (e.g., the *Prabandham* of the Tamil Alvars), and defines an early Bengali Sakta tradition opposed to, but functioning analogously to, the Caitanya tradition of Bengal Vaisnavas.[37] We must remember it is the collectors and preservers of the songs, however contingent the process of preservation, who have given us this discourse, not Ramprasad himself, who had no part in the collection of his own work. What was preserved was what was seen to be important and significant to them. And exploration of the reasons for this give more insight into the texts.

The task of the scholar now is to examine this body of material, the discourse, to see what it can tell us about this early stage in the Sakta tradition. Here Ramprasad functions as an exemplar of the true Sakta, and the mythological accretions also assume importance for their relevance to this function. So the story of Ramprasad's idling away his time writing religious verses in the account books of his employer is not one to be examined for its (probably doubtful) historical authenticity but noted for the ideal it upholds of a devotee singleminded in his devotion. This is how authorship functions here. It is the Ramprasad of myth, not history, that is important for the Sakta tradition then and now, although I am sure that many Saktas believe this Ramprasad to have been an historical figure.

Deconstruction of the concept of authorship as a factor in considering the collection of early Sakta *padābalī* is in fact a "construction" of a new and profitable way of interpreting the material. This new perspective forces us from the unprofitable (because unsuccessful) and perhaps misguided ways of the past, and opens up the way for new insights into the status, beliefs, and practices of the eighteenth-century Saktas of Bengal. It also opens up the work commonly attributed to Ramprasad as accepted by his followers, to a new and more fruitful form of study.

The situation we are now in is an improvement on the former. We now have an agreed-upon body of songs whose authority is no longer undermined by the intractable questions of authenticity, authorship, and so on, but instead waits for a new interpretation and new understanding. This is true not only of the songs but of their author too. The dead author comes to life again in a new way, not as an historical figure but in the meaning of the stories and traditions associated with him as the singer behind the songs. It is this Ramprasad which is the subject of the next chapter, while chapters 4 and 5 provide a new interpretive methodology.

THREE

# *Reading the Life of Ramprasad*

## *The Importance of the Legendary Tradition*

One of the most important texts to be examined in this study of Ramprasad is that which concerns his life. We have seen in chapter 1 that there is little in the way of factual evidence to support many of the claims made in the literature about Ramprasad's life. Does this mean that the large text of legendary material still being circulated in Bengal in written and oral form, and which is very widely known among the people, is of no use to the scholar and should therefore be dismissed?

I think not, as I hope I have shown in chapter 2, because this text, when read not as an historical account but as a record of the way his followers saw him, or as the way they wanted to present him to their own and subsequent generations, will prove to be very informative. It matters little that some Saktas did regard their accounts as history. The earliest biographer, Isvarachandra Gupta, saw himself as an historian who was attempting to recover the real Ramprasad. But even he admitted that much of the material he collected as early as the early decades of the nineteenth century was hearsay. But if all history is interpretation,[1] under any theory of history we need to examine the methods by which the history is constructed and the motives of its authors.

When our largely legendary text is approached with all this in mind I believe it comes alive in a new and very revealing way. This text was constructed and passed on by Ramprasad's followers—Isvarachandra Gupta was himself a Sakta, and was motivated to preserve the life and work of Ramprasad primarily because he was a Sakta poet. If we read this text with an eye to discovering the motivation behind it I believe we can begin to understand why it was constructed in the way it was, and learn some important facts about the whole tradition. Most important of these is that in my opinion what we have here is a life which is constructed or modelled on the life (factual or legendary, again it does not matter) of the great Gauriya Vaisnava saint and singer Caitanya. Ramprasad is therefore presented as a kind of "Sakta Caitanya," a leader who would be the central figure in a Sakta revival equal to the Vaisnava revival instigated by Caitanya. It is equally my contention that this was successful and lead to the ascendency of Saktism in Bengal well into the twentieth century. Of course Ramprasad was chosen for this role because he did have a number of exceptional qualities, as a saint and as a singer, which enabled this to happen, as we will see further in chapters 4 and 5 when we examine the text of his *padābalī*. But let us also note that the process involved in both cases discussed here, the Vaisnava and the Sakta, is very similar. It was his followers who constructed the biographies of Caitanya, in order to present him as a certain kind of person, and it was Ramprasad's followers who in a like manner constructed his biography.[2] So we must read Ramprasad's life in light of the lives of Caitanya, written in both Bengali and in Sanskrit by his followers, which were then and still are current in Bengal, and were well-known to the early Saktas.

## *The Lives of the Saint/Singers*

We must also bear in mind that there is a much wider genre of such literature on the lives of saintly figures, in Hinduism as in other religions, standing behind both Caitanya and Ramprasad.

> These collections of extraordinary and exemplary lives differ significantly from one religious community to another, and from subgroup to subgroup and period to period; but they bear family resemblances that are often striking. Indeed these various hagiographical traditions might be threads drawn from a single skein of yarn: the weavers of the larger fabric of tradition had different ideas about where a thread should go and

> how often it should be used, but once one knows what color to look for, one will almost always find it.[3]

Such exemplary lives are very important for the adherents of their respective religions or sects, serving a number of functions for their followers. They might serve as a foundational charter for belief or practice. For example, the saint might serve as a moral or devotional exemplar for devotees to follow, or might serve to strengthen resolve when a devotee's or the group's ardour is flagging. In the Hindu tradition they function especially as links between the groups of adherents and the metaphysical realm, the realization of a sort of union that is a basic goal of Hindu religious practice. The traditional ways of achieving union are through yoga and asceticism, through philosophical speculation and discrimination, but the rigor demanded by these methods does not lie within the capabilities or inclinations of everyone. Thus Hawley reminds us that, "Within each religion a powerful body of tradition emphasizes not codes but stories, not precepts but personalities, not lectures but lives."[4]

The lives of Hindu saints usually fit into the "extraordinary" rather than the "exemplary" category, and thus seem more detached from the factual details of history that tend to preoccupy Westerners. In fact, as Dimock reminds us, such factual details are often unimportant for the writer of such lives because he is more concerned with its meaning. For one of the writers of the life of Caitanya, Dimock says in a comment which could apply to Hindu lives in general, "[T]his type of fact was not important. There was little point in treating overt detail, for true significance lies in meaning, which only devotees can comprehend."[5] Here we see both that tradition is privileged over history, and the knowing reader is privileged over the ordinary one. So if the ordinary reader can point to errors of fact in a biography this is of no consequence for the point of the story is that it embodies Truth of a different kind, the kind that can be realized by the initiated. "[I]f people are bothered [by such factual errors], they have not understood the revelation."[6]

Dimock reminds us that the biographers of Caitanya were, of course, aware that they were treating people and often events that had actually occured, but because they were always primarily concerned with meaning they could move easily between the material and spiritual realms, and the blurring of the line between these two realms is a feature of the lives reported. And it is these Lives that are the immediate model for the followers of Ramprasad Sen.

## *Ramprasad as a Saint/Singer*

In reading the text of the life of Ramprasad I wish to examine in some detail the account published, in two parts, by Isvarachandra Gupta in 1853 and reproduced in the Appendix. It is still the basis for all the other accounts, much longer and more involved as some of these are, and it gains in importance by apparently being the first life account that we have. I also refer from time to time to a fuller and later book-length account purchased randomly from a stall at the Calcutta Book Fair, *Sādhaka kabi Rāmprasād* by Pranabkumar Dasgupta.[7]

When looking at lives, both Ramprasad's and Caitanya's, we follow a general pattern designated as "the lives of great men," with the inclusive subclass "lives of saint/singers in India." But there are a number of features in Ramprasad's life which are especially close to that of Caitanya, which lead me to think that it is modelled intentionally on it, and is not just another example of the same genre, because the similarities are not just coincidences.

### *The Calling of the Saint/Singer*

Gupta's biography begins, as is customary with these biographies, not with Ramprasad's birth but with what I will refer to as his "Calling," which amounts to a spiritual birth, or a birth into his life as a saint/singer. The story is probably the most widely-known of the stories about Ramprasad. He starts out as a clerk in the zamindari office of some (unidentified, see chapter 1) wealthy householder near Calcutta, but because of his intense spiritual nature he cannot settle to such a mundane existence and whiles away his time composing songs of praise to the Goddess, filling whole pages of his ledger with her name. Discovered by his superior he is hauled before his employer and accused not only with idleness but with being "mad or drunk." Examining the ledger the employer sees the song, "Make me your accounts clerk, O Mother . . ." and is moved to tears by the religious sentiment in this song. After some word-play over the idea of drunkenness—is Ramprasad drunk with the spirit of devotion, or the superior clerk drunk with worldliness?—his employer declares, "Ramprasad is no ordinary man, he is a holy man, an incarnate son of the Goddess," and given a stipend of thirty rupees per month to enable him to devote his time fully to the "path he has set out on."

The important elements of this story are (1) that because of his spirituality he is unable to live an ordinary mundane life, even to the extent that he appears drunk or mad; (2) this is recognized and announced formally by someone; and (3) Ramprasad abandons his previous life and sets out on his full-time religious vocation, he "went home and passed his time quite happily on his new stipend," and "immersed himself in a sea of Sakti bhakti and song singing."

I will return to these in a moment, but first let us notice two other interesting features. The first is the relationship between the story and the song. The song, as noted in chapter 1, takes as its central trope the idea of the good/bad accounts clerk, as a model of the good or bad devotee. Ramprasad cries that if he were made accounts clerk he would be a good servant of his master (in contrast, by implication, to his actual superior), as he is a good servant of the Goddess in his devotion. The intertextuality here is very interesting. Does the song confirm the story in which it is embedded, or does its existence in fact precede the story, to which it later gives rise? It is impossible to know, though the latter is certainly as likely as the former, especially as this kind of process is at work throughout the text. And this practice is even more pronounced in later lives, for example that of Pranabkumar Dasgupta, who constantly appeals to songs as evidence to support his tale.

The second notable feature is a tension between the story itself and other songs by Ramprasad that are roughly related. Ramprasad is given a stipend of thirty rupees, with which he seems quite happy. But Gupta comments, "with a wife and family he was not able to prosper domestically on so small an income, and his dependents began to nag him constantly to find some other source of income. . . . his family had no material goods and depended on the wealthy who came to hear his songs and *saṅkīrtans* and made presents to him." Now this tension is a curious one. Ramprasad was happy, and presumably the employer gave him a sum which he believed would enable him to survive without any other income, or the story begins not to make sense. It seems, on research into the times, that thirty rupees was a substantial amount and would have allowed him to live comfortably.[8] And Gupta claims later in his biography that he was also given a substantial grant of tax-free land by Raja Krishnachandra of Krishnanagore.

Why then the persistence of this tradition of family poverty? The reason is that here again the two textual traditions are working against each other. In the songs Ramprasad presents a persona of poverty, even referring to himself as "Poor (Din) Ramprasad" on a number of occasions. Now in my opinion this can be considered a literary conceit that serves two functions. On the one hand it allows him to identify with the numerous poor of his times, and they with him; the religious message of his songs offers a solace to the poor in need. On the other hand, worldly poverty serves as a metaphor of spiritual poverty, which every devotee admits as a precondition for the reception of the Goddess's grace. There is no paradigm for the rich saint/singer.

If this line is taken, there is no tension between the two texts. It is only if the povery of the songs is taken literally that a problem is perceived, one with which the biographer must come to terms. This also seems to confirm my theory that the songs came before the story, and are often the source of the legend rather than its confirmation.

Now let us return to the dominant features of the Calling narrative referred to above. These are very similar to events in the Calling of Caitanya. Caitanya's spiritual conversion, the cause of which is not known, "swept him off with its overwhelming force"[9] so that he was not able to continue with his work as a teacher. His behavior was described by the people as "the height of insolence."[10] "When he taught his pupils, the subject of his discourse was Krishna, [not as it should have been: Sanskrit grammar] and very soon he had to close his school."[11] His state is described as drunkenness or lunacy, but his true state is recognized by a small group of devout Vaisnavas and interpreted as spiritual ecstacy. They welcomed him "with hope and joy"[12] and thenceforth he devoted his time to singing and religious ecstacy—a practice which continued to be met with "scorn and ridicule."[13]

### *The Death of the Saint/Singer*

The next significant event to examine is Ramprasad's death. Here Gupta's account is based on what "the old people say." What they say is that when Ramprasad was a little over sixty, on the day set down for the ritual immersion of the image of the Goddess in the Ganges (presumably after Durga or Kali Puja) he announced that he too would be immersed with the Mother. He told the people to bring the image, then off they all went, singing the "farewell" songs he had composed. Pranabkumar Dasgupta relates how he slowly descended the steps into the river, taking the image with him, and the front cover of the book shows the commonly-accepted manner in which he did so, bearing the image on his head.[14] He died singing the song, "Tara, do you remember me any more," which ends with the line, "O Mother, now it's all over, I have done everything I can." As he sang these last words the *brahmarandhra* at the crown of his head opened and he died.[15]

This is no ordinary mortal death because a saint/singer like Ramprasad is no ordinary mortal. His was a miraculous death in which like/with the Goddess he is immersed in the holy Ganges. In it he is merged with the Goddess and becomes the Goddess. It is also once again strikingly noteworthy that the incident is linked to a specific explanatory song. The final (or any other) line of the song need not be taken as referring to his literal end, but here the tradition definitely interprets it as doing so. More striking, however, are the parallels again with the accounts of the death of Caitanya.

The biographers of Caitanya do not have a lot to say about it, but taken together there are three traditions concerning his death.[16] In one he merged into the image of Jagannath in the temple in Puri; in another he was drowned in the ocean at Puri when in a fit of ecstacy; and in another he injured his foot against a stone during frenzied dancing and died an ordinary human death six days later from the infection, presumably from blood-poisoning or something comparable. This latter account is now considered to be heretical by the faithful, who attempt to suppress it, because of its intimations of mortality and corruption of the body inconsistent with the end of an *abatār*. It is recorded by Jayananda in his *Caitanȳamaṅala* which Dimock says is "anathema to the pious."

> The paradigm . . . forbids mention of the subject's death; Jayānanda, interested in the particulars, tells us that Caitanya injured his foot in a spate of frenzied dancing, and, after suffering for six days, died from an infection of it. The presence of Jayānanda and other texts not yet censored out of existence by orthodoxy obviously suggests that exceptions must be made to . . . general statements about historical biography. But . . . they are considered heretical by the dominant orthodoxy. . . . [17]

The other two accounts are much more consistent with the image of Caitanya that the tradition wishes to project: in the one his body disappeared,[18] and in the other he merged with or was reabsorbed into Lord Jagannath. When we compare this with the account of the end of Ramprasad we find that it combines these two accounts. Ramprasad's body disappears into the Ganges (the sea) and it merges with or is absorbed into the image of the Goddess (the image of Jagannath). The similarities here absolutely defy any suggestion that they are just coincidental, and it seems obvious that the Ramprasad account is constructed on the basis of the Caitanya model once again.

### *The Miraculous Life of the Saint/Singer*

The accounts of both individuals' lives are dotted with stories of wonderful or miraculous events, descriptions of their deep devotion, ecstacy, spiritual powers, etc. Their similarities can be accounted for by acknowledging that both accounts in fact follow a general pattern of heightening the spiritual character of any saint/singer who is held up as a model for devotees to follow, or is the leader of a sect or movement. Extraordinary powers are taken as evidence of an extraordinary relationship with the deity, which confers extraordinary spirituality and marks the saint out for emulation.

There is, however, one such incident in the life of Ramprasad that is so similar to one recounted with respect to Caitanya, and one that is otherwise so unlikely, that again I want to suggest that the former is intentionally modeled on the latter. It is the story of Ramprasad and nawab Siraj-ad-daulah.

One day Ramprasad accompanied Maharaja Krishnachandra on a journey by boat down the Ganges. When their boat passed the boat in which the nawab was also traveling, Ramprasad was singing one of his songs. The nawab was captivated by the song when he heard it, and after enquiring who the singer was, commanded him to come to his boat to sing again for him. Ramprasad complied with this request and sang some songs he considered appropriate for the ear of a Muslim ruler, a *kheyāl* and a *gajal*.[19] The nawab however was displeased at this and told him to sing a song to Kali such as he had heard earlier. When Ramprasad did so the nawab was moved to tears, and immediately offered Ramprasad high rank if he would accept his patronage, an offer Ramprasad declined. The moral: "Let the reader judge what kind of man Ramprasad was and what a hard-hearted atheist Siraj-ad-daulah was; so could it have been by other than divine power that he should be so fascinated by those Bengali songs and utter such praise of them?"[20]

Now this could go down as merely one among the "inumerable such wonderful stories like this about Sen" if it were not so strikingly similar to a Caitanya story. In Caitanya's case there was a good deal of opposition to the ecstacy and fervor of his movement. "The aid of the Muhammadan Kazi of Navadvipa was invoked, but the sight of the Nagara-kirtana, [a snaking line of ecstatic singers] organized and lead by Caitanya himself, is said to have convinced the Muhammadan magistrate of its spiritual nature, and he acknowledged it by joining the party himself!"[21]

When discussing the "call" story above I noted the suggestion that Ramprasad might have been drunk, as well as the interpretation that this was a kind of divine intoxication of the saint. This idea is dealt with at greater length later in Gupta's biography. He recounts that Ramprasad once visited the Sanskrit school of the famous logician Balaram Tarkabhusan. When the pundit saw him he said to the assembled scholars, but presumably loudly enough for Ramprasad to hear, "See, there goes that drunkard."

The reactions to this comment are both interesting. The scholars remonstrate with the pundit, saying, "[He] is such a holy man, why do you ridicule him by calling him drunk," thus offering the divine-intoxication theory for his other-worldly behavior. Ramprasad himself replies with two songs. In the first he scornfully points out the utter irrelevancy of the pundit's logic, and ridicules the mercenary nature of his scholarship:

> Death draws near with matted hair.
> Whoever has Kali in his heart has no need of logic,
> Only one who recites scripture for money needs a pot or picture for his worship. . . .

In the other song he also turns to the cause of his condition:

> I haven't drunk wine (*surā*)
> With pleasure I drink nectar (*sudhā*).
> Today my mind is overwhelmed, and people say I'm drunk with wine.

Here Ramprasad puns on *surā*/wine and *sudhā*/nectar or ambrosia, that spiritually-intoxicating drink of the Gods, thus distinguishing his condition from that of mere drunkenness. But as we shall see below, there is probably another layer of meaning below the surface, making this a triple word-play. The pundit's call may amount to the cryptic "There goes one of those wine-swilling Tantrikas!" and Ramprasad's reply a tacit admission that the pundit is correct. If Gupta had provided the rest of the song[22] this interpretation might have been confirmed because Ramprasad says the nectar is distilled from what his guru, a known Tantrika, gave him: purified by the mantra "Tara." It is from drinking this nectar that his mind spins. Anyway, Gupta lets this pass and comments, not without some hyperbole:

> Here, in this beautiful verse, Ramprasad has expressed great learning and the highest spiritual sentiments. God has never before bestowed such wonderful power on anyone, Prasad alone has acquired such grace. The divine power of the Devi herself has possessed his throat, otherwise how could he express such uncommon sentiments.

This amounts to a claim that the divine-intoxication guarantees the divine inspiration of the songs. But the theme of divine-intoxication, or divine madness, has greater significance than this and occurs often in Ramprasad's work, with his claims that the Goddess herself is mad, or drunk, or both, and that he her devotee is happy to share this state with her (see chapter 4 below).

Linking madness to drunkenness however does add a new dimension to the claim. In India while drunkenness is not socially acceptable, madness is tolerated and allows the possessor of the state exemption from most social conventions. So by claiming to be mad (and here it means crazy not psychotic), Ramprasad, like many other saint/singers, is claiming both a state of divine possession and a reason for living outside the usual social conventions. In an excellent treatment of the subject, June McDaniel shows how Caitanya was the model for this kind of madness in Bengal.[23] His biographies are also full of examples of his ecstatic madness. She states, "[Ramprasad's] poetry proved that he was not mad, but rather inspired."[24]

Miraculous events soon color the lives of the saints in any religion and culture, and Ramprasad is no exception. Gupta recounts an incident which came to be part of the standard hagiography. The story goes that one day Ramprasad gathered together materials needed to fix the fence around his house and went off to get a builder to do the repairs. When he returned a few minutes later the fence was found to be already mended, and the materials used up. There was then an "uproar" among the neighbors who concluded, "[The goddess] Annapurna herself has come from Kashi and fixed Ramprasad's fence."[25]

From this story Gupta derives several morals. First, he himself regards this story as one of the "miracle-stories-of-the-saints" type because he comments "So many wonderful happenings like this are reported that if they were to be described they could not be contained in a single book." However, he rather tellingly also notes that Ramprasad himself never made any such claim lest these stories detract from interest in his songs. This I take to be a valuable insight into the character of Ramprasad, who in a quite modern (maybe even post-modern) way wanted his work to be appreciated in its own right, and not because it was associated with any miracle-workings. Such an association might in fact detract from the message of the songs.[26] The fact, noted by Gupta, that the songs soon became revered as magic-working mantras confirms at least part of Ramprasad's suspicion.[27]

Gupta also suggests another function for the miracle story: that it confirms Ramprasad's special relationship with the Goddess, which in turn puts a special seal on his songs as inspired by her. "[T]hey used to say that Annapurna used to come from Kashi every day and inspire his speech and he would compel her to listen to his songs."[28]

The final noteworthy occurence in the life of Ramprasad as recounted by Gupta is at first sight a strange one and concerns the holding of a poetry contest between Ramprasad and one Aju Goswami.[29] What takes place is a duel between two poets, the so-called *"kabir laṛāi,"* [30] in which two poets would extemporise verses against each other, often wittily, to entertain an audience, though there was a deadly seriousness in their intent to outsmart their opponents. Such contests were very popular in the eighteenth century, and Ramprasad was known for his ability to extemporise.[31] In the incident recorded here Raja Krishnachandra visited Ramprasad at his home in Kumarhatt, bringing Aju with him to engage in such a contest. Gupta relates how Ramprasad would sing a song, and then Aju would respond with a witty verse calculated to ridicule that of Ramprasad.[32]

Once again we can find a parallel story in the biography of Caitanya. In his account of Caitanya's life Kennedy states, "Equally irresistible was the might of his argumentation. . . . One incident reveals (all unconsciously) a touch of broad humour,"[33] and he then tells the story of a contest or disputation in which a notable Buddhist with a group of his disciples attempted unsuccessfully to defeat Caitanya in argument. "Humiliated and smarting under their defeat" they try to get Caitanya to eat a plate of unclean rice, and the humor enters when a bird swoops down, eats the rice, and drops the plate on the head of the unfortunate Buddhist notable, cleaving his skull in two.[34] The Buddhist's disciples all convert to Caitanya.

In Caitanya's biographies this incident makes some sense. It demonstrates the disputational skill of Caitanya (as the Ramprasad one does not), it leads to the conversion of many Buddhists (while the Ramprasad/Aju sessions seem to convert no-one) and is part of the myth of Caitanya's conquest of South India. It might seem that the only reason Gupta included the Aju Goswami story is its similarity to the story of Caitanya and the Buddhist (in spite of the differences), and I would not rule this out. Any reader of Gupta's story who was familiar with the Caitanya story could then draw their own moral, Ramprasad was able to impress the secular court of the Raja as Caitanya was able to dominate the disputations in which he participated. It is not sufficient to say Gupta recorded the incident because it happened. Many other things happened to Ramprasad which are not so recorded.

There is another more important reason why we find this recorded by Gupta. Aju Goswami was known as a fanatical Vaisnava who had no time for the adherents of other sects.[35] As Raja Krishnachandra was known to be a devout Sakta "who had no love for Vaisnavas,"[36] it is likely that in this case the contest was arranged not so much for entertainment but to show the superiority of Ramprasad's Saktism over Aju's Vaisnavism. Certainly in the exchanges recorded by Gupta, Ramprasad produces serious devotional songs, while Aju responds with verses which are certainly witty but amount only to doggerel. And Gupta concludes with the telling understatement, "Reading all these verses readers will be able to judge for themselves the disparity between the wisdom and other qualities of Sen and Goswami."[37] (Aju is only "half mad" while Ramprasad, of course, is "mad"!)

## *"Ramprasad" and His Times: Disparities Between Form and Content, Life and Message*

The effect of this account is to virtually deconstruct the life in which it is embedded. When it comes to the content of Ramprasad's message, readers can judge for themselves the wide disparity between that message and what the Vaisnavas have to say. It seems to be quite clear that what is implied here is that Ramprasad's message is vastly superior to that of Aju, and also vastly superior to that of other Vaisnavas, including Caitanya. So the circle is complete—Ramprasad is the model saint/singer as his life shows, compared with that of Caitanya. This life stands as an authority guaranteeing the message. Ramprasad is the model Sakta as his message shows, contrasted with that of Caitanya. This message stands as an authority vindicating the life. Thus in every respect Saktism is held to eclipse Vaisnavism.

Finally we have the strange overall portrayal of Ramprasad as a *prem-bhakta.* This is just assumed by Gupta, with no evidence adduced for it. There is certainly little warrant for this interpretation given in the songs, and Gupta knows this, for he also implies on a few occasions that Ramprasad is a Tantric *sādhaka.*[38] The only way I can see out of this problem is that there is enough ambiguity in the songs to be able to interpret them as advocating devotion to the Goddess ( I will return to this theme in chapter 7). Gupta seized on this to once again assimilate the life of Ramprasad with that of Caitanya, the *prem-bhakta* above all others.

Now with these last points we have also moved from the form of the message to its content. Before dealing with the content more fully below, I hope I have demonstrated sufficiently the proccesses involved in the construction of the life of Ramprasad, and shown how it is modeled after the life of Caitanya.

It remains now to answer the question: Why did the Saktas living in Bengal at this time want to construct such a life? To answer this question we need to look at the religious situation in late medieval Bengal.[39] From the eighth to the eleventh centuries Bengal was ruled by the Buddhist Pala kings. Their rule gave way to the Hindu Sena dynasty in the late eleventh century, and the process of Hinduizing Bengal began in earnest. The Senas were "ardent supporters of 'high' Sanskritic culture"[40] who encouraged the influx of brahmins to spread this culture and were responsible for the establishment of orthodox Vaisnavism and Saivism among the upper classes. Among the lower classes, however, popular indigenous religious practices continued largely unaffected by these "new" cults. When the two systems did come into conflict the indigenous practices continued largely in secret. Under the Palas a form of Tantric Buddhism had evolved in Bengal, and this also continued to flourish in secret.

From the beginning of the thirteenth century the Senas were themselves eclipsed by the Muslim rulers advancing from the west. There followed a period under Muslim rule in which even orthodox Hinduism was under a shadow, but indigenous religion continued to flourish, as can be seen from the large body of literature known as *maṅal-kābya.*[41] The many minor local *Purāṇas* devoted to various indigenous deities were produced during this time.

By the fifteenth century Bengal was governed by the Muslim Mughals, and converts to Islam had been made amongst low-caste people. Buddhism had virtually disappeared, though not without leaving some traces of the Vajrayana and Sahajayana kind. Within Hinduism Siva seems to have been popular, certainly among the merchant castes. The worship of goddesses seems to have been confined to women and low-caste people, and to have been conducted mostly in secret. There was Tantrism, practiced in secret as an underground movement, so that the exact extent of it is difficult to determine. De says, "Tantra, in both its Hindu and Buddhist guises, which were probably exotics in Bengal, . . . had at this time a wild and luxuriant growth on its congenial soil," and adds, "there can be hardly any doubt as to the wisespread character of Tantric teaching in Bengal."[42] There was also some Vaisnavism, but it does seem to have been somewhat moribund. The pandits seem to have been more interested in philosophy than anything else—Bengal had become the preeminent center for the new logic (*nava-nyāya*) school. The brahmins, in this post-Buddhist phase, seemed to have been principally involved in laying strong caste foundations and codifying the lawbooks which were the basis of Hindu social life. According to Kennedy, "Rarely, if ever, has any social order conferred on one group of men power over their fellows so far-reaching and so unlimited."[43] According to a contemporary, Vrindavan-das, "Religion was reduced to a mere form, and there was no faith in men."[44]

All this was to change. We know from the *mańal-kābya* literature that followers of the various goddesses were beginning to assert themselves, especially against the Saivites. They seem to have been largely successful, as it seems clear that by the eighteenth century Saivites were no longer a force to be reckoned with.

Meanwhile Vaisnavism was transformed, and so was Bengal, by the advent of Caitanya (1486–1533) and the Gauriya Vaisnava school. The emergence of goddess cults was slowed, and Tantrism was driven underground. Under the charismatic leadership and inspiration of Caitanya, Vaisnavism became a mass movement, sweeping up people of all castes and radically affecting Bengali society.[45] This transformation lasted until well into the seventeenth century.

Now there was still great rivalry between the different sections of the Hindu community. It is obvious that this was particularly strong between Vaisnavas and the followers of the Goddess tradition. As D.C. Sen records:

> Bengal was during this period [of the ascendency of Caitanya-ism] the scene of animated disputes between Saktas and Vaisnavas. The Vaisnavas would not name the *Java* flower

> because it was the favourite of Kali, the goddess of the Saktas. They called it *od*. The word Kali, which also means ink, they would not use as it was the name of the goddess; they coined the word *sahai* to signify ink. The Saktas, on the other hand, would vilify the Vaisnavas by all means that lay in their power. Narottam Vilas has a passage describing how the Saktas went to Kali's temple and prayed that she might kill the followers of Chaitanya Deva that very night. When the great Narottam Das died, a body of Saktas followed his bier clapping and hissing as a sign of their contempt for the illustrious dead.[46]

And because Vaisnavism was so strong, many Saktas (Goddess worshippers, Tantrikas, and so on) practiced in secret in what were called *gūhya* cults. A notable feature of Sanyal's account of the Vaisnavising of Bengal under Gauriya Vaisnavism is the ubiquitous presence of these secret cults.[47]

But by the eighteenth century Gauriya Vaisnavism had peaked and was declining. "The sixteenth and seventeenth centuries were the golden age of the Vaisnava song, the eighteenth and nineteenth centuries in just the same way were the golden age of the Sakta songs."[48] It had also lost much of its idealism, and there is evidence that caste discrimination, the banishing of which within its ranks had been one of its most appealling features, had once again become a feature within the Vaisnava community. It was an opportune time for Saktas to reassert themselves, for secret cults to emerge and claim popular support. Fortuitously, Ramprasad arrived on the scene with charisma and the ability to compose popular songs which caught the mood of the people, as Caitanya had with his *kīrtans.* And it is my contention that a conscious effort was made to portray Ramprasad as a Caitanya-like figure in order to generate a revival in Sakta fortunes similar to that gained during sixteenth-century Vaisnavism. Just why his songs made him such an appropriate figure for this task we will examine in some detail in chapters 4, 5 and 6. But I believe this does account for the attempt to construct the kind of life analyzed above.

There is one further point I wish to make about the life of Ramprasad, and it is a negative one. There is a school of thought which sees Ramprasad as attempting to effect a reconciliation between Vaisnavas and Saktas, a so-called *Śākto Boisnaba milan*.[49] I believe there is no evidence for this at all. I have indicated that there was rather much antagonism between these two sects. When we look at the content of the Ramprasad "message" we will see that it is strongly apologetic for Saktism, and all references to Vaisnavism, and they are few, are part of an assertion of an underlying monism based on the Goddess as the only Reality.[50] S.K. De sums the situation well when he says, "Throughout the history of the Sakta and Baisnab conflict we find, no doubt, the two sects directly antagonistic to each other and in Bharat Chandra, even in Ramprasad himself, we find the virulence of a militant sectarian zeal."[51] This is hardly a message which is likely to enthuse Vaisnavas. It is for this reason that I wish in this book to insist on the contrast between the form and content of the tradition. For apologetic purposes, Ramprasad is made to look more and more like Caitanya as a saint/singer and leader of a movement. But it is one of the ironies of the story that in content his message is completely different from that of Caitanya.

As Ramprasad has been made to look more and more like a "Sakta Caitanya" he has become less and less an historical figure. But this is the Ramprasad of popular tradition, a saint/singer, called to his religious task, inspired and miraculous, and finally merging into the Goddess who called him and whom he served. This is the Ramprasad of faith who is perceived as the author now of the whole Ramprasadi *padābalī* text.

# *Part II*

# *The Work*

# FOUR

# *Ramprasad's Mad Bitch Goddess*

We have seen that the biographies of Ramprasad, that of Isvarachandra Gupta and all those who followed, do not give us an accurate picture of a recoverable historical Ramprasad Sen. In fact they probably never intended to, because they were written to present the Ramprasad of faith, the faith of the Sakta community (though I am sure that many Saktas do not themselves make this distinction, and believe the biographies are the stories of a saint who actually lived the described life.) As a result when we turn to the songs of Ramprasad, the *padābalī*, we have a group of songs considered, in faith, to be the work of this Ramprasad, and it seems obvious that we should from now on refer to this author as "Ramprasad."

However, I wish to take the methodology employed one step further. Because the post-modern approach sees all authors as fictions we will apply this idea of a "post-modern fiction" to our author and refer to him henceforth as Ramprasad, bearing this fiction in mind. I also regard the body of songs now as the work of Ramprasad, whatever the form of the name given in the *bhaṇitā*. And while the songs are in many ways a diverse collection, with many themes dealing with different aspects of the Goddess's nature and her worship, I will argue that they can be seen as a consistent whole which presents a kind of charter for the devotion of the Sakta community.

## "Who Is This Woman" to Whom Ramprasad Is Devoted?

When we turn to the content of Ramprasad's work it is powerfully obvious that it is the work of someone devoted to the Goddess. As one reads through the songs the most striking feature is the extent to which the Goddess in one form or another dominates. I say Goddess (Devi) rather than Kali, or Durga, because even for the Goddess as his personal deity, his *iṣṭadebatā*, Ramprasad does not use a single name. He uses interchangeably Kali, Durga, and especially Tara, as well as many epithets like Compassionate One, Full of Brahman (*Brahmamoyī*), and so on. More important than the various names he uses, however, are the quite different aspects of the character of the Goddess pictured in his songs.

She is certainly no ordinary Goddess. Take this song, for example:

> Who is this woman with the wild loose hair,
> Who enters the battle with such hatred, accompanied by her frenzied friends Bhairavi and Yogini?
> She knows no shame as she laughs delightedly and dances on Siva's breast,
> Naked and drunk with nectar she becomes absorbed in the terrible fight
> She staggers about, laughing, and crying, "Catch me if you can!"
> Whose wife is she? I don't recognise her, but her half-exposed body entrances me.
> But who else to worship? Lose yourself at her feet,
> Her beauty lights up the whole world.
> How can I fight in the battle, I can't take my mind off her.
> Prasad says, Let's go to Kailash.[1]

Or this:

> Stop that dancing you mad bitch, it will injure Siva's chest.
> He's alive not dead, the Great Yogi is in a trance,
> And the force of your dancing feet will break his ribs.
> Drinking poison has sapped his strength, so when you touch him he loses his mind.
> Drinking the poison didn't kill him, he's closed his eyes to deceive you,

He achieved that dead look through his austerities, to get your feet to touch him.
He's completely stoned, that's why Siva looks like a corpse.
Poor Ramprasad offers this humble prayer,
Stop dancing, Mother, beloved of Siva.[2]

## *The Goddess as Erotic Warrior*

The first and most striking picture presented in Ramprasad's *padābalī* is of an erotic warrior Goddess who rampages through a battlefield, creating havoc and mayhem wherever she goes. As she does so she utters spine-tingling, roaring, intoxicated laughter, and from left and right she seizes her enemies and flings them into her mouth where she crushes them in her bloody teeth. Others she slashes at with her sword till the battlefield lies littered with severed heads and broken bodies. Even more remarkable perhaps is her appearance, because she is absolutely naked, and she seems to flaunt this nakedness which is both erotic come-on and defiant challenge.[3] This is an utterly shameless nakedness. Her loose hair streams like a tangle of snakes, her black body and lolling tongue stream with blood.

Sometimes the scene is different, but the impression is similar. We see her reeling through cremation grounds accompanied by jackals and demons, or dancing drunkenly on the prostrate body of her husband Siva. Around her neck she wears a garland of human heads, around her waist a band of severed hands, and her earrings are the bodies of dead infants. In her hands she holds a bloodied sword and a severed head.

This nude figure is also alluring, even erotic.[4] Through all the horror shines the beautiful nubile body of a sixteen year old woman at the height of her sexual powers which is absolutely irresistable to enemy, husband, and devotee alike. Something of this, and the ambiguity of her nature that this implies, can be seen in this song:

Look, whose wife is this who dances in so frightful a fashion?
Ah, who is this with body like a fresh blue raincloud?
Who is she who falls naked into the pool of Siva's heart?
Who has created this solitary figure
With feet more beautiful than a red lotus—and why is the earth so utterly destroyed?
I have this excessive burning desire to hold her with cords of love,

So she floats gently on the pool of my heart.
Who is she, reproached because her smooth soft thighs stream with blood,
Like angry lightning flashing from a cloud?
Her swelling stomach cradles a lotus like navel,
Her budding breasts thrust firmly upward, and bees drink honey from her mouth.
Her charms are displayed like a white lotus rising from dark water,
Her sensuous mouth and fluttering tongue have entranced Siva,
He seems confused and excited, as if drunk. . . .
Ramprasad says, It's no use fighting with this woman,
Under whose feet Siva lies pretending to be dead.[5]

This is no conventional picture of a goddess. And it is not just its Indian character which makes it so strange, even shocking. It must have seemed just as shocking, as repellent, to a great many people even in his own day when they heard it, especially those from the Vaisnava community

## *The Goddess as Good and Bad Mother*

The next picture Ramprasad gives us is of the Goddess as a good and bad mother.[6] Sometimes she is a kind, caring, providing mother, but sometimes she is a bitch[7] mother who inflicts pain and suffering on her son, laughing as she does so. For Ramprasad, Kali is certainly at times a loving mother—"She takes care of me like my own mother."[8] As such she tenderly takes her son into her lap when he cries—"When I beg her to prevent me from being reborn/ Mother, with a cry of affection, takes her weeping son to her lap."[9] She is a generous mother, who cares for him as if she were his own mother—"I know Mother gives food to her hungry child/ even if he doesn't deserve it,"[10] and she protects him day and night.[11] She is constantly appealled to as one who dispells fear and darkness, and grants release from rebirth and the four aims of life (*kāma, artha, dharma* and *mōkṣa*)—"Prasad says, Because she is a fount of compassion,/ If I meditate on her she will give me the four goals I seek."[12] She is like a boat which carries her son across the sea of suffering and rebirth—"Face the boundless ocean of existence without a trace of fear,/ Kali will effortlessly carry you across to the other side."[13]

She freely bestows her grace and mercy on her followers, and destroys Death, the great enemy. This aspect of her nature is summed up in this song:

> O earthly, birth-destroying Mother,
> You are the only boat on the vast ocean of worldly existence.
> Those blinded by ignorance distinguish between Durga and Siva,
> But both are the one undivided Paramatman, which is your true nature.
> You yourself are *māyā* and beyond *māyā*, assuming a body for the sake of your worshippers,
> Compassionate to the poor, granting them favours beyond their desires.
> One lingers in the garden of bliss through Durga's name,
> If one repeats it at the time of death one becomes Siva.
> Says Poor Ramprasad, Those who can appeal to no good works
> Durga, through her grace, delivers from the three worlds.[14]

But that word "*māyā*" is a worm in the rose. It contains an ambiguity that eats away at this cozy picture of the mother, and opens up a whole new attitude which Ramprasad reveals in many songs, to be set along side that just outlined. Here we find a dark and more menacing side to the Mother's nature—she is at times fickle, even dangerous and untrustworthy. Ramprasad accuses her of being a hard-hearted bad mother and wife—"Listen, to me, O Mother Kali, do I call you hard-hearted for nothing?/ . . . You brought Ramprasad into the world but caused him to be born blind."[15]

Not only does she cause his "blindness" to the real state of the world, she blatantly deceives her own child—"You gave me bitter *nim* to eat, saying it was sugar, and the sour taste remains in my mouth,"[16] she deceives him with her gifts and her promises—"O Mother you are a hard woman, I had found the greatest wish-giving jewel/ But you have turned to stone, deceiving Ramprasad,"[17] "You called me and took me on your lap and then dashed my heart to the ground? What a wonderful mother you are, won't everyone praise you!"[18] She rejects him when he turns to her in his distress—"You are everywhere called compassionate, but there's no trace of compassion in you Mother/ . . . the more I cry 'Mother, Mother', the more you turn a deaf ear to my cries/ Prasad suffers such kicks."[19] In fact she is quite unfit to be a mother, because she is mad, and prefers to get drunk or stoned with her husband rather than care for her children, "You're always fooling about with Siva, Mother, absorbed in pleasure/ You stagger about almost legless from drinking nectar,"[20] and, "Mother is mad, Father is mad . . . who has ever seen such a mad couple . . . Prasad says, I'm confused at the sight of it."[21] So bad is her behavior, and her neglect, that he wonders if he can stay at home any longer—"O Mother how can your son remain at home/ With parents who live under a tree their bodies covered in ashes."[22]

Not only does this mother ignore his suffering, she is in fact the cause of it, "In birth after birth, Mother, you have given me terrible suffering."[23] After complaining that she spins him about like a bull with a ring in its nose for eight million births he says, "There is many a good son, Mother, but never any good mother,/ Prasad is such a good son . . ."[24] For a son to criticize mothers in general and his own mother in particular in this way is very striking in an Indian context.

Anyway, this mother is so bad Ramprasad is sometimes prepared to reject her altogether:

> I will not call you Mother any more,
> You have given me, you are still giving me, such anguish . . . .
> I will not return to my mother's embrace,
> I called to her again and again, is she deaf and blind? . . .
> Ramprasad says, Why does Mother take this line, should a mother be the enemy of her son?
> Day and night I wonder what more she will give than the agony of repeated rebirth.[25]

This mother is not one that Ramprasad can have any confidence in. The worst aspect of her behavior is its inconsistency, which means he never knows what she is going to do next—"You're so two-faced, doing whatever takes your fancy/ To some you give great wealth, to others endless suffering."[26]

This behavior is rooted in her *māyā*, and the capricious play (*līlā*) which results from this aspect of her nature.[27] Ramprasad's understanding of the Goddess's *līlā* is clearly shown in a song which begins,

> All this is the mad Mother's play,
> The three worlds are deluded by her *māyā*.
> The woman's true nature is hidden by her *līlā*—
> She herself is mad, her husband is mad, his two disciples are mad.
> Which is her true form and which her disguise, what her true essence, no-one can say.[28]

Here we find three of the major features of the Goddess's *līlā*; that it deludes all the inhabitants of the three worlds, that it is a kind of game on her part, and that she appears to be quite mad. This is hardly the picture we expect of the divine Mother! And these are themes that are common in Ramprasad's songs. When he says that her actions are like a game, the idea he conveys is that the Mother is toying with her creation, she is playful but her game is unpredictable, it is like the game of a child. Yet the consequences of the game can have momentous significance, as one of the most famous of Ramprasad's songs indicates. Here her game is kite flying, competitive kite flying in which the strings of the kites have ground glass glued to them, the aim being to cut the string of the opponent's kite so that the kite is lost:

> Mother Syama flies kites
> (in the marketplace of the world).
> They are mind-kites, floating in the winds of hope, held by the strings of *māyā*.
> The frames are made from bones and sinews, covered in exquisite workmanship with her own attributes,
> Their strings are coated with the glue of worldliness so their cutting edge is keen.
> Of a hundred thousand of them only one or two break free, and you Mother clap your hands.
> Prasad says, They fly away on the southerly wind
> Over the sea of the world to freedom on the other side.[29]

The "game" here concerns the salvation of individuals, and most of them do not make it. Yet the Mother only laughs and claps her hands! The individuals concerned seem to be able to do nothing about this situation; they are held, deluded, by her *māyā*. Commenting on this song, Ramakrishna, another famous devotee of the Goddess, says, "She is full of play. This world is her *līlā*. She is wilful and full of joy."[30]

It is this willful, capricious aspect of her play that presents the difficulty. Because of it her actions are entirely unpredictable and take on a frightening nature, one even of madness. This is why she is cruel and heartless—"Prasad says, Everyone knows the Mother's *līlā* is cruel and heartless/ So proceed carefully, O mind . . . "[31] We have already seen her drunk, shameless, and half naked, laughing, shouting, totally out of control. In this guise she is almost unrecognizable as the Mother (though Ramprasad says he knows who she is). She completely deludes most people. She is a magician, a trickster, hiding behind a show of magic and pretense. Sometimes she even adopts the forms of other deities, she becomes Krishna and dances in the circle of gopis; in fact, "Siva, Krishna and Kali, I know they are all one," sings Ramprasad.[32] They are all forms of the Mother.

And this fickle Mother is the only mother to whom Ramprasad can turn:

> What a vain hope it was, coming into the world.
> I was deceived like a bee by a painted lotus!
> Mother you fed me *nim* saying it was sugar,
> Because I wanted sweets I had bitterness in my mouth all day.
> Mother, you said you would play with me, but your game has not fulfilled my hope.
> Ramprasad says, In the world's play what was to be has come to pass,
> Now it is evening, take your little child and go home.[33]

This is a very powerful song, with its sharply drawn picture of a mother whiling away the day till evening teasing her infant son. And the message is equally sharp. This mother lies to her own child, she deceives him and leaves him unsatisfied in his play and with a bitter taste in his mouth. Yet it was his initial hope that was misplaced, and what has transpired was inevitable, "what was to be has come to pass." He had no right to expect otherwise.

But most striking of all perhaps is the unexpected twist in the last line. Here is a mother who has just demonstrated herself to be completely untrustworthy, but the son begs her finally to place him on her hip and carry him home. Does he have any other choice? In fact, while Ramprasad does protest against the unfairness of his Mother's treatment of him—"I won't call you Mother any more/ You have given me, and are still giving me, such anguish . . ."[34] most often he displays a confidence and trust that seem to fly (like a kite?) in the face of his situation.

These songs show a vulnerability on the poet's part which is almost palpable even after two hundred years. He expresses the vulnerability of his powerlessness in the face of a Mother whose nature is so ambiguous, and whose behavior is so fickle and unpredictable. When contemplating this mad neglectful mother who roams about in cremation grounds, or stands on the prostrate body of her husband, his father Siva, he says, "I am bewitched at the sight of all these things! O Mother, do whatever you want, but you must destroy my fear of death!"[35] This bewilderment and uncertainty cause him pain which drives him almost mad;

> O Mother, who can understand your *māyā*,
> You are a mad woman, and through your *māyā* you have made everyone else mad.
> In this world suffused with *māyā* no-one realises the trouble they're in,
> This is all Kali's deception, and people think things are as they seem.
> This mad woman has created such confusion, who can know anything about her?
> Ramprasad says, All torment passes if she wishes to be merciful.[36]

This ambivalence and doubt almost tears him apart, "My mind is anguished being pulled in opposite directions."[37] And finally he seems to have been deprived of the one last refuge of the despairing, hope:

> The desires of my heart have not been realised,
> My mind is filled with sorrow.
> My life has been spent in suffering and misery, I no longer hope for any happiness.
> What can I say, Merciful One, with six senses that spoil all I do?
> Sri Ramprasad says, Mother I've racked my brains but am totally bewildered.
> I took refuge at your feet for re-assurance, and I've got the opposite.[38]

## *"Who Is This Woman . . . ?" The Sources of Her Nature*

What are we to make of this strange picture of the Goddess, erotic and militant, drunk, mad, and neglectful of her children, yet often tender and considerate? Ramprasad himself seems unsure. As we have already seen in the songs above, and as we find in a number of others, Ramprasad himself when contemplating his Goddess is prompted to cry, "Who is this woman?" This is a question which might be answered in two ways. The first kind of answer is an historical one—Where does this Goddess come from in terms of the religious tradition? What are the antecedents of this figure in the cultural traditions of Bengal? The second kind of answer is an interpretative one—What does this Goddess mean to her devotees, to Ramprasad, and to any hearer/reader of the songs today? I will in turn answer both of these questions, although here I will deal only with the first, deferring the answer to the second until chapter 7.

I contend that Ramprasad's greatest contribution to the development of Saktism in Bengal, and the reason he became such a prominent figure in that development, was that in his work he achieved a synthesis between the three traditions which are the sources of his picture of the Goddess. These are (1) the classical Puranic tradition, especially that of the *Devī Māhātmya* section of the *Mārkaṇḍeya Purāṇa,* (2) the popular or folk (*laukik*) religious tradition, especially the cults of local goddesses but also including the folk Siva, and (3) the esoteric and secret Tantric tradition.

## *The Goddess of the* Devī Māhātmya

The first source of this picture of the Goddess is the classical Sanskrit *Purāṇas,* and especially the *Devī Māhātmya,* which now forms part of the *Mārkaṇḍeya Purāṇa,* but probably in the first place existed, as it is used ritually and devotionally today by Saktas, as a separate text. In this text the dominant picture is of an erotic warrior Goddess engaged in cosmic struggles against the forces which beset the gods. The mythology centers around three incidents in which the Goddess fights with, and is victorious over, various demons. These are the famous slayings of (a) the buffalo demon Mahisa, of (b) Sumbha and Nisumbha, and the blood demon Raktabija, as well as (c) Chanda and Munda.[39]

In these accounts we encounter a Goddess who fights with all the powers and weapons at her command and almost singlehandedly defeats thousands of demons in the armies of her main foes. She hacks off their limbs, she cuts them in two down the middle, she slashes and disembowels, till the earth is littered with the dead and their entrails and blood flow through rivers. In the process she downs large quantities of wine till her eyes and mouth are reddened, and her drunken roaring and mad laughter cause the heavens and the earth to quake. The noise of this carousing and the twanging of her bow string strikes fear into the hearts of her enemies, to whom it seems like the howling of a hundred jackals (8.22). It even dries up the flow of the rutting elephants!

Sometimes she appears as a repellent emaciated figure clad in a tiger skin, with lolling tongue and garland of heads, her terrible laughter revealing "ugly teeth gleaming within her dreadful mouth" (7.18). Into this mouth she flings her enemies and grinds them to destruction. Eagerly she drinks the blood which flows from the blood demon Raktabija and his offspring and then dances intoxicated by this her favorite liquor.

Into this picture is introduced the theme of her erotic attraction, especially in the episode in which she confronts Sumbha and Nisumbha. She appears to them in all her alluring beauty and arouses in them a passionate desire to possess her. Such a form as hers "has never been seen anywhere by anyone," (5.44) "She is a jewel among women; with the most beautiful limbs" (5.45). The catch is that she can only be had by one who can defeat her in a fight. Sumbha and Nisumbha so desire to possess her that they take up the challenge, to their ultimate cost. They talk of "marrying" her, but the reteller of this myth, and the one in which she slays Mahisa in the *Devī-Bhagavata Purāṇa*, makes it explicitly clear that their desire is for "sexual intercourse" and that the so-called "amorous love sentiments" amount to lust and the desire to possess, by force if necessary (Sumbha & Nisumbha's servants are instructed to bring her by force if she will not yield voluntarily, "dragged by the hair, losing [her] dignity" 5.74). And it is spelled out that "battle" for her means sexual intercourse, it is "the fight of sexual intercourse" (*Devī-Bhagavata Purāṇa* V.XIV.1–12, 41–60, etc.).[40] Finally, out of this erotically alluring Durga figure emerges the terrible Kali, who fights with and kills in turn Sumbha and Nisumbha, thus bringing together these two aspects, the fascinating and the fearsome—the nature of the erotic warrior Goddess.

It is clear from the direct references to these myths in his songs that it is the *Devī Māhātmya* which is Ramprasad's principal source for his portrayal of the Goddess. In song 314 she "strides militantly through the battle/ With a menacing roar slaying Sumbha and Nisumbha."[41] In song 307 she wears the heads of Chanda and Munda in her garland.[42] In song 282 her feet "strike fear into the buffalo demon."[43] In song 62 Kali "kills Nisumbha and destroys all [his armies]."[44] In song 42 "The incomparably beautiful one uses her beauty to kill Chanda and Munda."[45] And in song 297 Ramprasad refers to

> . . . the words of the sage Markandeya
> Who has shown in the Chandi he wrote

Those bastard demons falling to the ground
Where the Mother tramples them underfoot.
At the touch of the Mother's feet the demon's body
Becomes as motionless as Siva in the battlefield.[46]

This *Purāṇa* is also the classical source of the ambiguities, not to say contradictions, which emerge in Ramprasad's picture of the Goddess as mother (though as we shall see there are other sources which are also important). Each of the myths in the *Devī Māhātmya* in which the Goddess emerges victorious over demons is accompanied by a hymn in which the gods praise her for the work she has done. In these hymns, which contain the essence of the "Glorification" of the Goddess, which is what "*Devī Māhātmya*" means, the two sides of her nature are clearly set out.

In the very first hymn (1:54–64) she is both creator of the world and its destroyer, she is great knowledge (*māhāvidya*) and the great illusion, and she is both terrible when she appears armed with all her weapons, and also "Gentle, more gentle than other gentle ones, exceedingly beautiful." In the second hymn (4:2–26) the picture is modified slightly. To some extent the terrible aspect is preserved for evil-doers and the gentle aspect for the good, she is "Sri herself in the abodes of those who do good. Alakshmi [ill fortune] (in the abodes) of those whose soul is wicked" (4:4). So when she appears to the buffalo demon Mahisa she appears with face "Slightly smiling, like the orb of the full moon, as pleasing as the lustre of the finest gold," but the sight of this face arouses Mahisa's anger so that he sees her angry face, "terrible with knitted brows" (4:11f). So her form is one which is "exceedingly charming (yet) striking fear into enemies" (4:21), and the gods pray, "With your gentle forms that roam about in the triple world,/ And with the exceedingly terrible ones, protect us, and also the earth" (4:26). In the third hymn (5:7–36) the dualities persist, she is "the auspicious great Goddess" and "the terrible one;" she is Durga and "likewise the black one" Kali; she is *māyā* in all creatures and also consciousness in all creatures, she is intelligence as well as "the form of sleep." In the last hymn (11:1–34) the theme of her being both deluding and revealing is continued, and related to personal salvation (*mōkṣa*), "Deluded . . . is this entire universe; you, when resorted to, are the cause of release right here on earth," (11:4) and the slightest hint of fickleness on her part is introduced, "When delighted, you destroy all afflictions, but when angered, you destroy all longed for desires." (11:28)

This is not the place to examine the sources of the ambiguities in the *Devī Māhātmya* itself,[47] but it may be briefly noted that it represents a final stage in a process whereby many goddess traditions become welded together into one Goddess tradition. There is perhaps an (unconscious?) recognition of this in Ramprasad when, after asking "Who is this woman?" he further asks, "Is she a goddess or a demon?"[48] This also has its origin in the *Devī Māhātmya* where in 1:58 she is called "the great Goddess (*mahādevī*), the great demoness (*mahāsurī*)."

It is also in the myths and hymns of this Puranic eulogy that we find par excellence the portrayal of the Goddess as the Great Power in the universe. In fact it could be said that the purpose of the *Devī Māhātmya* is just to establish the Goddess as the One, the Greatest power, creator, preserver, and destroyer, greater that any of the other great gods, even greater than all of them together, for on each occasion when the gods are bested by their enemies they are forced to come to her for rescue. And even in the accounts where her power to some extent derives from that of the various gods who endow her with some of the attributes, there is no doubt that the agglomeration of such powers makes her greater than them all. I will have more to say about this in the next chapter.

## *The Folk Goddesses of Village Bengal*

Meanwhile it is obvious that this Puranic material does not explain all that we find in Ramprasad's picture of the Goddess, particularly in her role as mother. Here an important source is the popular goddess, or perhaps the popular goddesses, of Bengali folklore. These goddesses, in their natures and their behavior, are modeled on the homely mothers of rural village life as it existed over a period extending from as early as the eleventh century, and is documented for us in folk traditions and stories which still exist today,[49] and especially in a considerable body of literature known as *maṅalkābya*.[50] Here we find the domestic picture of the Goddess as the house-wife of Siva, who is incidentally not the Puranic Siva but a popular folkloric Siva. And in the various goddesses who are the objects of worship in these tales we discover rather petty and vindictive beings who will go to any lengths to secure their worship.

The story of the Bengali folk goddess centers around her domestic arrangements as housewife and mother, and so must begin with her spouse, the folk Siva. This Siva is not the Siva of the *Purāṇas*, though he is in some ways similar and later becomes identified with him. This Siva may be found in the many *Śibāyans* of the *maṅal-kābya*, in local minor *"Purāṇas"* such as the *Sunyā* and the *Padma*, and in earlier texts such as the *Mṛigulabdha*, an early work which is a kind of proto-*Śibāyan*.[51] And inevitably he appears in the various goddess *maṅals* such as the *Chaṇḍīmaṅal*.

One of the earliest references to the folklorist Siva is a song, possibly from as early as the eleventh century, which was sung by village people as they husked rice:

> Siva won't grow old—he spends all his time
> High on bhang and datura—and making love.
> He takes bhang, datura and balls of siddhi
> And rolls about day and night in the harlots' houses,
> Siva, the lord of deception, among 1600 whores,
> Wasting no time in fulfilling their insatiable desires.
> Or else you'll find him in some cremation-ground or such,
> His body covered with ashes.
> —Everyone says he's gone quite mad.
> Sitting there, surrounded by ghouls.
> This is how he fritters away the year,
> Then pulling on his tigerskin and climbing onto his bull
> Off he goes again to the brothel quarter.[52]

In all the songs which reflect the earliest stratum of the tradition, Siva is portrayed as a farmer and a *bhaṅ*-addict, crude, lustful, lazy, and poor as a result. He orders his wife to plough his fields as if she is his wage-servant. His domestic situation is always far from untroubled, reflecting the strife that is inevitable when an old debauch is paired with a young girl, but in the *Śibāyans* the conflict is leavened with much earthy humor and not a little marriage-bed eroticism.[53]

The Siva who emerges in the later literature is not too dissimilar from this, he remains a domesticated deity, even when other Puranic myths are added. But even in the earliest stages there is evidence of a high devotional tradition associated with this ambivalent deity.[54] The Siva of the *maṅal-kābya* is a mixture of Puranic and folk traditions, the mixture made possible because the Siva of the *Purāṇas* is in many ways similar to the folk Siva—the folk Siva constantly resorts to prostitutes for gratification, the Puranic Siva is lustful and immoral.[55] The powerful persistance of the folk elements is noticeable in the *maṅal-kābya* tradition in the way the stories are incorporated. Take for example the story of

Daksha's sacrifice, a Puranic story well-known in Bengal at this time and incorporated into many *Śibāyans* and also Bharatchandra's *Annadāmaṅal.* The folk tradition is not so much conflated with the Puranic story as inserted in blocks, often creating inconsistencies in the complete work.

The story typically begins with the myth of Daksha's sacrifice, and moves on to the birth of Parvati/Gauri.[56] Once Gauri has been married to Siva, the Bengali material departs from the Puranic with the following stories.

Gauri leaves her comfortable natal home and goes off to live with Siva in his lowly farmer's hut, where she begins to suffer extreme hardship. Her husband is so lazy that she has to do the ploughing herself, but still the farming proves fruitless. Siva wants to abandon the farm, but can see no alternative. So he begs more land from Indra, and gets Visvakarma to turn his *triśūl* into new plough, yoke, and harrow. He tells Gauri to go and borrow seed from Kuvera, but she refuses and he has to go himself, promising that he will repay the loan when the harvest is completed. But in spite of all these efforts there is still not enough to eat and they continue in need.

Even while engaged in his farming Siva still hankers for a return to Kailash, his mountain home, and consoles himself with his prostitute friends. Parvati learns of his desire to leave her, and sends mosquitos, gnats, and flies to bite him and distract him from his plans. He smears himself with ghee to relieve the bites, and is then pestered by leeches. These events bring his mind back to farming, but not to his faithful wife.

So she disguises herself as a *bāgdinī*[57] and goes to the field where Siva is working, and begins fishing! Siva is attracted to this woman and proposes marriage to her, promising that if she will marry him he will flood the fields so that her fishing will be sucessful. The woman asks Siva to give her a brass ring, and in return Siva demands an "embrace." Pretending to oblige, the woman moves off on the path to Kailash, and as they reach there she reveals herself as Parvati.

Siva is highly embarrassed, and Parvati forbids him to enter the house. Just then Narada arrives and Parvati explains her husband's adultery. To help settle their quarrel Narada advises her to request from Siva a conch-shell bangle, the wearing of which will ensure that her husband remains always under her control. She does as he suggests. But Siva in Kailash is a mendicant, and no more successful at this than he was at farming.[58]

How can he get the price of such a bangle? He can find no way out of his troubles.

Her feelings hurt by Siva's failure to comply with her request, which may be interpreted as a refusal on his part to give up his philanderings, Parvati leaves and returns to her father's Himalayan home where Durga puja is in progress. Narada advises Siva to go after her, disguised as a conch seller, and himself place a bangle on her arm and bring her back. Having no option but to comply Siva does so, and when she sees the bangle Parvati is delighted. When she asks the conch seller what its price is, Siva replies, "Its price is surrender." Parvati then recognizes Siva, she holds out ten arms (that is, assumes her Durga form) and Siva himself places the bangle on her arm. Her hurt pride vanishes and they return to Kailash.

The inconsistencies in this story can be accounted for on the basis that we have here an accumulation of folk stories about the early farmer Siva. Elements from the much earlier tradition persist—Siva is a farmer, he is lazy, and unsuccessful. He resorts easily to prostitutes, and has no qualms about adultery with any woman he meets. Parvati's lot is so hard that she returns (or wishes to return) to her father's house. The marriage bond is cemented with a conch bangle. In the end it is recognized that the pair are Siva and Durga, but even as over time the Puranic elements become more dominant, the folk elements persist and remain very important.[59]

The goddess *maṅals* add another folk tradition to the picture of the Goddess. These goddesses, and there were many of them (Manasa and Chandi were probably the most popular; Bhattacharya lists the major ones[60]), were worshiped predominantly by women and the very low castes. Their cult was an underground one, practiced in forests or in secret in the home using waterpots with grains of rice and durva grass, with Tuesday a favorite day for the celebration of the vows (*bratas*) observed in these cults—"Tuesday" is "Mangal-day." Clear evidence for this is found in Mukundaram's *Chaṇḍī-maṅal*, in the story of Khullana and the lost goats. The goddess first sends a heavenly dancer, whom she has cursed, to earth for the purpose of introducing the rites to women. Then we find Khullana searching in the forest for her lost goats and, becoming tired, falling asleep under a tree. The goddess appears to her in a dream as she sleeps and tells her that if she performs the *brata* rites she will find her goats, and instructs her in the rites with the aid of eight demi-goddesses called Vidyadharis. Dasgupta, interpreting the story, says:

> We can see here that when Khullana went to the forest to search for the goats she saw other women performing the *brata* and came to learn of it. Then every Tuesday she would perform Sarva-manala's *brata* sitting at home.[61]

Interestingly, when her merchant husband Dhanapati returns home from the business trip during which all this has happened, Khullana's jealous, older co-wife betrays her to him. She says to him:

> Merchant, I have something private to tell you
> That young thing you are infatuated with has learned witches
> tricks
> Daily she worships the goddess Durga
> With gold pot of water, with long durva-grass on top
> And eight grains of rice inside
> Sandal-paste on its mouth, saffron, musk and betel
> She worships every Tuesday
> Offering rice, curd, fruit, flowers and such
> And with incense of sandalwood
> Blowing the victory conch your wife worships alone
> The friend of the One-eyed One (i.e., Manasa!)[62]

Dhanapati then smashes the pot, which seems in a special way to represent the goddess—an action exactly paralleled in the *Manasā-maṅal* by the merchant Chand when he discovers his wife Sanaka performing the same rite.

In these goddess *maṅals* we see also an attempt to reconcile these folk deities with the Puranic Goddess, but as with the Siva *maṅals* this attempt is rather unsophisticated. The story of Manasa, the snake goddess,[63] begins with the birth of the goddess as the daughter of Siva, conflict between herself and her rival, the goddess Chandi, who is Siva's consort but not her mother, which provides a myth of origin for the "new" goddess and links her with the traditional pantheon. Siva used to go every day to a certain lake to see a beautiful woman promised to him by the god Dharma. His wife Chandi suspected he was up to something and disguising herself as a low-caste *ḍōm* girl followed him one day. Not recognizing her, Siva seduced her, after which she revealed to him her true identity. (To get even, Siva disguised likewise himself, and going to her house, was seduced by her in turn.)

One day Siva went to bathe by the lake, and thinking of his wife discharged his seed which fell on a lotus,[64] ran down its stalk, and landed on the head of Vasuki the *nāga* (snake) king. From it his mother made a beautiful woman, named Manasa, who was given charge of the snakes and their poison. One day walking beside the lake Siva saw Manasa and began to lust after her. Manasa begged Siva to take her to his home, and after some time he reluctantly agreed. Siva hid her in a basket, but his wife Chandi discovered her and a row ensued in which she not unnaturally accused Siva of unfaithfulness. Manasa pleaded that Siva was her father but Chandi was not pacified and put out one of Manasa's eyes with a hot coal. Manasa then killed Chandi with poison from her poison eye but Siva pleaded with her to restore Chandi to life, which she eventually did, and then Siva and Manasa left the house.

They walked until Manasa tired and lay down under a tree to rest. Siva saw his chance to abandon Manasa as she slept, but as he did so a tear of remorse fell from his eye, and from the tear he created another woman, Neto, to be a companion for Manasa.

At the time of the Puranic churning of the ocean of milk Siva drank the poison from the serpent and fell down dead. Chandi then sent for Manasa to restore him to life. The two again argued, and Manasa again shot poison from her eye and killed Chandi. She then revived Siva with some mantras and as the poison came out of him collected it, giving half of it to the poisonous snakes and insects and storing the other half in her empty eye socket. At Siva's request she then revived Chandi again. Advised by the gods to do so Siva then had Manasa married, to a sage named Jaratkaru. They had a son, but Jaratkaru soon after abandoned her.

Here the "new" goddess has been linked with the traditional pantheon through her father, Siva, but is also linked with the snakes, of which she is Goddess, and with the underworld that is probably the original folkloric point of her origin.

Expelled from her natal home because of the jealousy of Chandi, Manasa now sets out to gain human worship, because the divinity of the gods depends on human recognition. The main myth in this respect concerns the Saivite merchant Chand and his wife Sanaka. Sanaka becomes a follower of Manasa and with her six daughters-in-law begins to worship her, represented by a pot, in her home. When he discovers this, Chand smashes the pot with a stick in a rage. A struggle then develops between Manasa and Chand, in which Chand's estates are razed, his six sons are killed, all his trading ships are wrecked, and he is reduced to utter destitution. When another son is born Manasa kills him too.

The conflict is finally resolved when Chand agrees reluctantly to worship Manasa, and in turn she agrees to restore his lands, his fortune, and all his sons. But Chand only agrees on condition that he be allowed to worship her with his back turned, and with his unclean left hand. Manasa agrees, imposing in turn the condition that Chand throw away the staff with which he had earlier smashed her pots. Manasa then accepts Chand's worship and blesses them all.

Bringing all these folkloric elements together we receive a picture of the Goddess as the downtrodden wife and mother, caring for her two sons Ganesh and Kartika under the most difficult of domestic circumstances, with no help at all from her lazy, drunken, and drug-addicted, adulterous husband. She sometimes joins him, and is portrayed as drunk, or mad, and living in cremation grounds with him. But she is also the jealous and vindictive bitch who will stop at nothing to secure worship from Chand, even causing her own devotees, Sanaka and her daughters-in-law, to suffer in the process. (Siva is not only the husband in this domestic menage, as a god also he is so lazy that he does not even come to the aid of his own followers. When Chand is tormented by Manasa he cries out to Siva, but Siva remains totally unmoved and allows him to be converted.)

So this is Ramprasad's "holy family," not an ideal one, but one that any Bengali villager could identify with; a human goddess with all the strengths and foibles of a human wife and mother. Ramprasad's Siva remains very much the folklore Siva, even when he becomes a symbol of Reality (see next chapter). But the Goddess, while retaining her folklore character is now identified firmly with the Goddess of the *Devī Māhātmya*, concerned for the world, and representing ultimate Reality. This combination of the homely village housewife with the Puranic Goddess of awesome power and world domination, so skillfully accomplished that sometimes when he describes this half-naked drunk staggering about in cremation grounds one can hardly tell which of the traditions he is appealling to, (e.g., song 99)[65] represents a decisive step in the growth of Saktism in Bengal. This Goddess is inseparable from Bengali folk culture, one who can be understood as sympathizing closely with the trials and tribulations of her followers, yet powerful enough to deliver them from all the vicissitudes and hardships of the world.[66]

*FIVE*

# *Ramprasad's Tantric Goddess*

## *The Goddess as Power: The Power of the Universe*

There is another much more abstract strain in Ramprasad's work in which the Goddess is portrayed as the Power of the Universe, a power that is also within each individual. This power is Sakti, the creating, sustaining, and destroying female power of the universe from which Saktas take their name as worshipers. It is no surprise then to find Ramprasad naming the Goddess as the *śakti-tattva*[1] or the *ādyāśakti*, [2] the basis of all forms of existence. As the power of Brahman she is also called "full of Brahman," *Brahmamōyī*.[3] Sakti is the creative power of Brahman, so she is acknowledged as the creator, but also as the preserver and destroyer because she acrues those powers also. Hence, "She creates, preserves and destroys with a mere glance/ She keeps the endless universe within her womb,"[4] and, "You are Mother and nurse of the world, you bear heaven, earth and hell in your belly."[5] This "*Brahmamōyī* exists in all things."[6]

Through this association with Brahman the Goddess herself attains ultimate status, because all reality is ultimately one, and so she becomes the sole focus of Sakta concern. "Says Ramprasad truly, you cannot know the mother's greatness/ The queen of the eternal form of conscious Brahman . . . ,"[7] "Brahman is the lustre of the one who is full of Brahman."[8] As Brahman is ultimately—indivisibly one, she *is* Brahman—"Kali's name is Brahman."[9] So "Tara's name is the essence of Reality, I have treasured it on the crown of my head,"[10] "Tara's name is the essence of all,"[11] "O Mother, only your name is reality,"[12] and "You are the *paramārtha* . . ."[13] There is another way to express this, "It says hundreds of times in the Eternal Veda that my Tara is formless,/ But Ramprasad says, Mother exists in everything."[14]

She is, as this reality, the power which gives or contains all knowledge, *Mahāvidyā,*[15] but she is also deluding *māyā* because it is *māyā* that hides the true nature of reality. The world she creates is both herself and reveals herself, and at the same time conceals her nature—"Poor Ramprasad . . . is bound with the rope of *māyā,* a device which you have made, Kali,"[16] "The madman and the mad woman bind beings with the rope of *māyā,* and think it's a game,"[17] "All this is your *māyā,* /Like a magician's illusion."[18]

Ramprasad employs another set of terms to express this same truth, one taken from the Samkhya system and long employed by Hindu thought in general, favored by Tantrikas. She is *prakṛiti* to the Absolute's *puruṣa,* "Primordial Kali the archetypal eternal *prakṛiti.*"[19] But once again as in reality the two are ultimately not two, she is both *puruṣa* and *prakṛiti*—"You are the world-mother, assuming the form of *puruṣa* and *prakṛiti,*"[20] and, "You yourself are *puruṣa* and *prakṛiti,* full of *gunas.*"[21]

This truth is expressed in mythological form when the two aspects of reality are personified as Siva and his consort/Sakti, a picture that runs through the songs both in the domestic depiction of Siva and the Goddess as husband and wife or father and mother, and in the depiction of the Goddess standing on Siva's prostrate body. "O Mother Tara, consort of Siva/ . . . I wanted the place at your feet but Siva has taken it."[22] This symbolises the relationship of the two powers—Siva represents the inert, inactive power of Brahman, and the Goddess represents the active creative power or Sakti. The symbolism here is given an added dimension. Siva is often described as a corpse, that is, inert.[23] But in a number of songs Ramprasad enhances the image by asserting that he is not dead. He appears to be, but in fact, "He's alive not dead, Mother, the great Yogi is in a deep trance."[24] Here the feet of the Goddess touching the body form the ambiguous point of connection of the two figures or powers, they are two but come together in a union. And Siva only "feigns death/ So that he might touch your feet."[25]

O Mother Shyama, get down from there, stop dancing you mad bitch,
He's alive not dead Mother, the great Yogi is in a deep trance.
See that power in your legs, if he hadn't uttered your name his ribs would have broken,
The old fellow took so much poison that you left him, Mother,
And now his bones are brittle.
But the poison didn't kill him, so why should he be dead now?
Ramprasad says, He only feigns death,
So that he might touch your feet.

The feet of the Goddess are the most important part of her body. The attainment of her feet, by the *sādhaka*, represents the attainment of union for Ramprasad, just as it is the attainment of the feet of Sakti that revives Siva.

## *The Goddess as Power: Within the Body of the Individual*

Now because all reality is one, it follows that the body of the individual is no different from the world, and the power in the individual is no different from the Power in the Universe. In fact the body may be thought of as a microcosm of the universe, a fact which has enormous significance for *sādhakas,* because they need look no further than their own bodies in order to attain release. This belief is the basis of song 317:

Come on, mind, let's dwell in Kasi,
See, Varanasi is in the heart-lotus.
The Varuna in the north is the *iṛā*, the Asi in the south is the *piṅalā*,
Manikarni is the *suṣumnā*, to the east curves the Ganges.
With the discriminating attitude of a *brahmacārī* it will be a city of satisfaction.
Siva is its king, and also its queen.
Prasad says, Pile up the *jaba* flowers at those feet.
Beneath the Mother's feet forget about Gaya, Ganges and Varanasi.[26]

Here the whole complex of ideas comes together. The sacred city of Varanasi may be found in the body of the practitioner, and the Mother, worshiped at Manikarni, the one who grants release to the dead, dwells in the heart lotus. But even as the *sādhaka* worships her there he realizes that she and Siva are in reality one, (remember, Varanasi is the city of Siva) and he passes into the trance state of the realization of the oneness of all. And in song 180 also, "Dwelling in the 16 petalled lotus, you will be revealed in the world,/ Ramprasad says delightedly, Tara hides herself within [lit, in the pupil of the eye]."[27]

Parry reminds us "that [Varanasi] provides for the attainment of all the goals of human existence (the *puruṣārthas*)," and insists, "*All* are fulfilled in Kashi . . . Hence, the desire for *mokṣa* no longer excludes the pursuit of *artha* or the pleasure of *kāma*."[28] This would no doubt be of some significance for a Tantrika, for whom "bhoga is yoga," but the significance for the Tantrika extends far beyond this, through a whole series of homologizations, such as the body to a tree, the axis mundi, which recalls the wish-fulfilling tree which also grants the four aims of life, and culminating in that of the *pīṭhasthāns* where the body of the Goddess is homologized to the world and to the body of the individual and to the *cakras* within the yogic body, and finally to Annapurna, the personification of the sustaining earth and granter of the four aims of life, who is also (as we will see in chapter 6) seen as Ramprasad's daughter.[29]

The *pīṭhasthāns* are an important part of the system which links the body of the Goddess to the body of the earth. They derive from the Daksha myth, in which Siva, disconsolate at the death of his wife Sati, wanders about with her dead body, refusing to surrender it for proper disposal. The gods become alarmed at this unnatural occurence, and fear for the fate of the universe if Siva continues to be distracted in this way. Finally they send one of their number to dismember Sati's body in order to remove it from Siva's grasp. The pieces fall to earth, and the places where they fell have become holy sites for Saktas known as *pīṭhasthāns*, important as pilgrimage places and often also centers of Tantric practices.[30]

These *pīṭhasthāns* often have associated with them important cremation grounds, reflecting the connection of the place with part of the dead body of the Goddess. They are also places where the important Tantric ritual of *śaba-sādhanā* meditating on a corpse is practiced. Addressing his own "mind" (again, see below for more on the significance of mind), Ramprasad says, "Unless you dwell within your own power, where will you find a *śabāsanā* [a corpse-seat]."[31] He draws these themes together in a song in which he claims that "all cremation grounds are *pīṭhasthāns*" and then, rejecting the personal aspect of the Goddess as Mother, symbolically performs his own funeral rituals and thus "gets to see her" (i.e., identifies with her) as Brahman, the power of the universe:

> Why do I so vainly call out Mother! Mother! I'll never get to see her,
> Or if I do it will only be when she comes to complete her work of destruction on me.
> All places of death and cremation grounds are *pīṭhasthāns*,
> Finally it dawned on me, it's futile to suffer this affliction.
> So going to the Ganges I burned my effigy on its bank,
> And completed the period of mourning with a *piṇḍa*. Now, mourning over, I'm off to Kashi.
> Dvija Ramprasad says, Why worry about this Mother,
> Mother has gone, now she's called Brahman, so I needn't worry about crossing to the other side.[32]

Here Ramprasad, by symbolically acting out his death, is identifying himself with the power of the universe (Brahman) in the same way that the institution of the *pīṭhasthāns* symbolically act out their identification with the Goddess as that same power:

> . . . the structural homologation of the cosmos, the *pīṭha,* and the devotee [is] startlingly effected by what seems a tragic act—the apparent "Death" of the goddess. This mythic act of self-inhumation, however, is implicitly ironical, yet quite consistent with the unending Sport or Play *(Līlā)* of the goddess; it is so whether she plays with her spouse *(Śiva)* in the thousand-petalled lotus *(sahasrāra)* or plays through the medium of the cosmogony.[33]

## *Kundalini, the Coiled Snake*

The Goddess is also symbolized as Kundalini, the serpent power.[34] Kundalini is the microcosmic form of the universal, macrocosmic power, Sakti, lying in latent form as a coiled serpent at the base of the *sādhaka's* spine in a center known as the *mūlādhāra cakra.* Ramprasad says, "Brahmamoyi lies sleeping within the body, awaken her to consciousness."[35] Through yogic rituals a practitioner awakens this power and causes it to ascend through a subtle channel called the *suṣumnā*, situated along the spinal column. (On either side of it lie two other subtle channels, the *iṛā* and *piṅalā*.) Situated along the *suṣumnā* are a number of other centers (*cakras*, symbolized as lotuses) through which the Kundalini rises. There are seven in all including the *mūlādhāra* at the base of the spine and the *sahasrāra* at (or above) the crown of the head, at the *brahmarandra*.

The aim of this practice is to raise the Kundalini to the *sahasrāra* where she unites with Pure Consciousness, symbolized as Siva, the consort of the Goddess. This union represents the sexual union of the two. During this process the practitioner identifies himself with the Goddess so that the union of the Goddess/Kundalini with Siva is experienced as the union of the individual self with Ultimate Reality, as the ultimate realization of oneness. This identification with the Goddess is achieved through ritual techniques like visualisation, the use of *mantras, yantras* and so on.[36] Part of the technique involves the *sādhaka's* identification of him or herself with this power, so that the Goddess is identified with the inner self of the *sādhaka*. The significance of this identification will become more obvious later.

There are many references to this power in Ramprasad's songs—"O Kulakundalini, pervaded with Brahman, You are Tara within,/ You are the Mother within,"[37] she is "Sakti-Kulakundalini,"[38] "The Mother, as eternal Brahman, is strung on the beautiful *suṣumnā*,"[39] and Ramprasad's duty is to "charm the snake, so don't neglect the mantra for it, or you'll be embarrassed when your father tells you to catch it,"[40] that is, to cause it to ascend by means of the requisite mantras and other rituals to the *sahasrāra*.

In the *sahasrāra* the Kundalini/Sakti/Kali unites with Siva in a union which symbolizes the union of the individual self with Brahman in the trance state. When this has been achieved "one becomes as if Siva."[41] In this process we see a typical instance of the method in which dualistic means are employed to attain the goal of oneness in which all dualisms are finally transcended.

This is the state Ramprasad yearns for, and it is obvious from a number of his songs that he employs Kundalini yoga to achieve this goal—"I have a longing in my heart, O Mother,/ I meditate on your Brahman-form in the *sahasrāra* at the *brahmarandra* with the letters h, l, ks . . ."[42] This is also what he is referring to when he says he wants to "sit at the confluence of the three rivers (the *irā, piṅalā* and *suṣumnā*)" to cool his innermost being.[43] In this song he draws on the mythology that locates one of Hinduism's most sacred sites at Prayag, the confluence of the Jamuna, Ganges, and Sarasvati rivers—the Goddess "attains great holiness at the confluence of the three rivers."[44] By implication, these three macrocosmic rivers correspond to the three microcosmic channels within the *sādhaka*, so that "The one revealed in the heart lotus I have kept in the *sahasrāra,*/ At the feet of Kulakundalini Sakti I have surrendered my life."[45]

In song 113 the Goddess is specifically homologized to the Kundalini, "O Kundalini Brahmamoyi, you are Tara within, you are the Mother within,/ . . . You sleep peacefully there as a red snake,/ Meditating on this a man is blessed."[46] Here also she is linked to the subtle physiology of the Kundalini yoga with its three channels, "Siva and Sakti are to right and left, as the Ganges and the Jumna,/ While Sarasvati graces the centre."[47] She is said to occupy the various *cakras* or lotuses associated with this system, "You are in the *mūlādhāra*, you are in the *suṣumnā* . . . ," "You gradually rise to dwell in the lotuses," and is said to exist in the form of letters, which are those of the mantras associated with the lotuses. And she is identified with the various other Saktis associated with the lotuses (and, incidentally, in the final couplet she is identified with Ramprasad's guru, Srinath—but more on this later).

All of this comes together in another song, in fuller and more systematic detail, presented almost like a textbook exercise. It is probably intended as a reader's guide to the ritual of the Kundalini yoga:

> I have a longing in my heart, O Mother
> I meditate on your Brahman-form in the *sahasrāra* at the *brahmarandra,* with the letters h,l,ks.
> I meditate on Maya Dakini in the earthly *mūlādhāra,* in the four petalled lotus, with the letters b to s,
> Where the Kundalini surrounds Siva with three-and-a-half coils.
> I meditate on Bhairavi Dakini in the six-petalled *svādhiṣṭhāna,* with the letters v to l, in the watery confluence of Varuna, Visnu and Siva.
> I meditate on Bhairavi Likini in the fiery triangular *maṇipura,* with the letters d to ph.
> I meditate on Bhairavi Kakini who sits in the hexagonal twelve-petalled *anāhata,* with the letters k to th, associated with the wind/air.
> I meditate on Sankhari Sakini in the vowels in the sixteen-petalled lotus *bisuddhā* where sits Visnu on an elephant.
> And in the two-petalled lotus of the mind, situated between the eyebrows where Siva's lingam is surrounded by yoni,

> and nectar flows from the moon, with the letters h and ks, I meditate on Hakini.[48]

Ramprasad yearns for this union, which is *mokṣa*—or at least sometimes he does. He says:

> Meditate day and night in your heart, O mind, on terrifying Kali,
> On Mother's naked dark-blue form with its streaming hair.
> Don't you know, mind, she frolics between *mūlādhāra* and *sahasrāra,*
> Always absorbed in the enjoyment of bliss, like a swan in a clump of lotuses.
> Set up in your heart the blissful Durga,
> Light the flame of knowledge, and you will see her true nature as Brahman.
> Prasad says, It is the devotee's hope and great desire to attain
> Union with her embodied form, what's the point of nirvana?[49]

Here he fully acknowledges the goal of union, the monistic state, but implies that he would, at least at times, rather enjoy the lower state, the bliss of devotion to the Goddess in the heart lotus (the twelve-petalled *anāhata*) or the *ājñā* (situated at the level of the eyes, immediately below the *sahasrāra*), sporting among the lotuses like a swan on a pond. The most graphic expression of this desire is found in the much-quoted line "I wish to enjoy sugar, not become sugar."[50]

## *The Goddess in the Lotus of the Heart*

Ramprasad also refers to the Goddess Kundalini Sakti as dwelling in the lotus of the heart, where he often wishes to attain her feet. In this picture she is imagined as standing on/in the *anāhata* lotus, situated at the level of the heart—"Poet Ramprasad says, On the lotus feet of Kali/ The yogin meditates in his heart for the state of liberation,"[51] "If she is enshrined in the heart, her black complection illumines the heart lotus,"[52] "Prasad says, My heart is an upright pure lotus,/ Establish yourself there and dance as the essence of mind [*manomōyī*]."[53] Again, the significance of the Goddess as mind will become clearer below.

There are two reasons for wanting to dwell at this lower level. First, it is believed that a practitioner cannot remain for long in the state of complete union (21 days is the traditional period of the limit of this experience).[54] Second, it is at the lower levels that enjoyment of the experience is possible. This enjoyment of the experience is a feature of Ramprasad's worship of the Goddess. The bliss of this experience of worship is likened to being intoxicated with wine, as he drinks the nectar which flows from her lotus feet:

> Oh, it's not wine I drink, it's the nectar I get when I cry, 'Victory to Kali,'
> This is the intoxication that's befuddled my mind, it's real drunkards who think wine has done it . . . .
> Ramprasad says, drinking that wine will give you the four goals.[55]

So the *sādhaka* is almost out of his mind, but like a drunk is still aware of the world around him and able to enjoy the experience, as one who is in a trance is not. And like the drunk he cannot get enough of his "wine."

> In my heart She [the One full of bliss] is playing, ceaselessly.
> In whatever state I find myself, I will never forget her name,
> And when I close my eyes I see that One with the necklace of skulls in my heart.
> I have lost my worldly wisdom, and everyone says I am mad.
> Well, let them say what they like, I have the Mad One in my heart,
> Sri Ramprasad says, Mother is there in the lotus,
> I have taken refuge at her feet, when I die she won't desert me.[56]

But we must remember that the Goddess thus worshiped in the heart is still the power within, the Kundalini in the heart lotus.

## *The "Mind" Songs*

The identification of the Goddess power within with the self of the individual is important for Ramprasad, and is the theme of a significant group of his songs (some seventy or so out of 321 in the S.N. Bhattacharya collection). I have called these songs the mind songs because the distinctive feature they share is a dialogue Ramprasad conducts with his mind or heart (*man*).[57] For example:

O mind, this is my humble prayer,
That you sing like a trained bird.
Learn what I teach you, mind, and you'll be fed,
But remember the saying, He who won't learn is beaten with a stick.
Learn to repeat the name of Kali, mind, and gain satisfaction at her feet,
Learn that and take refuge in your Self, mind.
Why take to the air and wander about the earth?
How long can you live off the fruit of other trees? Better to stay where you can enjoy the four fruits.
Prasad says, In one fruit-tree you will get this fruit, mind; listen to my plan,
Stay at home and repeat Kali's name, shake that tree every day.[58]

This is typical of these songs. In most of them this form carries through the whole song, though sometimes there is but a single reference to mind. This is however sufficient to identify it as a song of this type.

The most obvious way to interpret these songs is probably to understand the device used here as a metaphor for introspection; the poet is "talking to himself" or reasoning with himself. He does this "out loud," in a song, so that we are now privy to his introspection, because there is something in each song that he wants to teach us. This is an interpretation that I believe can be applied to all the songs discussed here. However, it is not the best interpretation, or the one to be preferred, because it misses the main significance of the mind in these songs.

## *The Songs of the Bauls*

Another interpretation for these songs, one which relates to the theme of this chapter, is that they bear a striking resemblance to another group of songs that have by general agreement been interpreted in a quite different way—the songs of the Bauls. In these songs the Bengali word *man* is universally taken to refer specifically to the so-called *maner mānuṣ* or "man of the heart." Here is such a song, by a Baul known as Lalan Fakir:

Mind, who is this you call your own,
Who is crying so deceptively?

Leave those worldly relatives,
That life-bird is not your own.
If you allow yourself to be deluded by *māyā*
    You will lose the treasure you have gained.
Search day and night for the Beloved one—
Many birds dwell in the one tree,
At the time of your going who will help you?
    Only that one within you [*deha-prān*].
Don't drink the wine of false *māyā,*
Don't forget the path you have found,
You won't come this way again—
    Don't fall into the coils of this Age.
Alone you came into the world, O mind,
And alone, O mind, you will depart.
Siraj Sai says, O Lalan,
    In whose dance do you caper so deluded?[59]

The interpretation of Baul songs, at least with respect to those that concern us here, is uncontroversial. The Bauls are a kind of *sahajiyā* group[60] of usually itinerant religious practitioners, well-known for their songs as the principle form by which they express their beliefs and indicate their religious practices. Like many other *sahajiyās* they often employ a coded language in their songs so that the real meaning is known only to initiates able to interpret the code. The main features of their beliefs, as outlined by Upendranath Bhattacharya in his book *Bāṅlār bāul ō bāul gān,*[61] are (1) that *sādhanā* takes place in the body, which is viewed as a microcosm; (2) that the relation of *sādhaka* and *guru* is particularly important because rituals are often practiced in secret. The *sādhaka* needs to be instructed in the form of these rituals and in the coded language the Bauls employ, and the *guru* consequently has a particularly high status; and (3) the particularly Baul belief regarding the so-called "man of the heart" or *maner mānuṣ.*

It is the latter that Shashibhusan Dasgupta holds to be the distinctive feature of their belief.[62] Its essence can be summed up in the words of a *dohā* cited by him,[63] "There is some one formless hiding himself within our body,—he who knows him is liberated." This "someone" is constantly addressed in Baul songs, as the eternal Beloved residing in the temple of the body,[64] as "another mind within your mind,"[65] and as an "unknown bird" within a cage, the cage of the body of the *sādhaka.*

> The life-long search of the Bāul is for this 'unknown bird', which is felt to be very near, singing within and enchanting us by its beauty and sweetness of song,—but which we are not able to find out. It is always playing the game of hide and seek, as it were. In the pang of his heart the Bāul says,—"Where has the 'Bird of Beauty' hidden itself by deceiving me? I roam about in search,—but cannot find it out,—it has flown far away . . ."[66]

It is a mistake however to search for the bird outside, for it is to be found inside the body. "It is the beauty or the Formless residing within all forms that has entrapped the heart of the Bāul" and which drives him "mad."[67] As such the bird/mind/"man of the heart" is acknowledged openly in Baul songs, as in the song:

> O my mind, let me tell thee,—the 'Man of the heart' is in the heart and search for Him there; why art thou roaming from country to country?—never have I seen a greater fool than thee.[68]

This song illustrates clearly another aspect of Baul belief and practice. On the surface this song is very dualistic. The singer addresses his "mind" as another, and speaks of the "man of the heart" as an other. There is also apparently a dualism between the mind and the man of the heart. But this dualism is only a poetic convention. The goal of the singer is the realization that there is only One, that the mind or man of the heart is the self within this body—and "he who knows him is liberated."

The *sādhanā* practiced by the Bauls to achieve this realization is another noteable feature of such groups, and it has distinctly Tantric overtones. The aim of Tantrism is to realize the oneness of reality. This aim recognizes that before realization is achieved there is duality, or the appearance of duality. Tantrism at both the theoretical and practical levels uses this idea of duality; in the former it uses the symbolism of duality, and in the latter it uses dualistic means—but in both there is implicit the idea that duality of all kinds must be transcended. The principle involved here is clearly indicated in the *Kulārnava Tantra,* when it says, "As one falls onto the ground, so one must lift oneself by the aid of the ground."[69] How this works is illustrated by Dasgupta:

> In Hindu Tantricism [the] two aspects of the absolute reality have been conceived as the *Śiva* and the *Śakti,* or the primordial male and the female. Again, one of the fundamental tenets of all the esoteric schools is to hold that the human body is the epitome of the universe, all 'truth' . . . is contained within the body. Consistent with this view it has been held that *Śiva* resides in the *Sahasrāra* . . . as the principle of pure consciousness and *Śakti* as the principle of the world-force resides in the other pole of the *Mulādhāra-cakra* in the form of a coiled serpent. Now, the *Sādhanā* consists in raising the coiled force from the one pole to the other and to unite her there with *Śiva,*—and this union of *Śiva* and the *Śakti* or the male and the female are contained within the person of every man and woman.[70]

Consistent with this, Goudriaan emphasises the importance of the body as the site of this realization, *sādhanā* being based on "the elaboration of a mystic physiology in which the 'microcosm' of the body is identified or homologized with the 'macrocosm' of the universe and the world of the gods."[71] Tantric *sādhanā* in all its forms has as its goal the realization within the individual of the integration or union of these forces, however visualized. Noteworthy are Kundalini yoga practices, mentioned by Dasgupta above, and the use of sexual yoga techniques for which Tantrism has become famous or infamous (depending on one's perspective). Both of these techniques were and are employed by the Bauls.[72] Another method involves the visualizing of the two poles as the individual self and the Absolute—represented by a deity such as some form of the Goddess. *Sādhanā* then takes the form of ritual which appears not dissimilar to ordinary devotion, or *bhakti,* but which actually is conceived somewhat differently, for the object of the exercise is to introject the deity within the body so that the union of the "two" might be realized there. As the *Gandharva Tantra* has it:

> A man should worship a divinity *(devatā)* by becoming a divinity himself. One should not worship a divinity without oneself becoming a divinity. If a person worships a divinity without himself becoming a divinity, he will not reap the fruits of that worship.[73]

This aspect of Tantric *sādhanā,* while less popular amongst Bauls, has been adopted by many Sakta devotees, and as we will see below is also important for the interpretation of Ramprasad's songs.

But let us now look more closely at the songs themselves, and at the parallels between the two groups of songs, those of the Bauls and the mind songs of Ramprasad. As an example of the former, consider the collection of songs by Lalan Fakir in Bhattacharya's *Bāṅlār bāul ō bāul gān,* where he lists 210 songs. Therein is a reasonable number of songs, by a reasonably well-known and representative Baul.[74] When we look at this collection we find that there are sixty-three songs in which Lalan addresses his mind *(man)* in a way that is so similar to Ramprasad that in many cases if the singer's name were removed from the *bhaṇitā* it would be difficult to tell which singer had written which song. So we can say that the first significant finding is that the same style or form is found in the songs of both singers.

## *The Place of the Body in* Sādhanā

There is a prominent place given to the body as a vehicle for the mind in the songs of Ramprasad. The two most prominent images are of the body as a house or room, with the orifices as windows, etc., and the body as a boat that carries one over the sea of life.[75] The image of the boat carrying the individual across the troubles of life is a common one in riverine Bengal, but the boat is usually the deity who provides salvation, not the body of the individual.[76] In these mind songs the boat and the house are definitely the body in which is to be found that which will save the *sādhaka.* This is particularly clear in one song, in which Ramprasad mentions the "body-boat" *(dehatorī)* that will carry the mind through the storm of the passions.[77] More common is the image of the house in which is hidden a treasure that must be found:

> If you find anything when you light the lamp in your darkened room
> O mind, then put out the light for you have gained a treasure.
> Wise one, you live in a palace, look within yourself,
> Ramprasad says, When you lift the net all you see is yourself.[78]

The message here is quite clear, the goal of realization takes place within the body, and one is to search within and not look to any external means. This is a theme clearly enunciated by Lalan—"Have I been deluded, mind,/ I have been looking outside for the treasure of the house."[79] But a much more prominent, and more famous form of this theme, is the likening of the *maner mānuṣ* to a bird in a cage, where the cage is the body of the singer/*sādhaka*. This allows the singer to speak of the *maner mānuṣ* as something elusive, like a bird that can fly away, but must be captured and kept within the cage.

> See how the unknown bird comes and goes from the cage
> within.
> In order to hold it I have placed a mind-fetter on its foot. . . .
> Mind, your only hope is to stay in the cage,
> The cage you have made of green bamboo.
> One day the cage will fall down,
> Lalan says, When the cage is opened
> That bird will fly away somewhere.[80]

Lalan is saying that the "bird" must be kept within the cage of the body until finally at the time of death the cage falls down and breaks open. Then the mind/bird/self is released. However, there is the hint in some songs that the bird is in the cage all the time, and it is the delusion of *māyā* that causes one to think that the bird has flown, as in song 27 cited above[81] and in song 50:

> When the moon is reflected in the water,
> Who can catch it in their hands?
> Just so it always remains, . . .

Here the moon is the elusive *maner mānuṣ*, present in the body (the water) but eluding Lalan's grasp.[82]

Most commentators emphasize that the search for the elusive *maner mānuṣ* or the "unknown bird" is one of the major themes of Baul songs. "By following the instructions of the guru, [the Baul] seeks to recognize the 'unknown bird' or the 'elusive Man' and to capture Him."[83] It is the basis for all Baul *sādhanā*. Dasgupta goes so far as to say, "it seems that out of their doctrines and practices their search for the 'unknown bird' *(acin pākhī)* that mysteriously comes in and goes out of this cage of the human body emerged as the most striking feature,"[84] and:

> [The 'Man of the heart'] is like an 'unknown bird' that comes within the cage of this corporeal form,—and it is the greatest wonder with the *Bāul*, how the 'unknown bird' is playing its eternal play of coming and going,—the play of self-manifestation and of returning once more to itself. Though the bird lives in the

cage of the human body, it floats in the boundless sky above. The life-long search of the *Bāul* is for this 'unknown bird', which is felt to be very near, singing within and enchanting us by its beauty and sweetness of song,—but which we are not able to find out. It is always playing the game of hide and seek, as it were. In the pang of his heart the *Bāul* says,—"Where has the 'Bird of Beauty' hidden itself by deceiving me? I roam about in search,—but cannot find it out,—it has flown far away . . . "[85]

There is clear evidence in Ramprasad's mind songs of the use of this image. For example, there is the recurring idea that the mind is a pet bird that is kept in a cage. The word Ramprasad uses for cage is *piñjar,* which also means ribs or thorax, so the idea of mind as the self within the body is clearly intended. That the bird is a pet or tame conveys the idea that effort has to be exerted to maintain control over it, and in two songs there is more than a hint that the bird might escape, or become "lost" and deceived:

Mind, don't you see what danger you are in . . .
You have tamed the bird in the cage, but who will guard it,
Don't you realise it has nine doors?
You have bad friends, six self-willed ones,
And you do what they say—What daring! . . .[86]

On whose advice have you forgotten, O my pet bird
That you live within me. Why do you deceive me?
I have kept you in a cage, to repeat the name of Kali.
O Mind, you deceived me, much to the delight of my enemies. . . .[87]

And in song 236, quoted above, we find the idea that the mind/bird has to be trained, lest it take off for some distant tree to eat the fruit of passion, which is contrasted with the "four fruits" *kāma, artha, dharma* and *mokṣa,* which it can enjoy if it stays "at home" within the body.

The *sādhanā* employed by the Bauls in taming the bird, or realizing the true nature of the *maner mānuṣ,* is heavily indebted to Tantric *sādhanā.* Though this aspect of the Baul tradition was, and to some extent still is, overlooked or deliberately ignored by many who appreciate Baul songs,[88] Tantric influence is undeniable. Upendranath Bhattacharya makes this abundantly clear, and it seems obvious from the songs. Obvious, that is, once one realizes that

Tantric elements are often referred to in a kind of code. Tantrism involves the use of many secret rituals and secret teachings, and a coded language, *sandhyā bhāṣā,* was employed to convey information about them to initiates, while concealing it from the uninitiated. Investigation has shown that the Bauls also practice secret rituals, and that there are coded references to these in the songs. Sexual rituals, *moithun* yoga, were the most secret rituals practiced by both Tantrikas and Bauls.

## *The Importance of the* Guru

Because so much in the Tantric tradition is secret or restricted to initiates, the *guru-śiṣya* relationship is very important, as it is the basis of the transmission of both teaching and practice. The *guru* has a very important role, and is given very high status.

In the songs of Lalan we find clear evidence of the Baul use of Tantric practices in *sādhanā,* and the tremendous importance invested in the *guru.* There is the underlying theme that the body is the place of *sādhanā* and realization, and there are more specific references to rituals like Kundalini yoga. In Lalan's song 204 the *maner mānuṣ* is referred to as a "golden man" or precious treasure. He says that "through the grace of his *guru*" he will be able to "know" or realize this man "in the two-petalled lotus" of the *ājñā cakra,* situated according to Tantric physiology, between the *sādhaka's* eyes. In song number 50, after a similar reference to the "two-petalled lotus" Lalan says:

> Have I been deluded, Mind, I have been looking outside for
> the treasure of the house.
> Siraj Sai says, Lalan will wander about
> Without any understanding of spiritual reality.[89]

Here Lalan is referring to the mistake one might make, when deluded, of pursuing spiritual reality or the treasure of the house outside of the body, either in the form of some conventional deity or by means of conventional devotion. The one who sees through the delusion, Siraj Sai, is Lalan's *guru.*

Ramprasad more than hints that the training of the mind involves Tantric practices. In song 317 the image is of pilgrimage. But Varanasi is in the "heart-lotus," the *anāhata cakra* of Kundalini yoga, so his mind already dwells there as the man of the heart. The body is seen as a microcosm, and the various *ghāts* at Varanasi are assimilated to the *iṛā, piṅalā,* and *suṣumnā* (channels in the body according to the Tantric physiology associated with Kundalini yoga). In song 236 quoted above,[90] the tree that produces the four desired fruits is the *suṣumnā,* the channel of the Kundalini, and to "shake" the tree is to activate the Kundalini by means of *sādhanā.* When in song 240 Ramprasad talks about his mind's inability to "catch the snake," he is again referring to the Kundalini. It is, he says, the mind's duty to charm the snake and one must not neglect the mantra needed to accomplish this. It is only by means of the mantra that one may grasp the "treasure" and banish ignorance. Song 286 is an excellent example of this theme, referring explicitly to the use of Kundalini yoga:

> O mind, you have escaped from my control,
> Abandoning the pure sweetness of the lotus flower, you have become intoxicated with the taste of earthly enjoyments.
> And you have not awakened, O mind, the Kundalini power (*śakti-kulakuṇḍalinī*), . . . [91]

Ramprasad also acknowledges the importance of his guru who, like Lalan, he names in one of these songs:

> Mind, if you want to take my medicine,
> From time to time take this *paṭal* juice given by Srinath.
> Renounce prosperity, and serve the conqueror of death [Siva],
> Ramprasad says, Only then, mind, will you be cured [lit. 're-leased,' *mukta* ] of the disease of birth.[92]

Here *paṭal* is both a bitter vegetable used as a medicine, and a *mantra* given by his own *guru* Srinath. His *guru* is seen as the great benefactor of his life, giving the *mantra* that will cure all his problems. In song 78 he calls on his mind to "repeat day and night the *mantra* given by the *guru*" . . . and the mantra is obviously Tantric.[93]

The *guru* is also the one who gives the treasure the *sādhaka* is seeking, characterized as "ambrosia" or "nectar" in 225.[94] In fact, in one song the *guru* is almost as important as the treasure itself:

> Come, mind, let's you and I sit together in a solitary place.
> United in mind and heart we will make a cage at the *guru's* feet,
> Hiding at those feet we will drink nectar, then what concern need we have for Death?

My mind wants to steal this treasure, but I don't understand the secret,
How can I spend that treasure the *guru* has given, his reassuring presence?
Sri Ramprasad's hope is to cut away the thorns and clear the way
To the city of nectar where, holding the *guru's* name in his heart, he may drink it.[95]

The "cage" here is the same cage in which the elusive bird dwells in songs referred to previously, so the idea here seems to be that the *guru* actually dwells within the *sādhaka.* "Sitting in a solitary place" refers to secret *sādhanā.* "Drinking nectar in the city of nectar" may be taken here as symbolizing the final state of blissful union. That such a state is the ultimate goal of the poet seems clear.

## *The Question of Devotion*

Ramprasad's mind songs also appear to contain hints of what sounds like theistic devotion, as in song 211:

Are you mad, mind, searching about for her in a darkened house?
You can only know her through ecstatic love (*bhāb*), what can you gain without it? . . .
You couldn't find her with the six philosophies, nor in all the Vedas and Tantras,
She enjoys the taste of devotion, ever dwelling blissfully in the house.[96]
To experience that the Great Yogi practiced from age to age.
When that emotion arises it draws one like a magnet attracting iron.
Prasad says, She I regard as Mother must I reveal openly?
You must understand her, mind, through signs and gestures.[97]

Here Ramprasad seems not only to be introducing the idea of theistic devotion with references to Vaisnavite love-devotion, but also to be renouncing any allegiance to the Tantras. How are we to explain these apparent inconsistencies?

I believe he only "seems to be" renouncing allegiance to the Tantras because it is possible to interpret his references differently.

He may be adopting the same position noted among other fringe groups, like the Bauls, who in their orthodox scriptural forms reject all traditions, including the Tantric, substituting for them instead an eclectic tradition based on the *guru* as authority. A person will get nowhere relying on any sect or scripture, Vedic or Tantric. Ecstatic love of the Mother will be realized only if one listens to the "hints and gestures" of the *guru* (although *mantras* are probably implied by these "hints and geatures," or possibly Tantric coded language, *sandhyā-bhāṣā*.) It is part of the convention of madness that Ramprasad adopted that allows us to interpret his work outside any strict orthopraxy.

The second question is, how are we to interpret his apparently theistic, devotional references? I believe the answer again lies within rather than outside of the Tantric tradition. Although there is a strong emphasis in Tantric *sādhanā* on yogic discipline, including Kundalini yoga and secret rituals (sometimes of an extreme kind), there is also considerable emphasis on Goddess worship, or *pūjā*. But this is not to be confused with what we find in *bhakti* cults like the Vaisnava ones. They might appear to be similar to the casual observer, but what is going on is quite different.

The *pūjā* aspect of Tantric ritual is well-described by Sanjukta Gupta[98] who begins by stressing that *pūjā* and *yoga* are of equal importance. If this aspect of their *sādhanā* is not prominent in Tantric texts, it is possibly because "the theology of the Goddess-worshipping Tantric religion had already firmly imprinted its precepts, code of religious behaviour and duties on its followers long before these were recorded in Tantric texts" around the fourteenth century.[99] Popular forms of the Goddess worshiped in this way by Tantrikas are Kali and Tara.

*Pūjā* of the Goddess takes three forms, internal or mental *pūjā*, repetition of mantras (*japa*), and actual offerings to the Goddess. Thus three important areas of Tantric concern are employed, namely body, speech, and mind.[100] We can note here that all three involve, or are confined to, the body. And we can note also the importance of mind, because the emphasis here is predominantly mental. *Japa*, the repetition of mantras or of the name of the Goddess, may be performed with the aid of a rosary of beads, but ultimately this aid should also be dispensed with, and the repetitions performed only in the mind.

The mind comes into its own at the mental stage of the ritual, when "the votary interiorizes the deity and envisages her as identified with his own self . . . The worshipper interiorizes the whole of the external pūjā with a strong tendency to idealize its concrete elements by transforming them into ontological abstractions . . . "[101]

> '[W]hatever sensual pleasure (the Tantric) derives by using any of his senses, he attaches the pleasures to the supreme Being and it becomes an item of offering (to the deity)'. This very assertion [by Abhinavagupta] that there is no distinction between the votary's own sensation of pleasure and the pleasure of his deity makes the monistic (advaita) stand-point clear to the Tantric. The whole point of performing *āntara* [internal or mental] *pūjā* is to gradually establish this notion in the mind of the Tantric and keep him constantly aware of it.[102]

Gupta then makes it clear that the purpose of this *pūjā* ritual is that the *sādhaka* should experience the complete identity of his *iṣṭadebatā*, his *guru* and his own self. One step in this process is to envisage his own self as the Kundalini, and as a manifestation of the Goddess, rising to the *sahasrāra* lotus where the supreme Being and his *guru* are already situated in union. There his own self also becomes part of this union. This lotus contains within it nectar, or *amṛita*, which is identical with the Goddess. Thus "the Tantric indirectly gets a taste of that bliss, which is represented by the more or less actual sensation of being bathed in, or saturated with, *amṛta*."[103]

This explains, I believe, the famous saying of Ramprasad (from one of his non-mind songs, "I want to enjoy [the taste of] sugar, not become sugar."[104] It is also very interesting that one hundred years later Ramakrishna, who was very fond of quoting the line about "sugar," interpreted song 211 discussed above in roughly the same way we do. After singing the song on one occasion, he is said to have gone into a trance. When he regained consciousness he said, "Ramprasad . . . is talking about knowing the one whom the Vedas call Brahman—that one I call Mother. That which is *nirguna* is also *saguna*. That which is Brahman is also Sakti . . . If you love her you will realise Brahman."[105]

Perhaps the reason that Ramprasad provides such vivid pictures of the Goddess is because one of the most important techniques of realization is the technique of visualization. Eliade in his book *Yoga: Immortality and Freedom*, talks about a *sādhanā* of several stages of which the first is "to 'visualize' a divine image, to construct it mentally or, more precisely, to project it on a sort of inner screen through an act of creative imagination."[106] This is followed by the important step of "identification with the divinity [the visualisation] represents." But as Eliade points out this is no mere "mental exercise." "To identify oneself with a divinity, to become a god oneself, is equivalent to awakening the divine forces that lie asleep in man," which leads in turn to the discovery of "the ontological unreality of the universe and its 'gods'."[107] The Goddess then represents a reality very like the *maner mānuṣ*, and the visualization technique comes to look very much like that of Kundalini yoga.

Here again I think the difference between Lalan and Ramprasad is more apparent than real. In song 192 *bhakti* is seen by Lalan as a ladder he must seize and ascend. In song 204 the "man" becomes a "golden man" in the two-petalled lotus, one who must there be worshiped if he is to "cross over" to the other side. In song 62 one "receives consolation" in devotion, and Lalan holds up as examples Prahlad's devotion for Krishna and Lakshmana's for Rama. But the references are by no means so common, nor so specific. In song 45 worship (*bhajan-sādhanā*) is rejected. And in songs like 204 one is left in no doubt that realization comes solely by means of discipline within the individual (*mānuṣ-bhaja*). So when devotion is mentioned it is to be taken to mean *pūjā* of a Tantric nature, not conventional dualistic *bhakti*.

In all Tantric sects or those influenced by Tantrism it must be remembered that deities are present more for what they represent than for what they are. Their presence allows for a devotional attitude to be adopted by the *sādhaka* that seems to be akin to Vaisnava *bhakti*, but for the true initiate traditional *bhakti* is not involved because the intention of the Tantric *sādhaka* is quite different from that of a *bhakta*. After listing all the yoginis, gods and goddesses in the *Tantrasār*, and there are many, Bhattacharyya says:

> It should be noted . . . that these deities have only a symbolic significance in Tantric cults—their names are used to define some special positions in the *cakras* and *yantras*, each of them representing a typical attribute, or quality, or element and not the concrete person of the sectarian god.[108]

## *From Underground, the "Secret" Cults Emerge into the Light*

To further account for differences between songs that are otherwise similar in style and content we need to go back to a period earlier than that of either Lalan or Ramprasad. In his book *Bāṅlā kīrtaner itihās,* H. R. Sanyal describes the situation in Bengal at the time of Caitanya (1486–1533) and the rise of Bengal Vaisnavism, a situation in which there was a proliferation of esoteric, secret cults (*gūhȳasampradāy*) that now represent the ever-present "other" against which the self of Gauriya Vaisnavism was formed. (I have already argued, in chapter 3, that Gauriya Vaisnavism was the "other" against which in turn an emergent Saktism asserted its selfhood, strengthened in its effort by the life and work of Ramprasad.)

Among the groups Sanyal mentions are Buddhist and Vaisnava Sahajias, Nathpanthis, and Vamachari and Kaula Tantrikas.[109] These movements tended to be anti-caste and even to accept untouchables,[110] and for this and other reasons—such as their use of the *pąčamakāra* (including sexo-yogic rituals),—they were considered quite beyond the pale by polite orthodox society, and so flourished as underground movements. Another distinctive feature that most of them shared was their belief in the human body as microcosm:

> All these secret sects employed left-handed Tantric or *siddha*-yogic methods in their *sādhanā*. There were variations in practice among these sects but the basic philosophical outlook of almost all of them was the same. They were human-centred [*mānobbādī*]. They believed that within each human individual the whole world lay mysteriously hidden, therefore if in *sādhanā* the individual had recourse to the body it was possible to pass beyond individuality and attain the whole universe . . . .This is the highest knowledge. According to the Tantra-sastras this undivided universality is attained by following the path of sexo-yogic *sādhanā*. *Puruṣa* and *prakṛiti*, man and woman, appear to be different. But through this yoga one passes from a state of dualism to the enduring state of blissful union.[111]

Because these groups were largely secret by nature it is hard to determine how many people followed them, or what their sociological makeup was. But while they would obviously appeal to low and out-caste people, there is evidence that they appealed to members of the higher castes as well.[112] It also seems that they were very popular.[113]

Sanyal also notes that among the followers of secret cults there was later a tendency to incorporate elements of *bhakti*, no doubt because of its growing popularity above ground, and because of its emotional appeal. In such a diverse body of groups one could pick and choose from a wide selection of beliefs and practices, which accounts for both the similarities and the differences to be found between them.

This was the mileux out of which both Ramprasad and his brand of Saktism, as well as the Bauls later, emerged. They can both be seen as having roots deep in this underground soil, and both adapted differently to its varied influences. But the common elements come from this shared background. That they do represent different developments of some common ideas is seen in the rather obvious fact that Ramprasad does not employ any direct mention of the *maner mānuṣ*. This omission shows that Ramprasad placed emphasis more and more on the symbolic figure of the Goddess, a direction almost entirely absent from Baul songs, possibly because of Buddhist Sahajiya or Muslim influence.[114]

## *Ramprasad the Tantrika*

In conclusion, Tantrism is the dominant strain in the work of Ramprasad. If Ramprsasad showed great skill in combining the classical Puranic with the popular folk traditions, he showed genius in then conflating this with the existing Tantric tradition, albeit underground in Bengal. The picture of the Goddess as the great Primordial Power, the one who creates, sustains, and destroys the universe (as described at the beginning of this chapter) can be identified with the Goddess in the *Devī Māhātmya:* "You are sakti . . . as is written in the Chandi,"[115] but she is also more than that. Tantrics were fond of using the Samkhya terminology to express the dualistic nature of reality as it is before oneness is realized, and in song 136 Ramprasad brings many of these ideas together. Mother Tara is daughter of the mountain and the consort of Siva; these two reveal themselves as *puruṣa* and *prakṛiti.* She deludes but also bestows grace and delivers from death, and she resides in the *mūlādhāra.* This power is also to be identified with the mind of the individual *sādhaka:*

> O Mother, merciful deliverer, give me refuge at your lotus feet,
> You who banish the fear of approaching death.
> O Tara, wife of the merciful Lord, in the form of the *praṇaba*
>     you are the boat which carries one across the ocean of existence,

You are *saguṇā* and *nirguṇā*, gross and subtle, the uncaused cause of all,
Dwelling in the spotless *mūlādhāra* lotus.
Mother of the universe, beyond all scriptures [*āgama nigama*], as *puruṣa* and *prakṛiti,*
You play like a swan within all beings, O daughter of the mountain,
Manifest three-fold as creator, destroyer and sustainer.
The nectar-filled name of Durga is the only place one may realise identity with the Absolute [*koibalȳadhām*].
The ignorant continually suffer a three-fold affliction, drowning in a well of poison,
Says Ramprasad loudly, I know what that poison does.[116]

It was the work of Ramprasad more than any other that popularized and legitimated this tradition for the common people. The general public was afraid of and ignorant of what went on in secret Tantric circles, and even brahmins who practiced *śakti-sādhanā* followed a Vedic or Puranic path. It has been said that "no-one could write a song about this secret *sādhanā.*"[117] Ramprasad could and did, and his songs became the primary vehicle for the spread of this *sādhanā*. They were prized for this quality, as Gupta noted in his biography. Because of Ramprasad's work, fear and ignorance about this practice were dispelled such that these practices became commonplace among all levels of society.[118]

Tantrism up to the time of Ramprasad was not only a secret esoteric cult, it was largely a Sanskritic one, and therefore inaccessible to ordinary Bengalis.[119] It was probably during Ramprasad's time, and at the court of Raja Krishnachandra, that one of the most popular of these Tantric digests, and one which influenced the work of Ramprasad,[120] the *Tantrasār*, was translated into Bengali by Chandrakumar Tarkalankar. The links between this work and the court of Krishnachandra are strong, and one of the court pundits, Ramanandatirtha, prepared a revised version of it.[121] The Tantra itself is a Sanskrit work, compiled probably about 1580 by Krishnananda Agamabagisa, a "massive digest [which] deals with all important topics of Tantra," including descriptions of numerous gods and goddesses, and the modes of their worship.[122] Banerji says, "Krishnananda is credited with the conception, for the first time, of the Kali image current in Bengal. He is also believed to have introduced the worship of this goddess in the province."[123]

Just how strong Krishnananda's influence on Krishnachandra himself was can be seen from the tradition "that Mahārāja Kṛṣṇacandra . . . of Nadia ordered all his subjects to perform this worship on threat of punishment. As a result more than ten thousand images of the goddess came to be worshipped on this occasion every year in the district of Nadia."[124]

Ramprasad's popularized Tantrism by combining it with the classical Puranic and popular folk goddess traditions. That this was successful can be seen in the way it was to dominate the nineteenth century in Bengal, an age which, religiously speaking, can be seen as the age of a popular Tantric Saktism. Confirmation can be found in the tremendous importance of certain *pīṭhasthānas* at this time,[125] and in the importance of figures like Bama Ksepa[126] (who was associated with one of the most famous of them—Tarapith) and Ramakrishna.[127] This Tantric influence extended also to Rammohun Roy and other members of the Brahmo Samaj.[128] Even the picture of the Goddess described in the previous chapter, the martial and erotic Goddess, has Tantric elements that Ramprasad added to the picture given in the *Devī Māhātmya.*

Ramprasad's *Bidyāsundar* may be seen as a Tantric *maṅalkābya* devoted to the glorification of Kali. Sundar accomplishes many of his exploits through the use of powers acquired in Tantric *sādhanā,* and the work ends with the glorification of Kali in a celebration of the corpse ritual *śab-sādhanā.*[129] This is one of the most Tantric of all rituals, symbolizing the Tantric idea of facing the final enemy, and the ultimate indication of our own mortality, death:

> Sometimes erotic imagery is made more striking by being mixed with paradox. The mystic likens himself to a high-born individual who has gone mad and become corrupt and uncouth, who united with a partner equally grotesque enjoys an erotic dance in wild and hideous yet blissful abandon. Beauty and the grotesque are juxtaposed on equal terms to convey the transcendant.[130]

The Tantric elements in Ramprasad's work are easy to miss today, but to miss them is to miss the most significant thematic aspect. To ignore this aspect of his work would result in a misunderstanding of Ramprasad's historical importance as the pivotal figure in the development of Bengali Saktism, and a misunderstanding too of the existential message or meaning of his songs. It is this Tantric strain that is fundamental to his work and in which his other themes are combined to form a unity.

If I am right in my interpretation of these songs, then almost every song attributed to Ramprasad is either completely Tantric or has some reference within it that can be interpreted as Tantric. Here are all the tell-tale signs: the Goddess as Sakti, and thus as a symbol of the world; the Goddess as the Kundalini, the power within each individual and the basis of Tantric yoga; the Goddess as mind, the bird within the cage as the body or center of ritual practice; the *guru* as giver of the secret mantra; rituals in cremation-grounds, *pīṭhasthānas*, corpse sadhana; and visualizations of the Goddess for the performance of worship. All this is interwoven with themes from the *Devī Māhātmya* and from the domestic Goddess of the folk tradition of Bengal, and as such it is obvious that the ground bass in this polyphony is the ever-present theme of Tantrism.

# SIX

# The Goddess as Ramprasad's Daughter

## The Bengali Goddess

Ramprasad's Goddess is enormously popular in Bengal today. Her annual festival is one of the great religious festivals of the world. Each autumn in a ten day ritual she is worshiped as Durga Mahisasuramardini, Durga the slayer of the buffalo demon, celebrating the myth of the apotheosis of the Goddess in her triumph over demonic forces as recorded in the Chandi, the *Devī Māhātmya* section of the *Mārkaṇḍeya Purāṇa*. For this festival, images of the Goddess slaying the demon are set up throughout Bengal,[1] holiday is declared and gifts are exchanged, and for the principal three days of the ritual, crowds throng the streets as they move from image to image to offer their worship. For three days the *ḍhākīs* scarcely pause from their drumming.

The Chandi's account of the exploits of the Goddess is central to this celebration, and the recital of this Puranic account is central to the ritual.[2] But careful observation of the festival reveals some interesting features, the explanation of which take us away from the classical Puranic text. The Goddess Durga is always portrayed in a family tableau, surrounded by her four children, Kartika, Ganesh, Lakshmi, and Sarasvati, and with her husband Siva, usually depicted by the presence of a small head situated above and behind the Goddess. She is thus portrayed as the mother and is always recognized as Ma Durga.[3]

## *The Daughter Returns to Her Natal Home*

In the minds of most Bengalis, however, Goddess Durga is not celebrated as mother in this great festival, but as daughter. *Puja* time is the time when the Goddess leaves her married mountain home and her husband and visits her natal home. Here she is welcomed with great joy and much celebration and feasting. At the end of the festival it is with great sorrow that her devotees bid her farewell as she sadly returns to her husband. Sadly because Siva is no model husband, and life with him in his Kailash home is one of hardship and sorrow. But because she is a good and dutiful wife, she must return. To soften the pain of her departure, she is reminded that she may return to her natal home again next year.[4]

Thus does the great Mother Goddess become the archetypal Daughter Goddess, the form that many Bengalis continue to recognize and worship today. The origins of this aspect of the celebration lie deep in the folk roots of Bengal Saktism. It is a still-observed social custom that a young bride leave her natal home to live with her husband and in-laws, then return to visit her natal family once a year. This is an occasion the young bride and her natal family look forward to with eager anticipation. Devotees celebrate the coming and the going of the Daughter Goddess in song. The welcoming *āgamanī* songs are very tender and the *bijayā* farewell songs are some of the most poignant of all Bengali songs.

> On the fourth day of worship, in the evening, the image of the deity is immersed in a tank or river. In the morning, worship is offered on a small scale with offerings which resemble food and other things given formerly to a daughter on the occasion of her leaving her father's house for her husband's. Durga is looked upon as one's daughter, and she comes to the house of the worshipper, her father, annually for three days. And during the worship, she is to be treated like one's own daughter as much as the supreme Mother. One witnesses really a pathetic scene when the image of the deity is taken from the place of worship and members of the family of the worshipper gather round with tears in their eyes.
>
> Touching songs, called the *vijayā* songs, were composed in Bengali from the eighteenth century onwards commemorating this occasion. Deep paternal care is also reflected in what are called the *āgamanī* songs, which hail the deity, the daughter, coming to the house of her father after a year's stay in the house of her husband.[5]

Medieval folk traditions regarding the Goddess as daughter are found in the *maṅal-kābya* literature, and in stories of minor goddesses currently still worshiped. In the *maṅal* of Manasa, the snake goddess Manasa is the daughter of Siva, born of seed which Siva involuntarily discharges while seated by a lotus pool thinking of his wife. His seed lands on a lotus[6] and runs down the stalk to the *nāga* (snake) world below where a beautiful girl is fashioned from it. Siva is thus unaware of the identity of his divine daughter, and later when he sees her in all her beauty he lusts for her. Manasa persuades him to take her to his home, concealed in a basket. When she is discovered, tension and rivalry develops between Manasa and Chandi, Siva's wife, a rivalry which continues until the story takes up its main theme, the glorification of Manasa and her securing of the worship of humans.[7]

When this story is compared with that of Chandi herself in the Chandi *maṅals* we can detect parallels between the two goddesses, and it is plain that all are but forms of the one Devi.[8] Thus the identity of the Goddess in relation to Siva is blurred, she is both his wife and his daughter. This ambiguity can also be seen in the stories associated with other goddesses.

## *The Story of* Jōgādyā

Stories of goddesses like Manasa involve goddesses who are daughters of gods. There are, however, relevant instances of a goddess being the daughter of a human individual. There is such an instance in the Bengali tradition concerning the goddess Jogadya (or Jugadya),[9] still worshiped today in various places in the Bardhaman district, especially Kshirgram. Her story is known from the *maṅal-kābya,* from Manik Ganguli's *Dharmamaṅal,* from the *Śibāyans* of Ramesvara and Ramakrishna, from Chaitra *gājan* songs, and from songs sung at an East-Bengali Siva festival, *Nīl-pūjā*.[10] The story draws heavily from the folk religious tradition in which divine beings display local human characteristics, in this case the Bengali woman's love of bangles cut from conch shells (usually indicating that the wearer is married), a custom still observed in modern days of plastic bangles.

One day, in the faint light of early dawn a conch-cutter approached the village of Kshirgram, calling out his wares as he approached, "Who'll buy my bangles? Who'll buy my bangles?" As he entered the village he saw an exceptionally beautiful woman bathing at the steps descending into the village tank. This woman answered the conch-cutter's cry, and he placed two bangles on her tender young arms. Then, wearing the bangles, the woman pointed to a nearby temple, saying that if the conch-cutter went there he would receive from her father payment for the bangles—the exact price would be found in a basket (*jhāpi*).

The conch-cutter went to the temple and recounted the incident to the astonished priest, who begged the conch-cutter to take him to the steps to see this goddess in the form of his daughter (*kanyārūpiṇī debī*). But when they reached the tank all they saw was two arms adorned with bangles rise above the still dark waters and then disappear again in its depths.[11]

In Kshirgram there is an image of this goddess, Jogadya, that is kept submerged in the tank and taken from the water annually for special worship. This worship consists of a mixture of Aryan and non-Aryan elements,[12] as might be expected, but whatever her history she is now associated with Durga *mahiṣāsuramardinī*, the slayer of the buffalo demon—the main form of the goddess worshiped in Bengal today,[13] or with Bhadrakali, another popular form of the goddess.[14]

## *The Story of Annapurna*

While there is no direct link between this story and Ramprasad, Dasgupta definitely sees this as a model for the story of the "Mother as daughter 'repairing Ramprasad's fence'."[15] As we shall see, there are links with Ramprasad's story and that of Annapurna, the form of the goddess that is supposed to have repaired his fence, according to the traditional lives. The story of Annapurna was also well-known in Ramprasad's time, especially from the *Annadāmaṅal* of Bharatchandra, Ramprasad's contemporary and fellow court poet at the court of Raja Krishnachandra.[16]

Bharatchandra's story has some notable features. He begins by relating the well-known Puranic story of Siva and his wife Sati and the destruction of the sacrifice of Sati's father Daksha. But the story is given a very *laukik* flavor. Siva is the folk Siva, a bad husband who makes his wife's life a misery. The conflict with Daksha is seen in terms of village son-in-law/father-in-law rivalry.

The story then moves on to the subsequent marriage of Siva to Gauri, following the death and dismemberment of Sati (a dismemberment of particular importance in Bengal, of course, because the places where the dismembered parts of Sati's body fall to earth are the *pīṭhasthānas* so important in Tantric worship (see chapter 5). The folk style again dominates. Siva resorts to begging to support his wife and two sons, Ganesh and Kartika, with a notable lack of success. Gauri resolves to return to her natal home with her two sons, but Durga reminds her that this would be a very shameful thing to do and would cast a bad light on her father's house. She advises Gauri to resort to Annapurna, to set up an image of her and keep what food she has near it. When unsuccessful at begging, Siva will have to come to her, thus making him beholden to her while glorifying the goddess. This is what happens, and when Siva's hunger is appeased, he commands a temple to be built in Kashi with a golden image of Annapurna established in it. The gods come and worship her, and her worship is sanctioned by this. The goddess is pleased by this and announces that anyone who worships her will receive the four fruits, *dharma, artha, kāma* and *mokṣa*. Of note here is the fact that the worship of Annapurna is established by Siva, not by some human individual as in other *maṅals*, and that it is the other gods who worship her and spread her story.

However, Bharatchandra is not content to stop here. He goes on to recount two more stories that glorify Annapurna, the stories of Vyasa and Harihaur. In the story of Vyasa we once more find Annapurna appearing in disguise to Vyasa, although he eventually realizes she was the goddess. More importantly, the story revolves around antagonism between the worshipers of Siva and those of Vishnu, no doubt reflecting contemporary attitudes in this matter. The tone of the story is also remarkable. The venerable Vyasa, the author of the *Puranas* and the *Mahābhārata*, is held up to such ridicule that in his introduction to the first part of Bharatchandra's work, the editor Kartik Bhadra is at pains to explain it. Such a "completely frivolous" picture of Vyasa can only be accounted for because Bharatchandra "had no faith at all in any deities or divine powers."[17] Even though the second and third parts of the *Annadāmaṅal* are not religious, I think many would find it strange that an atheist poet would devote so much of his work to religious themes such as the glorification of a goddess.[18]

Nonetheless, I believe this story accurately reflects the ethos of the court of Krishnachandra, including the attitudes of many who attended it; the religious ambience was strong, but many earthy, bawdy elements of folk culture were also common. Editors like Bhadra and many other scholars are at pains to explain away the embarrassing "coarseness" of the times. For example, Siva is portrayed as a dope-smoking lay-about so randy that he is constantly lusting after women, hardly caring if they are wives, neighbors, prostitutes, even daughters! But this was an age when gods were modeled more on humans, and such behavior was found in many a village and town. In this atmosphere a "religious" poet such as Ramprasad would not have felt like a stranger. He himself wrote a *Bidyāsundar* which is today regarded either as erotic or pornographic, depending upon whether the regarder approves or disapproves.[19] Dasgupta shows his understanding when he concedes that whatever one thinks of the popular elements in these goddess stories they "[D]o not completely obscure the glorification of the Goddess; it's as if the Goddess's glory becomes more lovingly appealing in these human displays—more like ourselves."[20]

Bharatchandra returns to the Goddess and her attempts to spread her worship among humans with the story of Harihaur. This story is much more like the conventional *maṅal-kābya*. The story involves Basundhar, an attendant of the god Kuvera, who observes a woman engaged in sexual intercourse when out collecting flowers to be used for worship. For this offense he is cursed to be born as the mortal Harihaur, the son of a cow-dung cake seller so poor he cannot even clothe himself properly.[21] Harihaur in turn grows up in his father's footsteps and attempts to support his parents selling cow-dung cakes. One day the goddess Annapurna sees him at his work. Disguising herself as an old woman she appears before him with a basket full of dung cakes and firewood. As he is returning home empty-handed she asks him to carry her basket, which he gladly does.

When they reach his house the old woman asks if she may stay the night, and Harihaur becomes worried, for he knows they haven't even two handfuls of rice to feed themselves—but he cannot refuse. The old woman, recognizing their plight, tells them that if they invoke Annapurna's name rice will come into their bowl. They do as she says, and the bowl is completely filled with all kinds of delicious food. The astonished Harihaur then wants to know the woman's identity, but she just offers him another dung cake to sell. When he takes it in his hand it turns to gold. This is too much for Harihaur and he faints. When he becomes conscious again he senses danger in these happenings, his hand trembles, and tears flow.

The Goddess then smiles and reveals herself as Annapurna. She has come to grant him a favor—his house will now be filled with rich sons. In return he is to worship her on *śukla pakṣa astami* night in the month of Chaitra. Harihaur does as he is bid, spends his days worshiping Annapurna with the deepest devotion, and is happy ever after. He becomes rich enough to become a respected member of society.

A kind of parallel sub-plot follows involving a brahmin called Bhabananda Majumdar, who is really Kuvera's son Nalakubar, cursed to become a man because he persisted in having sex with his two wives when he should have been worshiping Annapurna. This sub-plot is ostensibly to secure the return of the cursed Basundhar/Harihaur to heaven, but serves also to extend the worship of the Goddess to the higher castes—a common *manal-kābya* theme. This the Goddess achieves indirectly, through the agency of a poor Ganges boatman, to whom she appears in disguise.

Arriving at the river on the way to Bhabananda's house, she calls the boatman to ferry her across. When he enquires who she is she replies in such high and elaborate language that the illiterate boatman cannot understand, and he guesses that she is some high-caste wife who has fled as a result of some domestic strife: "These *kulīns* are always quarreling," he mutters to himself. As they cross the river the woman dangles her feet over the side of the boat. Fearing she might come to some harm, for which he would no doubt be held responsible, he asks her to pull them in. When she does so her foot strikes the bailer, which turns to gold. The Goddess then reveals her true nature to the amazed boatman, and tells him to ask a favor of her. He does; "Just give me enough milk and rice for my son."

The Goddess then disappears, the boatman goes and tells Bhabananda all that has happened, and Bhabananda goes to the temple where he sees a golden basket on the floor. Just then a voice, that of Annapurna, speaks from heaven telling him to keep the basket (*jhāpi*) carefully and never open it and her blessing will stay with his family. Bhabananda then also spends his days in happiness and in devotion to Annapurna.

There are a number of features of these tales that are relevant to Annapurna's relationship to Ramprasad, and contribute to a coalescence of the various goddesses concerned. The first is that Annapurna appears to and gives material assistance to the poor who are usually found at the lowest levels of society. I say "usually" because the cases of Siva and Vyasa are obvious exceptions, but when Annapurna appears to them they are both in a state of utter destitution. Associated with this is often found the idea of domestic strife, to which extreme poverty no doubt contributes. (I think the comment of the boatman in the last story, that "These *kulīns* are always quarrelling" is just Bharatchandra's joke, but maybe it does reflect a malaise in his society.) That Annapurna gives material relief to those in need is to be expected, because as her name suggests (Anna-da means "giver of rice/food," Anna-purna means "replete with rice/food") the giving of such bounty is what she represents. She is a young goddess who is recognized as a manifestation of Durga, but who is not recognized as a Mother goddess herself.

Given the tradition of Ramprasad's poverty, reflected in Gupta's biography, as well as the rumors of domestic unhappiness,[22] it is perhaps not surprising that she appeared to assist him materially (though not with gifts of food). And that she comes in disguise is typical of all the stories related here. She appears in whatever feminine guise she chooses, so her appearance as a daughter is not surprising nor, because of the story of Jogadya, unusual.

At first glance the stories of Annapurna would seem to be quite different, but there are a number of features that allow us to link these two. One of these is the curious basket (*jhāpi*, a small wicker basket usually with a lid, the same word is used in both stories) that appears in connection with both. In the Jogadya story it is the place where the payment for the bangles is to be found, in the story of Bhabananda it seems to represent in some way the source of wealth given by Annapurna. Both are kept in the temple.

Both these goddesses are seen as manifestations of Durga. In the case of Jogadya, however, it seems that a minor local goddess is transformed from one who inspired fear, as the story recounted above indicates, to one who gains wider acceptance and a more benign image. Both are, in some sense, seen as consorts of Siva; Annapurna is considered a spouse of Siva[23] and Jogadya becomes such through her identification with Durga or Bhadrakali.[24] As we have seen, her story is retold in the context of the Saivite *Nīl-pūjā*. Both also have fearful aspects as well as benign aspects. In the case of Annapurna, she manifests a Bhairavi aspect, according to the *Tantrasār*,[25] a form which is nevertheless identified with the benevolent Annapurna.

It is also worth noting Annapurna's nature as an earth goddess. Her benevolence is thus symbolic of the bounty of the earth, producing rice and other food. She may therefore be seen as a form of *śākaṃbharī*, "she who supports with vegetation."[26] Dasgupta links Annapurna to the earth through an all-encompassing conjunction of Annapurna, from the "*śākaṃbharī* Devi" of the *Devī Māhātmya*, to the Devi Basundhara, another form of the earth who as an attendant of the god Kuvera is linked with Annapurna in the story of Harihaur in Bharatchandra's *Annadāmaṅal,* back to the Vedic earth goddess Prithvi, and forward to Durga whose worship in Bengal is also known as *śaradiyā pūjā* or autumn *pūjā*. The nine plants *(nabapatrikā)* used in Durga *Pūjā* represent the harvest of the earth and link Durga directly with the earth. He concludes that, "A conscious effort has been made to link the Puranic Durga in every way with this harvest-goddess."[27]

In the *Tantrasār,* Annapurna's image is described: "Engaged in giving food, she is always adorned on her two sides by Earth *(bhūmi)* and Lakshmi *(śrī)*."[28] These represent the earth itself and good fortune in general. Linking this with the image of Annapurna Bhairavi, we might say that the Goddess is made to symbolize the earth in both its beneficent and destructive aspects, whether as mother or as daughter.

## *The Goddess as Ramprasad's Daughter*

In his songs, Ramprasad refers to the Goddess appearing as his daughter to mend his fence, but the references yield little but the bare facts—"Mother, you came to your devotee as his daughter, to mend the fence of his house/ . . . Those who meditate single-mindedly will realize Kalika Tara/ Come out and see her as his daughter mending Ramprasad's fence."[29] There is barely enough here to form the basis of a legend. The direct references to Annapurna in the songs are not much more helpful. All seven refer to the Annapurna who dwells in Kashi as the wife of Siva, and who provides the food/spiritual blessings that the impoverished/ spiritually-impoverished Ramprasad craves. But in the most suggestive of the songs Annapurna seems to be failing him—"Dvija Ramprasad says, How people slander me! They say/ If Annapurna is your Mother, why has your father's house no food?"[30] Here Annapurna has become his mother, not his daughter.

Ramprasad has also left us some *āgamanī* songs that celebrate the return of the Goddess from the mountain home of her husband Siva to her natal hearth. In the background lies the destitution and hardship she has left, but the songs focus on the joy of welcoming home again the Goddess, as Uma or Gauri. They are a skillful blend of classical story and the singer's own family intimacy, wherein the Goddess is both mother and daughter.

O Queen, get up, there is uproar in the town,
Your daughter is almost here,

Come on, come with me to welcome her home.
Jaya, what wonderful news you bring,
I'll be in your debt for the rest of my life,
All I have, up to my life, would not adequately reward you for it.
The queen drifts around, her hair still not done, floating on waters of love,
While her companions console her, Gauri is nearly here!
Out on the road the chariot arrives, and seeing Uma's face
People cry, Mother comes! Mother comes!
Little Mother, have you forgotten your mother, says her mother.
Sankari gets down from the chariot and greets her mother,
Over and over again she consoles her.
Sri Kabiranjan Das says tenderly, Has there ever been such a wonderful day.[31]

Even in translation this song conveys feelings of joy, expectation, and intimacy generated by the welcoming of the Goddess as a daughter. The song has a greater significance for the interpretation of Ramprasad songs because in it he blurs any hard-and-fast distinction between the roles of mother and daughter. In line eleven the words I have translated as "Little Mother" and "mother" are in fact the same—*mā.* So taking lines ten and eleven together there is no linguistic difference between *mā* as Mother (Goddess), *mā* as an ordinary mother, and *mā* as daughter (here translated as Little Mother to make the meaning clear). The reason that this is possible is that in Bengali it is common to address one's daughter as "*mā*" because she is potentially a mother.

So when Ramprasad addresses "*mā*" in a song it might be the Goddess as mother or as daughter. In many songs one can tell from the tone of the poet's voice that the Goddess as daughter is intended. This is most obvious when he appears to be gently scolding his wayward daughter, for example for running about without any clothes on:

Get dressed, Ma, put your clothes on!
Then I'll place a red hibiscus with sandal-paste at your feet.
Standing there with bloodied sword, a garland of heads round your neck,
Just look down, Ma, you're standing on your husband!
Everyone says you're mad, Ma, and you're driving others mad,
Ramprasad had gone mad too, longing for your feet.[32]

This conjures up the picture of a father rebuking a naughty child—"Get some clothes on, look at you! Look at the state you're in, and just look where you're standing! No wonder people say you're mad. And you expect to be treated like a goddess." Sometimes the father is so enchanted himself by this favorite daughter that he wants to join in her game:

> What a dance, Ma, for a battlefield!
> What an appearance, with your hair streaming and dancing naked on your husband's chest. . . .
> Your smiling face shines like a lotus,
> You radiate beauty like a rain-cloud, how beautiful the red of your feet,
> Prasad says, My mind skips about too, I can't keep my eyes on you.[33]

In another song of the same theme she is specifically referred to as a daughter who dances on Siva's chest, shaming him with her nakedness, although the display creates pleasure rather than anger on the earth.[34] And there are many references to her as the "daughter of the mountain," that is, Daksha's daughter, a common appellation of Durga—thus linking this image back to the folklore image so well-known throughout Bengal.[35]

There is an obvious intimacy created by this tender affection for a wayward daughter, without the deference that must always be part of the son-mother relationship. This mood is described well by Sanjukta Gupta;

> The common Tantric image of the Goddess as . . . the young daughter of Himalaya, inspired devotees to experience a love for the Goddess akin to that of a doting father for his daughter. Poets like Ramprasad Sen have often described the deity as a loving little daughter, understanding, sympathetic and even docile to Her adoring devotee, as a daughter to her father, her power expressed in a manner more persuasive than coercive.[36]

But too much should not be made of it, for it is just one of a number of conceits employed by the poet. In fact, "The Mother may be found in any house/ . . . As mother, daughter, wife, sister, or any other,"[37] an idea taken up later to mean that all women are embodiments of the Mother. But for Ramprasad the daughter has a special place, and anguish fills his heart when she must depart:

O mountain lord, my body trembles with fear,
What terrible things I hear that turn my day to darkness.
Mahakala sits on his tiger skin outside the door,
Calling again and again for the mother of Ganesh to come out.
Your body is stone, and it must have a stony spirit within
To have endured it so long.
A daughter is another's treasure, how hard that is to accept,
Alas, thus does the Creator mock us.
Thus says Prasad, As the *cakōrī* bird at dawn despairs for its nectar,
So does the mountain lord's queen [for her departing daughter].[38]

Finally, even as daughter the Goddess must depart. Even as daughter, the Goddess represents both presence and absence, both joy and sorrow.

> [The Bengali girl] is auspicious and delights all by her presence but she must have a sense of shame about her very being. She is the accessible form of the goddess yet she is also a contradiction: accessible but fleeting, enduring but easily hurt.[39]

And so she leaves, and the poet finds himself once again alone in his house.

Several writers have suggested that this adoration of the Goddess as daughter might have been borrowed from the *bātsalȳa bhāb* of the Vaisnava cult wherein devotion is channeled into the attitude of his mother Yasoda for the infant Krishna.[40] But I see no need to resort to such a hypothesis. I believe its roots can be found deep in the soil of Bengali culture, in the deep bond of affection between parents and daughters, and in the feelings associated with a daughter's marriage—the deep sadness as she departs for her husband's home, and the joy and excitement that accompanies her return to her natal home when she comes to visit each year.

Another strong root of this tradition lies in indigenous Bengali folk religion, centered on the numerous goddesses worshiped probably long before Vaisnavism ever reached Bengal. In these cults, as we have seen in the case of Jogadya and Manasa, the Goddess appears either as mother or as daughter, and in the latter role she brings joy and auspiciousness to the devotee as a daughter does to a family. It is in just such a way that Annapurna comes to Ramprasad, in the form of a daughter, to mend his fence. And his *āgmanī* and *bijayā* songs celebrate the feelings associated with her coming and departure.

Finally, there is certainly some connection with the Tantric practice of virgin worship, *kumārī pūjā.* In this ritual, practiced long before and long after Ramprasad, young pre-pubescent virgin girls are worshiped as images of the Goddess. In the *Kulārnava Tantra*, for example, nine such girls are to be employed with ages ranging from one to nine years old, and the worshiper is to procede "considering all these as deities. . . ."[41]

In fact, not only do I think it is unnecessary to go outside of traditional Bengal to find the origins of this belief, one is prompted to ask, what could possibly have been added to such an already rich tradition by any Vaisnava *bātsalȳa* idea?

SEVEN

# Reading the Songs of Ramprasad

## Saktism and the Importance of Ramprasad

Understanding Ramprasad's songs means understanding what they mean or meant for the people who sing them or listen to them. And when we consider this audience we are considering a large number of people over a long period of time, from Ramprasad's contemporaries in the eighteenth century to the modern citizens of Bengal. This in itself indicates one important feature of Ramprasad's work, that it has retained its appeal and is as meaningful today as it was two hundred years ago.

It is not possible to say with certainty what Ramprasad's work meant to his contemporaries, but we can make some guesses, based on the record left by Isvarachandra Gupta[1] and the nature of his songs. It is obvious from Gupta's account that Ramprasad's songs were eagerly seized on and treasured by an emerging Sakta community. This community would have been enormously strengthened by the combining of the classical Puranic stream of the Goddess tradition, an all-India tradition based on the Sanskrit *Devī Māhātmya*, with the enormously popular local folk goddess tradition stemming from the vernacular *maṅal-kābya* tradition. This process was a reciprocal one whereby the folk tradition was strengthened and elevated by its association with the orthodox Puranic tradition, and the orthodox was broadened and popularized by its links with the popular goddesses who then came to be seen as manifestations of the one Goddess. This alone would have ensured the popularity and importance of Ramprasad.

But his skill and his genius in blending this in turn with the previously secret and underground Tantric tradition was Ramprasad's most significant contribution of all. Tantrism had been present in Bengal for a long time, but just how long and how widespread its practice was is impossible to tell because it was a secret cult suffering the disapproval of "good" society, both religious and secular.

It does seem to have had a considerable following in spite of suffering social censure. Buddhism was influenced by it, as well as a branch of Buddhism developed in Bengal, the *vajrayāna*—devoted to a Tantric influence—the most notable result of which was the domination of Tibetan Buddhism still seen today.[2] Even the Caitanya movement was significantly influenced by it, with several of the leaders of the Navadvip or Bengal branch of the movement (as against the more orthodox Vrindaban section) obviously under the influence of Tantric belief and practice.[3] The so-called Sahajiya movement also attests to its widespread influence on Vaisnavism.[4]

The paradox of Tantrism at this time is that in spite of an obvious popularity it continued to be a largely secret cult, suffering considerable social and religious censure. There is evidence that attempts were made to change this situation, and it does seem that Ramprasad's sometime patron, Raja Krishnachandra of Krishnagore, was attempting to emancipate it. He seems to have encouraged Tantrism, and it was probably under his patronage that the popular Tantric digest, the *Tantrasār*, was translated into Bengali. No doubt this patronage encouraged Ramprasad, and it was largely through his work that Tantric beliefs and practices emerged into the light of day and became an open and important feature of Bengali Saktism. It is also probable that some features of the cult continued to be practiced in secret, and it is also true that it continues to receive strong disapproval from the orthodox and the morally straight-laced, but that a revolution was brought about by the work of Ramprasad can be seen in the fact that the two dominant religious figures in nineteenth-century Bengal, Bama Ksepa and Ramakrishna, were both to a degree Tantrikas and could openly discuss and recommend Tantric practices.[5]

Isvarachandra Gupta records how much Ramprasad's songs were treasured by the early part of the nineteenth century. He found people hesitant in yielding up copies of songs to the collector, reluctant often to even let him see them. He records how many were destroyed by the devotion lavished on them, as people worshiped them with flowers and sandalwood paste, traditional ingredients of *pūjā*. It is obvious that they were used in rituals but we can only guess at the nature of this use. He mentions how they were copied and passed from hand to hand so that mistakes crept into the text.[6]

## *The Nature of the Goddess*

What did Ramprasad's songs mean to ordinary Saktas? I believe they were treasured for qualities they possessed beyond their historical importance. Their tunes were popular, we know, but there must have been something about the basic poetic message that appealed to the deeply-felt needs of people's lives. The biographies confirm one thing: Ramprasad's identification with the poor and needy, and release in the Goddess, were popular themes. Bengal in the late eighteenth and early nineteenth centuries suffered hard times, and there were many poor and destitute among the common people. Some of the effects of British expansion were very disruptive; the economy was strained by the decimation of the textile industry, and then further weakened by basic patterns of land-holding and use through the Permanent Settlement. There were invasions by marauding Marathas, and there had been a disastrous famine that had wiped out as many as a third of the people. Bands of armed *sannyāsīs* roamed the countryside, demanding support from the destitute populace.[7] Their favorite deities were also outside of the pale of orthodox religion, so they were religiously poor and outcaste as well.

We now need to look deeper into Ramprasad's message. What was the nature of the release offered through the Goddess in his songs? I believe the answer lies in his establishing the Goddess, through orthodox and popular religious imagery, as a symbol of the world in all its ambiguity, and as a symbol of life in general with all its vicissitudes, including its ultimate demise. It seems quite clear that for Ramprasad the Goddess is a symbolic representation of the world. In seeing her this way Ramprasad takes up one of the major themes of the *Devī Māhātmya,* one that provides the classical Sakta charter for recognizing the universe as her body. She takes the form of the world at its creation, she is primordial *prakṛiti* characterized by the three *guṇās* (1. 57–9; 4. 6; 5. 7). She is said to subsist in the form of the world as earth and water, she constitutes all living beings and has the nature of the universe that she upholds (11. 3–6, 31). She supports the world so that when the rains come the vegetation grows out of her own body so that she is known as *śākaṃbharī* (11. 43f).

This language is echoed in the songs of Ramprasad, "The Mother's belly is the universe, no-one knows its size,"[8] she is "the earth, [she is] water,"[9] she is "archetypal *prakṛiti,*"[10] she is "With qualities and without (*saguṇā nirguṇā*), gross and subtle, the uncaused root cause of all."[11] Ramprasad says, "O Mother you are suffering and you are bliss, as it is written in the Chandi,"[12] thus indicating that he sees the dualities of the Goddess's nature as the dualities of our universe, sometimes threatening and sometimes benign, sometimes inspiring hope and at other times despair, sometimes beautiful and sometimes terrifying, sometimes revealing its nature to us and at other times totally deluding. We live in a mad, drunken bitch of a world which at the same time we need to sustain us, whose meaning we at times cannot penetrate. And we cannot choose another, because this is the only world we have. This is an emphatic rejection of escapist religion.

The only choice open to the individual is to make something of this world themselves by coming to terms with its true nature, by not deluding themselves that it really is different, or that there is some way to escape its worst features. The only choice is to embrace the world in all its ambiguity and acknowledge it as Mother, by believing that thus one will experience the personal transcendence that enables one to overcome the world, and to confidently confront the worst it has to offer. And the worst it has to offer is the inevitable fact of our own finitude and ultimate death.

Ramprasad expresses such confidence in the way he confronts this Mother and remonstrates with her. In spite of her fickleness and all the suffering she dishes out he returns to her bosom and acknowledges he is her son. This gives him special knowledge of her, a special insight into the world, and a confident faith in the face of his own mortality.

This mortality is a constant theme in his songs. Ramprasad knows his hold on life is precarious, he is like one of the kites the Mother flies that may at any moment have its string cut and be freed, or be held bound in her hand forever.[13] The Mother's wild dancing is the dance of death, whether performed in the battlefield or in the cremation ground. And time and time again he refers to the final meeting with Yama, the god of death who personifies the inevitable final moment. Employing conventional religious imagery in one song Ramprasad directly addresses Yama:

> Prasad says, Get out of here, aren't you afraid?
> Look at my Mother with her necklace of heads, today I reckon she'll have yours![14]

In another he says:

> Who is this dark woman who comes to the battle,
> Naked, hair dishevelled, a sword in her hand, exultantly slaying demons?
> The weight of her feet makes the earth tremble with fear,
> And the sight of it makes Siva fall at her feet on the battleground.
> Dvija Ramprasad says, Why then need I fear?
> Yama is easily conquered in life, in death and in battle.[15]

It is knowledge that gives the Sakta freedom, a common Hindu theme. The realization achieved by the *sādhakas* enables them to personally transcend the world and all its vicissitudes. This knowledge is insight into the nature of the universe because it is knowedge of the nature of the Goddess. Conversely it is ignorance that creates the kind of fear that makes life depressing and burdensome. This idea that knowledge is what saves one even in the midst of life is a traditonal theme, found especially in the *Advaita* tradition. But it is almost as if Ramprasad in turn demythologizes this idea as well.

Ramprasad's victory over his own death, represented by the visit of Yama, is achieved by his acceptance of the destructive nature of the world, represented by the Goddess. In one of the most remarkable of all his songs he clearly states this:

> Why do I so vainly call out Mother! Mother! I'll never get to see her,
> Or if I do it will only be when she comes to complete her work of destruction on me.
> All places of death and cremation grounds are *pīṭhasthāns*,
> Finally it dawned on me, it's futile to suffer this affliction.
> So going to the Ganges I burned my effigy on its bank,
> And completed the period of mourning with a *piṇḍa*. Now, mourning over, I'm off to Kashi.

Dvija Ramprasad says, Why worry about this Mother,
Mother has gone, now she's called Brahman, so I needn't worry about crossing to the other side.[16]

Here Ramprasad first confronts the fact that there is really no Goddess as a mother goddess to be seen, she is only that world with which he will finally be united at his own death, when he returns to that "Mother" from whence he came. She is nothing other than the whole of reality ("now she's called Brahman") and he can forget about the traditional business of crossing to the other side; crossing the stormy ocean of this painful existence to the other side to dwell in bliss with some deity. It dawns on him that all cremation grounds, where the individual is finally disposed of, are *pīṭhasthāns*, those places sacred to Tantrikas where pieces of Sati's dismembered body fell to earth, thus representing the earth as the Mother's body.[17] Once this realization dawns on him the poet does not end his life in suicide but performs a symbolic ritual. He goes to the Ganges, on whose banks Hindus desire to die because such a death confers instant *mokṣa*, and effects a symbolic death by cremating a straw effigy of himself.[18] This is the act by which *sannyāsīs* ritually renounce the world, so here Ramprasad is symbolizing the death of his old unenlightened way of life and its suffering, and beginning a new life of freedom, enlightenment, and transcendence. He does not actually become a renunciant in the literal sense, a *sannyāsī*. But he does effect a true union with the Mother, he gains a true release in life, and off he goes to Kashi. Only symbolically, of course, for we have already seen in song 317 (chapter 5, page 70) that Kashi is to be identified with the body and there is no need to go to the geographical Kashi at Varanasi. But "off to Kashi" because according to the mythical complex Ramprasad is utilizing here, Kashi is the only place that survives the destructive holocaust of the *pralaya*, the final dissolution of the universe.[19]

## Reading Ramprasad Today

Ramprasad's understanding of this realization and his attitude toward death give his work a poignant modern resonance. It is as if he is calling for a realistic albeit painful acceptance of the true nature of existence, including an honest confrontation with a mortality that rules out any kind of escapist avoidance, secular or religious. In Isvarachandra Gupta's biography of Ramprasad, he chose the time of his death and entered the Ganges singing a song of acceptance;[20] this act may be taken as confirmation of his confidence. And it is just when he is most modern in these respects that he is most Tantric.

The Tantric tradition does not, as the Advaita school does, see the world as illusion. Though "[t]he Mother Cult preaches 'monism' as the final goal of *sādhanā*. It prescribes worship through dualism to achieve monism."[21] It has been called a "concrete monism" in which in "the reality of the objective world, creation is conceived of as a process of emanation or real self-manifestation of the Absolute."[22] Consistent with this, the Tantric tradition does not seek to avoid the negative aspects of life (five forbidden things [*pạcatattva*], the negative aspects of one's own personality, and so on), but seeks to confront them, deal with them, and use them positively. The search for the self is to be found in the world, not in escape from it. One uses the world to transcend the world; the freedom attained is freedom in the world rather than from the world. Or as Ramprasad himself puts it, one seeks union with the Mother, not nirvana—"Prasad says, It is the devotee's hope and great desire to attain/ Union with her embodied form, what's the point of nirvana?"[23] In this respect we can note that Ramprasad has no interest at all in any after-death state of any kind. This is significant given the emphasis on such an afterlife in other forms of religion, for example devotees who go to dwell in bliss with Krishna in the Vaisnava *bhakti* tradition as discussed in chapter 3, which provides much of the context for Ramprasad's work. Ramprasad's concerns seem to be entirely this-worldly.

What I find particularly modern about Ramprasad's attitude to these things, and what makes his work relevant to someone like myself, who is neither part of his religious tradition in any way, nor a Bengali, is the strong element of doubt that colors it, or rather the constant oscillation between doubt and certainty. The Bengal of Ramprasad's time was as I have already noted one of great uncertainty, with the decline of Mughal rule, the growth of British influence, and the economic upheaval that entailed. There were periods of great scarcity, and the land was under constant threat from the invading Marathas. This is reflected in the tone of many of the songs and strikes a resonance with many readers today. An important factor is the chance element in life that makes absolute certainty impossible and the sense of powerlessness that results from it. If we are like kites in the Mother's hand, some of which fly away and some of which do not, and if we do not know to which category we belong, how can there be certainty? The nature of the Mother gives no ground for certainty—she merely "laughs and claps her hands" when some of the kites are released.[24]

The idea of madness also symbolizes the unpredictability of life. Conventionality makes for predictability. The behavior of someone who is mad is totally unpredictable, "All this is the mad Mother's game. . . . Which is her true form and which her disguise, what is her true nature, no-one at all can say." She does not even keep her word, "The bitch promises to be impartial to all, but changes her mind when the crunch comes." But Ramprasad's knowledge that this is the way things are is a liberating knowledge, enabling him to end this song with the lines, "Stay on that raft floating on the world ocean,/ Float up with the flood tide and down on the ebb."[25]

These last lines redeem the song. Doubt does not lead to outright despair. Ramprasad refuses to give up in the face of all this madness and unpredictability; there is enough good in this flawed world for us to want to remain involved in it and seek our "salvation" in it. But doubt does constantly plague Ramprasad and is a prominent motif in his songs;

> Loose me, Mother with the loose hair,
> In this world I suffer day and night.
> You have handed me over to Death, Mother—Have you forgotten me?
> Tara, how long must I remain bound by terrible Death's noose?
> Prasad says, What's the point of going to Kashi,
> Father, with my stepmother in his hair, lives in the cremation-ground there![26]

The reason for this is the nature of the world and existence in it, expressed in terms of the Mother's *māyā*, that aspect of her nature which is unfathomable and confusing:

> It's all because of your *māyā*,
> Like some show produced by a magician....
> Day after day passes, Mother,
> And I still haven't found the right way.
> The terrible darkness approaches, Tara,
> And I grope about unable to find my way.[27]

This theme of the Mother's *māyā* is found in many of the songs, but Ramprasad never loses sight of the fact that the Mother also dispells the ignorance created by *māyā* and is the only one who can. She also bestows many favors, including the four aims of life *(cāturvarga)*—that embrace worldly life as well as release. Ramprasad expresses the transcendence this enlightenment brings through the metaphor of release in life:

> Do I willingly perform your worship, O merciful One?
> If they had no fear of Death,
> Who would willingly do so?
> Where are you Mother, Primordial Power *(ādyāśakti)*?
> In your name there is release in life,
> Who else has such power,
> Except you, Three-eyed One.[28]

This is summed up well by Kinsley who says,

> It seems that Kali's boon in some way has to do not so much with directing man's vision to liberation after death as to granting liberation before death. It seems that she is religiously efficacious not simply insofar as she scares man into rejecting the physical world by conveying its dark aspects. To her devotees she has also given a playful freedom in this life, painful though she reveals it to be. And this boon of freedom is not, . . . the boon of ignorance—an ignorance of the way things really are and a childishness based on futile hope. It is a freedom based on release from ignorance, a freedom that comes to one who knows himself to be mortal, a freedom that enables him to revel in the moment, to accept the fulness of life as a gift to be reveled in rather than a curse to be gotten rid of.[29]

The paradox of this situation is keenly felt—"Ramprasad says, Mother exists in all spheres,/ O sightless eyes, look at the Mother, in the darkness she utterly destroys blindness."[30] And in another song, which also plays on the contrast between light/enlightenment/transcendence and darkness he says:

> Meditate on Kali, don't worry about anything else,
> The night of delusion is over, day has just dawned.
> The dawn sun has destroyed the darkness of illusion
> Just as it causes the lotuses to open. . . .
> In the marketplace of bliss no *guru* or pupil studies,

Those who join in the play will realise the nature of reality.
The enlightened hero-devotee, he can enter that town,
Ramprasad says, My delusions are gone, who can contain fire.[31]

## *Problems of Interpretation*

Two problems relating to the interpretation of Ramprasad's songs need to be cleared up. The first of these problems, which probably contributes to the variety of meanings that have been applied to the songs, involves the apparent contradictions in the songs and the strongly ironic tone that I believe underlies many of them. Ramprasad appears sometimes to condemn all scriptures[32] and at other times to support them.[33] In some songs, as we have seen, he expresses confidence, in others doubt.

To solve this problem we must realize that we are dealing with a poet, and poetry (or at least good poetry) in any language is highly multivalent. It is always open to more than one interpretation, there is no one "reading" that is the "correct" one (which is not to say that any reading is a legitimate one, or that there is an infinite number of possible interpretations). This is certainly true of Ramprasad's work.

I believe that the contradictions in Ramprasad's songs are often more apparent than real. We must bear in mind that we are dealing here with a poet and what he says is usually not to be taken literally. Let us take for example the case of whether or not one should "go the Kashi," the famous pilgrimage place on the Ganges. There are many songs that praise it—"Blessed is Kashi . . . If a person dies there he is merged with Siva's body"[34]—and others which say it is futile—"What's the point of going to Kashi . . . ?"[35]—and they apprear to contradict each other. But a close reading shows that there is no contradiction, because the point is that both songs (and all others dealing with Kashi) suggest that it is futile to go physically to geographical Kashi because figuratively speaking one's own body is Kashi, the three mystical channels of the body are the three rivers of Kashi, and so on. So one can obtain all the benefits of the pilgrimage to Kashi by practicing Kundalini yoga (see my analysis of song 317 above, page 70). If we recognize the Tantric basis of Ramprasad's songs then all that he says, even the apparent contradictions, is perfectly consistent. We must remember that for Tantrikas the word of the *guru* is superior to the authority of any scripture, even the Tantras of which he is the authoritative interpreter.

The same can be said for the supposed contradictions regarding whether or not Ramprasad advocates or desires union with the Absolute, or seeks to remain in the dualistic state from which devotion to the Mother is possible. It is possible to find statements in many songs to support both views. But if we consider the problem in the context of Tantric belief and practice, it evaporates. This can be demonstrated by examining song 54 which begins, "This time, Kali, I will eat you up . . . /Now you must eat me or I will eat you, and the two will become one . . . " and goes on to describe the meal in detail. This may be taken as referring to the merging of the individual in the Goddess. But then he says, "I say I will eat you but I won't really swallow you,/ I will set you up in my heart-lotus and worship you mentally." The mention of the heart-lotus once again situates the whole discussion in the context of Kundalini yoga and eliminates any contradiction, because the heart-lotus is a way-station on the way to the *sahasrāra* where union does take place, but a way-station where a *sādhaka* may choose to spend time while on the journey. The famous claim by Ramprasad that he wants to taste sugar but not become sugar, often taken as a charter for dualistic devotion, must also be interpreted in this way. The whole question about apparent contradictions in Ramprasad's songs may serve as a warning to not take anything he says literally or out of its Tantric context.

The second problem concerns the ambiguity of the language and imagery he uses, something we find with all good poets, but which in Ramprasad takes on an additional significance because he is a Tantrika. Hence much of the imagery used by Ramprasad may also be interpreted in other ways than those argued here as main intentions. There is the possibility of interpreting his work through conventional theistic devotional spectacles, that is, taking the symbol for reality and seeing the Goddess as a conventional deity. An excellent example of this is the interpretation of the image of the "feet" of the Goddess. There are many references to the poet longing for the feet of the Goddess that may be taken as implying devotion, because a common form of obeisance is to bow one's head to the feet of a person one wants to honor. But I think we must take this image in context, and the context is one in which the poet longs for the feet to be placed in his heart, or more specifically in the "heart lotus." This places the usage firmly in the context of the Tantric Kundalini ritual, in which the Goddess is nothing but the power within the body of the *sādhaka*. The other reference to the feet of the Goddess has the feet situated on the body of Siva, and once again the context is decidedly Tantric. So even when this figure seems conventionally devotional, it almost certainly is not meant to be, although I have a feeling that Ramprasad would not have been bothered if his work were interpreted in this way. Indeed we might well ask with Biardeau: "[D]o hymns of praise and accounts that glorify the god [or in this case, goddess] belong to the sphere of bhakti or to that of tantrism? Any attempt to delineate the two would be absurd, since both are indifferently used by bhaktas and tantrikas alike."[36]

What I am concerned to assert in the face of this ambivalence is the strongly Tantric nature of Ramprasad's songs. Within the education system in West Bengal Ramprasad is regarded as a *sādhaka*, a term with strong Tantric overtones, or a *kabi*, a poet, and not as a *bhakta*.[37] Even when his picture of the Goddess is most orthodox, based on material from the *Devī Māhātmya*, it is colored by Tantric elements. For example, in most of his songs there is the theme of the militant goddess standing on Siva, as she does not in the *Devī Māhātmya*. The erotic Goddess is specifically aged sixteen in several songs, a detail found in the *Tantrasār* but not in the *Devī Māhātmya*.[38] When his Goddess seems most to be the kind of personal deity who might be the object of a devotional cult, she is linked to the Tantric Kundalini yoga, or is assimilated with the whole of nature. And we know from Gupta's biography, Ramprasad was known as one who took wine. This probably refers to the ritual taking of wine in the Tantric *pạcamakāra* [39] ritual; and as to the possibility that his domestic problems were caused by his participation in Tantric sexo-yogic practices, the fifth of these rituals, we can only speculate.[40]

We also need to bear in mind that Tantrikas have a penchant for using traditional religious language, but intend untraditional meanings.[41] The difference is known by the initiated, guided in their interpretation by their *guru*. And interpreting Ramprasad's songs as expressions of what is traditionally known as *bhakti* leaves the problem of how we would then interpret his expressions of doubt, and how to interpret the many injunctions against scriptures,[42] images,[43] pilgrimage,[44] and devotion ("You give doubled punishment, Mother, to those who flatter you/ By calling out your name and singing hymns of devotion [*bhakti*]"[45]) that form a much larger part of his work than do the others. We must also bear in mind that the songs existed as separate entities for a considerable time after Ramprasad's death, even after being written down. As late as 1835 there are no collections other than Gupta's, and his contained only a few songs; many more were carefully treasured by those who owned them and often hid them away from the eyes of others. So it would be possible to ignore songs one did not agree with, or rather to collect and treasure only those with a direct personal appeal, that is, the more "theistic" ones if that was where one's preference lay, or the more Tantric ones if one's preference lay in that direction. I believe many people do interpret him as more of a conventional *saguṇā bhakta*, ignoring the overt Tantric elements.[46] A song such as 223 for example advocates a form of *bhakti* while rejecting, at the same time, external forms of worship. And the fact that it is one of his mind songs leads me to read it as advocating a mental worship of a Tantric kind that identifies the Goddess with the world, as she is *Jagatmōyī:*

> O mind, you're still making the same mistake,
> Don't you know who Kali really is?
> My *Jagatmōyī* Mother, she has no equal in the world,
> Why do you want to make an earth image, and worship that as Mother?
> A person should have confidence in being her son, not in anything else,
> Do you think you can make her happy by killing a kid?
> Prasad says, O stupid mind, worship only with devotion [*bhakti*],
> You show off to people your worship of Kali [*Kālīpūjā*] but she won't accept your bribe.[47]

## *"Devoted" to the Goddess . . .*

It is against this background that I want to address in more detail the question of *bhakti* and what it means to say that Ramprasad was "devoted to the Goddess." In doing so I will rely to a considerable extent on the work of Krishna Sharma[48] who seeks to clarify the meaning of the term *bhakti* in the Hindu tradition and remove some of the misconceptions that have come to surround it. She begins by asserting that the predominant understanding of *bhakti* in academic circles is one that is defined in terms of the Vaisnava as faith in a personal God, derived from the teaching and practice of the followers of Caitanya. In this sense, "It is defined in terms of a belief and attachment to a personal God. Spelt out thus it is deemed as an emotional religious cult."[49] She then argues very convincingly that this is not the only meaning of *bhakti,* and that there are forms of *bhakti* that are very different from this Vaisnava model.

In fact, she argues, "Although bhakti is a generic term, it has acquired a restricted and technical meaning in modern scholarship. The common man in India understands the word as religious devotion in a general sense, regardless of the differences in the forms of its manifestation, caused by variations of beliefs and practices."[50] The term *bhakti* in fact encompasses a range of meanings as wide as the English word "devotion," and ". . . the bhakti of the medieval bhaktas did not present any uniform pattern of ideas, beliefs and practices."[51] Thus we can say, for example, "John is devoted to Mary," meaning that he loves her and implying probably that he has union with her as the goal of his devotion. If "John is devoted to Eric," then another rather different set of implications is probably entailed. But we could as well say, "John is devoted to his studies," meaning that he has given up considerable time and effort to them in order to pass his exams, though he may even dislike his studies.

Sharma calls the Vaisnava *bhakti* taken as the model of devotion *saguṇā bhakti.* It is characterized as intense, emotional attachment to a personal God, and demonstrated by acts of worship, service, and love to that personal God. This must be contrasted with another widespread kind of devotion called *nirguṇā bhakti,* which takes the form of contemplative and yogic practice leading to recognition and knowledge of a God defined as impersonal, with which the *bhakta* seeks to merge. These two forms of *bhakti* are described in, respectively, the *Nārada Bhakti Sūtras* and the *Śāṇḍilya Bhakti Sūtras.*[52] Examples of the *saguṇā* form of *bhakta* are Caitanya, Tulsidas, Surdas, and Mira Bai, while examples of the *nirguṇā* form are Kabir, Nanak, Dadu, Raidas, and Dhana.[53]

But there are not just two forms of *bhakti.* Sharma says, "[T]he word bhakti, when used in the religious context, can acquire particularity only when the name or the notion of the deity to whom it is directed is mentioned along with it."[54] She then demonstrates, in Supplement I, how this is so in the case of the various forms of Siva-*bhakti* that embrace a number of positions within the range of different kinds of devotion. Kashmir Saivism is a monistic form of *nirguṇā bhakti,* the Saiva Siddhanta is a form of *saguṇā bhakti* very similar to Vaisnava *bhakti* though directed towards a different deity, and Vira-Saivism contains elements of both kinds.

It follows from this that Sakti-*bhakti,* the kind of devotion that attains its particularity as it relates to the Goddess, must be considered as a type of its own and not assimilated with Vaisnava *bhakti*. And it is my contention here that Ramprasad's devotion is different from both *nirguṇā* and *saguṇā bhakti* as I, following Sharma, have just described them. What makes it different is the particular object of the devotion: the Goddess as understood in Ramprasad's songs, and the Tantric thought that underlies it. I think it is of great significance that Isvarachandra Gupta describes Ramprasad as a Tantrika when he refers to his devotion, calling it "Sakti-*bhakti*."[55]

The object of Ramprasad's devotion is a Goddess described in personal terms, but not personal in the same sense as Krishna is for Caitanya Vaisnavas. In terms of the *saguṇā* and *nirguṇā* models it is neither personal nor impersonal, because the Goddess always stands for something other than a mere personal female form of deity, although for the purposes of devotion "she" is conceived of "as if" such a deity.[56] The different names for the Goddess (Tara, Kali, Durga, Annapurna, Uma, Parvati, etc.) and the epithets applied to her (*mahāmāyā, mahāvidyā,* etc.[57]) indicate different aspects of what is a very complex symbol, and not different personal deities or aspects of a single deity. On the other hand, unlike the case of the *nirguṇā bhakti* of Kabir, Ramprasad does not reject all ritual and externalized forms of the Goddess such as images and pictures. These personal forms may be utilized in devotion, but only so long as it is realized that this devotion must eventually carry the devotee beyond these forms, because ultimately the individual is not different from the Goddess. Theologically speaking, this represents the idea that dualistic means may be used to attain the non-dualistic goal that lies at the heart of the Tantric position, to which I have referred above and in chapter 5. While on the one hand *saguṇā bhakti* recognizes some form of dualism at all times, and on the other hand *nirguṇā bhakti* denies any kind of dualism, Sakti *bhakti* employs dualistic means but supersedes them in its attainment of a unified state.[58]

There is no doubt that Ramprasad speaks of devotion to the Goddess, of setting her up in his heart lotus, of his desire to worship her "with form." But he also says, "Why worry about this Mother,/ Mother has gone, now she's called Brahman, so I needn't worry about crossing to the other side,"[59] and, "Devotion and release, they give me a headache,/ Now I know Kali's name is Brahman I've given up all religious practice [*dharma* and *karma*]."[60] Then he seems to combine both types of devotion when he says:

Set up in your heart the blissful Durga,
Light the flame of knowledge *[jñana]*, and you will see her true nature as Brahman.
Prasad says, It is the devotee's *[bhakta's]* hope and great desire to attain
Union with her embodied form, what's the point of nirvana.[61]

It is obvious that here we are not dealing simply with *saguṇā* or *nirguṇā* devotion, but a rather different kind that combines aspects of both. In this, Ramprasad's position is almost exactly like that found in the Tantras. For example:

O Devī Tārā, attained with difficulty,
I take refuge with Thee.
Thou art beautiful with form both amorous and charming.
Thou art *Bindu* and the half-moon,
Whose substance is *Hrīm* and *Phat*,
Thou art *mantra* and the shelter of all.
Thy forms are threefold—
Gross, Subtle, and Supreme.
Thou art beyond the reach of Veda.[62]

The Tantras are replete with this form of devotion in which the Goddess is invoked in personal form to become the object of ritual devotion, although it is acknowledged that this is but one of her forms. In the *Kulārnava Tantra* we read, "Although Bodyless, consisting of Pure Intelligence, Immeasurable, and Attributeless, yet the Form of Brahman has been imagined for the benefit of the Sādhakas," (6.72) and, "Dhyāna (Meditation) is said to be of two kinds, i.e., Gross and Subtle. Meditation upon a Form is said to be Gross, while Meditation without any Formal object is Subtle. The Gross kind of Meditation is resorted to for the steadiness of mind, The mind becomes steady by the Gross Meditation and also the Subtle, that is both kinds of Dhyānas promote the same objective . . . " (9.3f).[63] It is obvious then that these most Tantric forms of practice are here called devotion.[64]

The ritual side of devotion, with its corollary of *sādhanā* within the body, is obviously important for Ramprasad, however much at times he appears to reject it. Here Ramprasad's devotion is again somewhat like that of Kabir, in that while Ramprasad addresses his mind as if that were also a form of the Goddess dwelling within the *sādhaka,* Kabir uses the term *bhākti* in the sense of a *bhava* which is a state of mind.[65] So for him realization is something that occurs in the mind, and thus in the body. Kabir, of course, would reject the many disciplines of the Tantric body *sādhanā*, which only goes to show that Ramprasad's devotion is also different from Kabir's.

Finally, Ramprasad's relationship to the Goddess is hardly one that may be characterized as loving. Even when she is his mother, she is the kind of mother who is rebuked, criticized, and sometimes rejected. She is even a "mad bitch" who neglects her own children, or lies to them, and then laughs at her treatment of them. There is no way any Vaisnava would describe Krishna in such terms, and this difference in attitudes about their respective deities was no doubt one of the points of contention in the fighting between Saktas and Vaisnavas at the time. Even when Ramprasad treats his Goddess as the "good mother," trusting himself to her and crying out to her to save him, he does not describe his relation to her as loving. This lack is particularly striking if one wishes to attribute to him a kind of devotion based on the Caitanya model where the most intense love-relationship is implied.

## *Explaining Tantric Devotion*

Ramprasad's attitude about the Goddess and his worship of her will strike many as unusual, or at least in need of further explanation. If I am correct in my reading of Ramprasad, his form of Tantric religion is amazingly close to Feuerbach's theory of religion. Or conversely, Feuerbach's theory seems to explain what is going on in Tantrism, and the work of Ramprasad (and the Bauls too, perhaps) illustrate this well. Feuerbach's theory involves a reduction of religion to a human-centered and nature-centered vision, a reduction of theology to anthropology. It is a theory in which the religious recognize that God (or the Goddess) is a symbol for human natural qualities and aspirations, and the human becomes the center of it all.

The *Tantrasār* specifically treats deities in this way, and the homologization of the Goddess with the power within the body of the *sādhaka* (the Kundalini) recognizes in a very Feuerbachian way that the Goddess is not some objective deity "out there" onto whom the *sādhaka* has projected the perfection of human qualities. The Tantrika recognizes the "divine" qualities as qualities of the individual, of nature (i.e., *puruṣa* is *prakṛiti* ) and seeks to integrate these qualities through the various rituals Tantrism employs. The enlightenment and freedom that result are similar to the self-conscious understanding that Feuerbach holds is the goal of religion (properly understood). The Tantrika thus overcomes the alienation, the disuniting, of the individual from him or herself that otherwise results from the projecting of these qualities dualistically on to some Wholly Other Being out there.

In his own day, the Christians to whom Feuerbach was primarily appealing rejected his theory. It was too hard for them. It took away from them the external prop onto which they had projected all power and perfection, and to which they looked for salvation from their imperfect world. Perhaps this reveals something of why the Tantric way in India is not a popular way, not quite orthodox and acceptable. It is too hard a way, it throws the *sādhakas* too much back on themselves. And perhaps it is because they have accepted this responsibility for themselves, and rejected the easy way of devotion and grace, that people like Ramprasad were regarded as more than a little crazy.

Ludwig Feuerbach published his groundbreaking *The Essence of Christianity* in 1841. It was an immediate success, and has remained influential for the interpretation of religion although the theory contained in it has since been revised, supplemented, and updated (even by Feuerbach himself in the second and subsequent editions of the work).[66] In it, Feuerbach set out a new atheistic interpretation of religion, together with a devastating criticism of Christian theology. His aim was to present religion as a materialist anthropology, centered on human beings and their concerns, rather than a supernaturalist theology centered on a God "out there."

> If therefore my work is negative, irreligeous, atheistic, let it be remembered that atheism—at least in the sense of this work—is the secret of religion itself; that religion itself . . . in its essence, believes in nothing else then the truth and divinity of human nature.[67]

It was not his intention to do away with religion immediately, although because Feuerbach saw religion as a necessary stage in the development of human self-consciousness I think his theory implied that it would eventually be superseded. But for the present he wanted to re-interpret religion radically and preserve all that was positive in it. He believed all that was supernatural could be reduced to what was natural, and that the beliefs of religion could be taken as symbols for natural realities. He believed that if these symbols were rightly understood, religion could be recognized for saying something about basic human needs and concerns. Religious doctrines[68] would be seen as profound insights when interpreted as anthropological truths, or contradiction and error when taken as objective theological propositions. In fact human well-being depends on such an interpretation, because as it stands religion is alienating and escapist.

Feuerbach believed that religion did reflect the needs and desires of its human subjects, but in a perverse way religion inverted these needs and projected them onto a supernatural being called God.

> The divine being is nothing else than the human being, or, rather, the human nature purified, freed from the limits of the individual man, made objective—*i.e.*, contemplated and revered as another, a distinct being. All the attributes of the divine nature are, therefore, attributes of the human nature.[69]

God is thus a reification of the "constituent elements of [human] nature,"[70] reason, will, and love. He is humanity stripped of all its limitations and weaknesses. In this process, humans compensate for the lack of these elements in their own lives by projecting them absolutely onto God. So "man affirms in God what he denies in himself," and creates an illusory fantasy world of wishful thinking. "To know God and not oneself to be God, to know blessedness and not oneself to enjoy it, is a state of disunity, of unhappiness."[71]

Religion thus projects a perfect Person who in his perfection can offer help and salvation to humans in their weakness and imperfection. In fact, in this process essential human qualities are taken away from individuals, and the focus is on human sin, imperfection, depravity, in a way that is profoundly alienating. People no longer seek to improve their own humanity, they merely remain in it awaiting rescue from "out there." And the "perfections" that have been absolutized in God "we shall know only in the future—that is, after death."[72] There is a viciousness in this alienation because of the constant debasement of humanity as it is contrasted with supernatural perfection, and people are divided from the basic constituents of their own natures, their minds are "perverted and crippled by a superhuman, *i.e.*, anti-human, anti-natural, religion and speculation."[73]

> ... the more, by reflection on religion, by theology, is the identity of the divine and human denied, and the human, considered as such, is depreciated. The reason for this is, that as what is positive in the conception of the divine being can only be human, the conception of man, as an object of consciousness, can only be negative. To enrich God, man must become poor; that God may be all, man must be nothing.[74]

> Religion further denies goodness as a quality of human nature; man is wicked, corrupt, incapable of good; but, on the other hand, God is only good—the Good Being,[75]

One example that Feuerbach gives is of the nun who weds herself to God, thus giving herself a heavenly spouse, a process that then denies purity and holiness to human conjugal relations, embuing them only with carnality and sinfulness.

Alienation is best summed up in the sacraments:

> For as that which is or is supposed to be imparted in the water, bread and wine, over and above these natural substances themselves, is something in the imagination only, but in truth, in reality, nothing; so also the object of religion in general, the Divine essence, in distinction from the the essence of Nature and Humanity,—that is to say, if its attributes, as understanding, love, &c., are and signify something else than these attributes as they belong to man and Nature,—is only something in the imagination, but in truth and reality nothing.[76]

The task for religion then is to see itself in its true nature, to reverse the alienating process, to see its beliefs not as objective realities but as symbols which refer to the human subject, to human nature:

> Hence the historical progress of religion consists in this: that what by an earlier religion was regarded as objective, is now regarded as subjective; that is, what was formerly contemplated and worshipped as God is now perceived to be something *human*.[77]

And in a passage that sums up his work's intention, and gives us the reasons for its critical reception from traditional religionists, he says:

> Hence I do nothing more to religion . . . than to open its eyes, or rather to turn its gaze from the internal towards the external, *i.e.*, I change the object as it is in the imagination into the object as it is in reality.
>
> But certainly for the present age, which prefers the sign to the thing signified, the copy to the original, fancy to reality, the appearance to the essence, this change, inasmuch as it does away with illusion, is an absolute annihilation, or at least a reckless profanation; for in these days *illusion* only is *sacred, truth profane.*[78]

Feuerbach knew little about religions other than Christianity, but he accurately saw that his general theory could be applied to all religions. The case of Tantrism shows, I believe, how right he was. It is my contention that Tantrism, and the songs of Ramprasad, do take the doctrines and deities of their religion as symbolic of human nature and human concerns. And I believe the Tantric rituals that use the *pạcamakāra* function in a way that is exactly opposite to the Christian sacraments that Feuerbach criticized as alienating. The Tantric Kundalini doctrine recognizes the identity of the individual and the world, thus overcoming alienation from it, and the Kundalini ritual may be seen as fulfilling the intention of Feuerbach when he said, "In the religious systole man propels his own nature from himself, he throws himself outward; in the religious diastole he receives the rejected nature into his heart again."[79] And in a remark that might be applied as response to the more off-putting aspects of Ramprasad's work, and of Tantrism, Feuerbach says:

> He who earnestly believes in the Divine existence is not shocked at the attributing even of gross sensuous qualities to God. He who dreads an existence that may give offence, who shrinks from the grossness of a positive predicate, may as well renounce existence altogether.[80]

Feuerbach wanted to turn people away from concern with the supernatural to their own concrete situation in the real world. He saw value in religion, but only if it served this end, and only if it was recognized as a symbolic system whose true meaning was related to human existence in the way outlined above. That this did amount, in western religious terms, to an atheistic interpretation of religion, lead to its rejection by Christianity. I am not so sure that Tantrikas, had they heard of it, would have done the same.

## *The Importance of the Reader*

I believe the Goddess in Ramprasad's (largely Tantric) Sakta picture of her should be read in a Feuerbachian way. On the other hand, because Ramprasad does picture the Goddess in a very human way as part of this symbolic process, it is possible to see her as the object of devotion, one who will rescue her faithful servant from the pain and suffering of the world, who will be the vehicle for bearing one across the ocean of *saṅsār*.[81] The two streams of interpretation were obviously well-established by the time of Isvarachandra Gupta's researches in the first half of the nineteenth century, and he himself seems to think that both interpretations are valid. He says Ramprasad "immersed himself in a sea of *Śakti bhakti*," and that his "real internal attitude" was one of "true *sahaja*," a term with obvious Tantric connotations.[82] Then he says, in a passage that combines the two interpretations, "Most of his songs are filled with the *rasa* of *prem-bhakti*. He made no distinction between uttering the name of the formless Brahman and the name of Kali, for him there was no difference between *puruṣa* and *prakṛiti*, or *Parameśvara* and *Parameśvarī*, for him the meaning and purpose of *bhāba, rasa, bhakti* and *jñānā* were the same."[83] Gupta acknowledges the Tantric nature of the "descriptions of Durga in battle" that are in the "heroic mood—*birarasa*,"[84] and after listing thirteen of the songs says, "Those who are sincere Tantrikas or who have deep intuitions in the matter will gain real appreciation of these immortal songs which those without will not have. This is a difficult matter, especially as there are so many deep meanings in Ramprasad's songs, and there are few people left who can understand and explain these meanings." This is a very clear, and very important, statement of the Tantric significance of these songs, and an oblique comment that they are now interpreted in some other way by people with no knowledge of this esoteric meaning.

Add to this the fact that very often in Ramprasad's work one can detect a mood that is almost cynically ironic, as if he is saying, "Well, there you are, take it which way you will." The work is basically Tantric, but if you cannot follow that path, because it has always been recognized that the Tantric way is a difficult way, and is not for the many, then take it how you please.

So wide is the appeal of Ramprasad's songs today that we may include among those who appreciate his work many who are not even believers as well as many believers who are not Tantrikas. Sanjukta Gupta reminds us that:

> [N]ot all Tantric poetry is confined to a ritual context. All over India poet devotees, whether Tantric or not, have left behind a rich body of devotional songs on Tantric themes, the emotional appeal of which is still alive. These compositions stand on their own feet as poetry and music even if one disregards their religious relevance. . . . [I]n Bengal, Rāmprasād Sen . . . composed songs to Kālī. . . . [T]hese collections of songs enriched the general tradition of classical Indian music, and are as popular with non-Tantrics as with Tantrics.[85]

One might say then that neither of these readings is ultimately an incorrect reading of Ramprasad; you may take him how you find him. The choice is yours. It is even possible to read distinctions such as those between darkness and light, ignorance and knowledge, and bondage and freedom in his songs in cultural terms that are not religious at all, as signifying a dictinction between nature and culture. And who is to say that is incorrect?[86] That is Ramprasad's greatest strength and the reason for his continuing importance. And it outweighs his still considerable historical importance as a pivotal figure in the development of Bengal Saktism. Ramprasad is alive, not dead.

Yet when interpreting any text it must be borne in mind, perhaps even more clearly after the heady days of the extremes of Deconstruction, that the possibilities of meaning in the text while often manifold are not endless. Eco reminds us that this business of interpretation goes on between two extremes of possibility:

> On the one side it is assumed that to interpret a text means to find out the meaning intended by its original author or—in any case—its objective nature or essence, an essence which, as such, is independent of our interpretation. On the other side it is assumed that texts can be interpreted in infinite ways.[87]

Neither of these two extremes is open to us. Barthes and Foucault have shown that we can put little store in the intention of the author, and I hope I have show in chapter 2 that this is particularly so in the case of any "historical" Ramprasad. But nor does the text provide an infinite number of meanings. If, as I argued in chapter 2, the *oeuvre* of "Ramprasad" that we have reflects the interests and intentions of a community that preserved the songs, then I think we can confidently say there is a consistency about this body of songs, this "universe of discourse" marked by its association with the legendary "Ramprasad," that points us strongly in the direction of a particular range of meanings.

In this regard Eco also points out that, "[F]rom the moment in which the community is pulled to agree with a given interpretation, there is, if not an objective, at least an *intersubjective* meaning which acquires a privilege over any other possible interpretation spelled out without the agreement of the community."[88] I hope I have been able to show that the community that stands behind this text is a Tantric-Sakta community, and that the intersubjective meaning, this "privileged" meaning, is a Tantric-Sakta meaning, however much others may prefer to see it as something akin to Vaisnava *bhakti*. I hope also that I have been able to demonstrate some of the "pleasure of the text," Roland Barthes's *jouissance*,[89] that may be experienced even by the modern reader of these songs, from which there is undoubtedly a good deal of pleasure still to be had.

# *Conclusion*

The figure of the historical Ramprasad remains tantalizingly shrouded in mists seemingly impenetrable to the methods of historical enquiry. Even so, human nature being what it is, it is tempting to continue the search for this important figure, and to speculate about what he was like. There is some evidence to indicate that there was a Ramprasad Sen associated with the court of Raja Krishnachandra at Krishnanagore, and that he was the author of a work called *Bidyāsundar,* a work containing both erotic and Tantric elements. Was he then a sophisticated and perhaps dilletantish courtier, enjoying the patronage of the Raja, who semi-secretly practiced Tantric rites and who wrote his *Bidyāsundar* to appeal to the jaded tastes of his patron and fellow courtiers? The question of patronage is difficult to decide. There is evidence that he received significant grants of land from the Raja, but traditions continue to insist that he was poor and unable to adequately support his family.

There is also the question about whether it was this Ramprasad who wrote all the songs or *padābalī* that are associated with that name. There is evidence that connects this Ramprasad to poetic duels with a renowned Vaisnava named Aju Goswami, and the songs supposed to have been composed extempore by this Ramprasad certainly feature in the song collections. But there is enough evidence to suggest the possibility of at least one other Ramprasad who lived far to the east in Dacca, and that this Ramprasad was a brahmin, not a *boidya* as Ramprasad Sen was. And as many of the songs contain the authorial signature "dvija Ramprasad," a term usually indicating a brahmin, the possibility is underscored.

We are forced to conclude then that the historical evidence does not allow us to see any historical author of the songs with anything like the clarity and certainty that a photograph would provide. But if we turn away from this historical quest we find prominently before us a portrait of another Ramprasad, a portrait in vivid colors composed from the copious legends that in time surrounded this figure and the songs attributed to him. Moreover, this portrait is at variance with some of the historical evidence that suggests that its painters were not too concerned with details of mere "history." He is pictured with his Goddess, the deity to whom he was so dedicated, so dedicated that he was almost oblivious of worldy affairs, unable to hold down any job, and perhaps unable to adequately support his family. In fact he is seen rather as a crazy saint-singer who wandered the countryside singing of his devotion and then finally one day walked into the river bearing an image of his Goddess on his head, never to be seen again.

The songs he sang were popular and powerful and treasured by his followers who regarded them like sacred mantras. They were so powerful that they even impressed the Muslim nawab, who drew his passing boat to the shore that he might hear Ramprasad praise his Hindu Goddess. They enabled him to defeat Aju Goswami and the Vaisnavites in contests, thus demonstrating the superiority of Saktism over Vaisnavism. His devotion was so powerful that the Goddess herself appeared to him in the form of his daughter, and performed miracles on his behalf.

But there is also a dark side to this portrait. It is expressionistic in style, and the colors used strike some viewers with discomfort as they turn nervously away from it. The Goddess shown with Ramprasad, this Mother with whom he seems to have been so preoccupied, is sometimes a grotesque figure, covered in blood and striding drunkenly through a battle field—yet at the same time disconcertingly erotic in her appeal. Or she sits under a tree in a cremation ground with her husband Siva, both of them so stoned as to be almost oblivious to the world. Her attitude to her children when in this state is neglectful, and she seems to care little.

Even when she accepts her role as mother she is sometimes a poor one. She is fickle and unreliable in her dealings with her son, she offers him sugar then gives him bitter *nim;* just when he wants to throw himself at her feet she forces him back on himself. But he knows this is all a game, and he knows it will eventually come to an end. Her son's attitude at times is strongly colored by anxiety and doubt about the nature of this mother. Yet if she is no ideal mother, she is one he must accept and come to terms with, for she is his mother and his only mother. That is what life is like, that is the way the world is.

Like many paintings this one tells us as much, or perhaps even more, about those who painted it than the subject of the portrait. It was executed by the Saktas of late eighteenth and early nineteenth-century Bengal, a community emerging from a long period when Gauriya Vaisnavism had dominated the religious landscape and forced them on the defensive. Now they were seizing their chances, coming out from underground so to speak, asserting their sometimes strange beliefs and practices openly, claiming they too had a saint just as devoted as Caitanya. So Tantrikas linked up with those who had worshiped the folk goddesses in the forests when husbands were not looking. The lower classes of society brought these goddeses with them and joined with brahmins who had followed the Sanskritic goddess of the *Devī Māhātmya.*

The dominant lines of the portrait then are first the ancient Puranic line from the *Devī Māhātmya* which, while it shows a Goddess who is a rather unorthodox figure, nevertheless shows her as the foundation power of all existence and the sustainer of the world, and at the same time miltant and alluring. The second line is composed of Tantric elements that tend to dominate the portrait. They point to a Tantric understanding of the self and the world. They indicate the performance of Tantric rituals and a Tantric understanding of release from the vicissitudes of worldy life on the part of her followers. This is a dark line. But the picture is lightened by the bright colors of the third line that introduce the goddesses and traditions of the deep current of Bengali folk religion. This Goddess is one that all can identify with; she understands their domestic woes, she comes even as their daughter with all the joy that her visit engenders, even if her departure brings sadness. Together they proclaimed, "This is our Goddess. This is what she is like. And these are the ways we worship her." And the people responsible for this portrait could at last hold up this image with pride and show their Ramprasad and their Goddess openly to the whole countryside.

Their crusade was successful. The traditions spread and grew as they did so. The worship of this Goddess became ever more popular. One hundred years after the death of Ramprasad one of his greatest admirers, Ramakrishna Paramahamsa, was visiting one day the house of a devotee in Calcutta:

As it was . . . the night of the full moon, Ramakrishna went with the devotees into the room where Durga was being worshipped. The Mother had been decorated with sandalwood paste, flowers and flower garlands and she possessed a wonderful splendour. A priest was seated in front of her, and lights were burning all around. Ramakrishna gave one of the devotees some money and told him to offer it to the Goddess, because all who come to worship are required to make some such small presentation. Ramakrishna then remained standing in front of her, with the devotees behind him, his hands folded together. He stayed like this for a long time, gazing at the image.

Then as he was looking at it he went into deep trance. He stood silently like a stone image, his eyes glazed. Some time later he uttered a deep sigh, and broke his trance. Then, as if still intoxicated, he said, "Mother, I'm going now." But he couldn't leave—he remained standing in the same attitude. . . .

Then Ramakrishna went with the devotees into the drawingroom. When he came in he stood in the middle and said, "Mother, come and stay in my heart." Jadu Mallick [the owner of the house] was sitting there with his relatives. Ramakrishna was still a little in a trance, and he sang this song—

O Mother, you are full of bliss,
Do not deprive me of all joy.

When he had finished the song he was still in a state of emotional fervour and said to Jadu, "What shall I sing now? Shall I sing 'Mother I'm no prematurely-born weakling'?" Then he began to sing—

Mother, I'm no prematurely-born weakling,
I'm not afraid of your anger.
Those crimson feet of yours which Siva holds in the lotus of
his heart are my treasure,
But when I ask for my property you try to deceive me.
I keep in my heart the ownership document, signed by Siva,
So now I'll take legal action, and get judgement in my favour.

If you oppose me you'll find out what kind of son I am,
I'll submit to the hearing the document my *guru* has given.
What a scandal this dispute between mother and son will
create, says Ramprasad,
But I'll leave off when you take me quietly in your lap.[1]

Today Goddess worship dominates the religious life of Bengal. The main holiday season is centered on the great Durga Puja, celebrated with enormous happiness and ceremony in private home and public pandal alike, while throughout the land, in roadside shrines and in the great temples, people offer their worship every day. Such devotion is still accompanied by the chanting of the Chandi and the singing of Ramprasadi songs. People's attitudes have no doubt changed over the last two hundred years, and who is to know how so many individuals now understand this tradition?[2] But undeniably the songs and traditions of Ramprasad are as alive today as they were then, sustaining the life of the Saktas of Bengal.

# *Appendix: Isvarachandra Gupta's Biography of Ramprasad*

The Bengali text may be found in Bhabatosh Datta, ed. *Isvaracandra Gupta racita kabijībanī,* Calcutta, Calcutta Book House, 1958, 47–82. The translation is my own.

## *Kabiranjan Ramprasad Sen*[1]

It was in the daily *Prabhākar* in the month of Aswin that we first revealed a few songs composed by the great Kabiranjan Ramprasad Sen. Any reader of them would be completely filled with the bliss of love, because never before has anything comparable been published in Bengali by any poet. Among those poets born in Bengal Ramprasad Sen will be worthy of consideration as the greatest because of his spiritual qualities as devotee and *jñānī,* and these spiritual qualities shine through his verse in such a new way that when singers sing them they ravish the ear of the listener. Also Ramprasad has such a command of musical form, and has introduced new musical elements into his songs too. It does not matter even if these songs are performed unaccompanied, they instantly captivate the mind of the listener, and grasping the central idea he will be completely filled with pleasure to the extent that he reckons these the most beloved things on earth. Any of Ramprasad's verses are so skilfully composed both in terms of musical quality and religious sentiment that the effect is like a bright ray of sunlight which dispells the darkness and opens the heart's lotus so that one is overwhelmed with the fragrance of its nectar.

As a poet Ramprasad had such uncommon ability and supernatural power, as anyone can see, that when his heart was moved he would compose a song at once, not waiting till he could sit down with pen and inkpot. The words poured from his mouth in verse. He was one of the foremost travellers on the spiritual path, a man whose mind dwelt constantly on God, to the extent that he was utterly careless in matters of food and clothing. So he was not able to accumulate a good fortune, even though he was an exceptional poet and there were a number of very rich people in the country. He could easily have become a wealthy man had he desired to be. But all these things seemed utterly insignificant to a mind which thought only on Kali's name.

Ramprasad's songs were so noble and distinctive that they became known as "Ramprasadi Songs," songs with the ability to destroy danger and lift men from their misfortunes.

Ramprasad Sen started out as a clerk for an accountant in some wealthy household in Calcutta or nearby, but as he was not able to apply his mind closely to such worldly affairs he had no liking for such labour. So he would neglect his work, entirely oblivious of the fact of his master's dissatisfaction, and every day he would take up his place at his desk, open up his account book and fill whole pages with nothing but the name "Durga Durga." Finally one day he sat down and wrote this song:

> Make me your accounts clerk, O Mother,
> I will never betray your trust.
> Everyone else plunders the treasury of your feet, and I cannot bear it.
> You have left it in the charge of the forgetful Siva,
> He is fickle and gives away your property, yet still you trust him.
> He receives half your body as a grant, as well as a good wage,
> While I work without any wages, wanting only the dust from your feet.
> If you remain with your father, then I am lost,
> If you stay with my father, Siva, then I will receive my due, Mother.
> Prasad says, Let me die at those feet of yours which dispel all misfortunes,
> In that position I will be safe from all dangers.

When the accounts clerk saw this poem on the last page of the book he was very angry and said to his master, "Sir, this mad or drunk fellow who at first inspired faith through his work has now ruined everything! See, he has completely spoiled this beautiful new book, there isn't a single figure in it, only this lunacy. . . ." On hearing this his master looked at all the pages of the book, and as he read again and again the poem "Make me your accounts clerk, O Mother" a strange mood came over him. He was so moved by it that tears came to his eyes and he said to the cashier, "Who are you accusing of being mad or drunk? This fellow hasn't spoiled a good book, you are so drunk with the wine of worldliness that you haven't been able to grasp the true sentiment of this song. Ramprasad is no ordinary man, he is a holy man, an incarnate son of the Goddess." Then he addressed the Kabiranjan with words of devotion and said, "Ramprasad, as long as you remain on the path you have set out on nothing but trouble will befall you. So as long as you wander in the forests of this world I will give you thirty rupees per month stipend,[2] there is no deed for you to stay here any longer, go now to your house and keep up your good work."

Ramprasad went home and passed his time quite happily on his new stipend, but with a wife and family he was not able to prosper domestically on so small an income, and his dependents began to nag him constantly to find some other source of income. However he took no notice of that either and immersed himself in a sea of *Śakti bhakti* and song singing. As a result his family had no material goods and depended on the wealthy who came to hear his songs and *saṅkīrtans* and made presents to him. But because he himself was generous and benevolent whenever he saw anyone who was poor and needy he would immediately give them everything he had, so his own pot was never full and his family were constantly bewailing their want of food. Yet because he was such an open-handed person he did not waste away in utter poverty, When his wife or son or daughter became very annoyed at him he would call God to mind and compose some song such as:

> You have done me a favour, Mother,
> By not giving me worldly things.
> You've given me no earthly possessions at all.
> You gave me nothing so you received nothing back, and as you won't give me anything you won't get anything.
> So what can I lose?
> Let the game continue, I'll agree to that, but now the game is nearly over.
> O Mother, if you had given to me I would have given to you, I would have taken and eaten what I earned as your labourer.

But now I am no worker of yours, so how can I ask for wages?
I haven't the power to force them out of you.
So where are we in all this, my protesting seems futile, and is tiring me out,
Yours is a tortuous way, and this distress of mine is unbearable.
O Mother in this dark midnight my mind remains awake in yoga, what you are doing is cruel,
I am in danger in this world and the next, the *cakōr* bird receives no nectar.
O Mother, I pull towards the calm waters, but my mind draws me back, so great is the bondage of my *karma.*
Ramprasad says, That pot-bellied mind of mine is dying, being pulled in two directions.

Ignorant people might perhaps question whether Ramprasad was in an excellent state of mind when he composed this song. He who can grasp its hidden meaning will be happy. It is by no means an easy matter to keep an even temperament in times of great want and hardship, but if one can attain a state of ease in such a situation he will know true ease.[3]

Here are a few more songs which give an indication of the poet's real internal attitude:

My pride is hurt, Mother,
At what you have done to me,
You've made me poor and needy by saddling me with a family like this.
You even quarreled with Siva because he was a beggar.
No doubt knowledge is considered the highest *dharma,* but giving is better still,
Even Radha didn't go to Mathura without a gift.
You play at being poor, Mother, by covering yourself with ashes,
Where have you hidden your treasure?
So be gracious to Prasad, Mother—why are you being so stingy?
If you keep me at your feet I can escape adversity at every step.

Also:

At the name of Tara all prosperity vanishes,
Only my patched knapsack remains,

And that won't last long.
As a goldsmith steals gold and flees leaving base metal in its place
So your name removes all I have and leaves me destitute.
When a man, beset by many fears, utters Durga's name in his house
O Mother, you awake within his heart, knowing it is time.
When the parents live under a tree, covered with ashes,
Mother, it's doubtful if the son can live in a house.
Tara has encircled Prasad, it's difficult to find him,
O brothers, friends, don't hold out any hope for Ramprasad.

Every now and then some relative would come to Ramprasad and say, "You've passed so many days in sadness, why don't you enjoy yourself a little," but he would give no answer to this, he would just sing a song, the song being his real answer. For example:

O mind, don't hope for any comfort
If you want to dwell at the Mother's dependable feet.
Siva is in a state of utter poverty even though he is the wise Lord of the gods.
To those in distress she is compassionate, those who hope for comfort feel only hardship.
Yuddhisthira, who dwelt in glory, lost the dice game and departed for the forest,
Disaster comes in the midst of merry-making, mind, don't be angry at this,
Oh, in pleasure there is pain and in pain pleasure, as the saying goes.
O mind, you thought you would get what you wanted with insincere devotion
She'll take every last cent, she won't leave you a thing.
If, O mind, you are Prasad's mind, why act so like a rustic?
Work hard, and you will get the pearl of greatest price.

So in this way there arose an abundance of wonderful stories. Once the Kabiranjan, in order to fulfil the family tradition, went to the Sanskrit school of the famous logician Balaram Tarkabhusan. When the proud pundit saw him he said, "See, there goes that drunkard." Many respectable and learned people who were there were astounded at this and remonstrated with him, "Master *bhaṭṭāchārya,* what have you said! Ramprasad Sen is such a holy man, why do you ridicule him by calling him drunk?" Ramprasad said nothing at all to the scholar, he merely smiled. He put his answer in a song:

> O tongue, proclaim the name of Kali
> Death draws near with matted hair.
> Whoever has Kali in his heart has no need of logic,
> Only one who recites scripture for money needs a pot or picture for his worship.
> Bring your tongue under control and taste the sweetness of Shyama's name,
> Sing to her, drink your fill, you are good enough for that.
> Kali's name is full of sweetness, the only place of liberation,
> So repeat her name, is that such a terrible thing to do?
> Fill your ears with her praises, don't listen to any other name,
> Prasad says, Through that name you'll overcome your difficulty.

Also:

> I haven't drunk wine,
> With pleasure I drink nectar.
> Today my mind is overwhelmed, and people say I'm drunk with wine.

Here, in this beautiful verse, Ramprasad has expressed great learning and the highest spiritual sentiments. God has never before bestowed such wonderful power on anyone; Prasad alone has acquired such grace. The divine power of the Devi herself has possessed his throat, otherwise how could he express such uncommon sentiments.

Once on the last day of the month of Chaitra Ramprasad Sen went with several friends to a pole-swinging *(caṛak)* ceremony. As the *caṛakī* swung round and round, suspended from the pole, someone said, "Look, what a beautiful sight." Prasad smiled at him and said, "Brother, that's just an ordinary *caṛak*. Day and night I whirl round on a *caṛak* that can't be compared to this!" They asked him what kind of *caṛak* that was, and immediately, in the presence of a great crowd, he sang aloud this song:

> O mind, you whirl about like a *caṛakī* in this terrible world,
> The great Lord of Yoga laughs in amusement and you don't recognise him.
> Those two self-born Sivas on the young woman's breast, O mind,

Worship them with *bilba* leaves.
Inside the house the young woman speaks, outside in the *gājan* festival the drums beat,
The pole turns and the drums beat again and again.
Climbing the tall scaffold of desire you fell and broke your ribs,
O mind, the pain you felt is insignificant, your good fortune is great,
You have put all your hope in the *caṛakī* tree, choosing that as the best.
O mind, what you call love is the cord of *māyā* with the hook tied to it.
Prasad says again and again, Out of the worthless comes that which is best.
O mind, when you die you will receive a horn, use it to call the Mother.

When the people heard this holy man, filled with love and devotion, they were immediately charmed and began to chant, "*Sādhu, sādhu, sādhu.*" Here I must thank those people for recognizing the deep spiritual qualities of the man and his songs. Otherwise what a disaster would have befallen us, because we are not able to see this great spirit in person. That time was like the real Golden Age, while this is the Kali Age and can in no way be compared with that age, it's certainty is difficult to come by these days. That time into which we are born as men is the real time for us. Today people prefer darkness to the liberating light. Today, where is the freedom of that age? Where is that pleasure? Where is that *dharma*? Where is that *karma*? Where is that wisdom? Where is that spiritual discipline? Where is the scholarship? Where is its poetic talent? Where is its respect and reverence? And where are the determination and devotion? Time has swallowed them all up. Now no-one wants to hear about Rama, no-one wants anything to do with Krishna or Yuddhisthira, no-one mentions king Vikramaditya, that great patron of learning. All we can remember is the time of Maharaja Krishnachandra of Navadvip, and how happy we are if even one percent survives from that time. The Maharaja at least held learned scholars and great poets in high esteem, and rewarded them with his patronage. There were also in Bengal at that time afluent landowners who supported scholars and poets as much as they were able. Today there is no sign of those times. Today there are many excellent scholars and poets, but regretably no-one respects them or encourages them, let alone reward them for their abilities. If any teacher shows great scholarship, or some poet great poetic ability, then rather then laboring to discover their inner mysteries people with a mocking smile consign all those excellent things to hell. Today mediocrity rules and excellence is neither recognized nor praised. Those whom God has made wealthy do not use their wealth for good works, they only use it for their own display. Scriptural discourse has completely disappeared and people spend their time pursuing false pleasures. No longer do people take pleasure in worthwhile literature ancient or modern, which they can't in the least understand; their greatest delight comes from being invited to their friends' houses to watch the farces of the *jatrawallahs* and listen to the nonsense they sing....

What can one do? Blessed is the man who can find real happiness in such times. On all sides are the bazaars of hypocrisy and deceit, nowhere is there a fruit shop in sight. In this kind of atmosphere scholars and men of quality are saddened, for who is there to recognize their qualities? In the land where men wear no clothes, the washermen do not eat; where there is no recognition of worth how can one sell virtue? No-one makes any effort at all to pursue some worthy cause. If, moving in some rich society we see people who are wise, learned, refined, civil, courteous, we are pleased and consider ourselves fortunate. If the whole of society was like this there would be no limit to our happiness. But unfortunately in Bengal this pleasure is very rare, there are few places where such people can be seen. However, quality is more important than quantity. And I have been engaged in writing about one such piece of good fortune, so please prepare yourselves for a feast.

At the court of Maharaja Krishnachandra Ray Bahadur, there resided many men learned in the scriptures, many poets such as Bharatchandra Ray Gunakar, and many men highly qualified in other matters. But even in the company of such men the people were greatly pleased to listen to the work of that descendant of a *boidȳa* (physician) family from Kumarhatt, Ramprasad Sen, the *Kālīkīrtan*, *Kṛiṣṇakīrtan* and *Bidȳāsundar*, and thought him the greatest poet of all. There was a *kīrtan* singer called Bala Phenchata who used to sing Ramprasadi *Kālīkīrtans* who went one day to the Krishnanagore palace and stole everyone's hearts with his singing. The Raja himself was enraptured and said to the singer, "Balaram, for a long time you have been known as Phen-chata [Frothy-lips], now I will give you the name

Madhu-chata [Sweet-lips]." Balaram, very pleased at the Raja's favour, saluted him and said, "Maharaj, I am pleased that you as Raja have removed the froth which comes from my fits but have not removed my lips." This pleased the Raja who then gave the singer a suitable reward. The Navadvip ruler wanted Ramprasad to remain with him in his service, but this was not to be as by this time Ramprasad had no concern at all for worldly desires. What Ramprasad wanted, and what the Maharaja agreed to, was that he would come to Halisahore from time to time and set up court in his house for a few days in order to listen to his songs. Everyone was so delighted by what they heard that he gave him the title 'Kabiranjan'. Ramprasad then composed his *Bidyāsundar* in response to the royal favor of the granting of the title. In this matter there is clear proof that the Maharaja, after seeing Ramprasad's *Bidyāsundar*, gave orders to Bharatchandra to compose one too. This he did and became famous for the beauty of his work. As he had not written his work as a result of any patronage Ramprasad's *Bidyāsundar* may not be in every respect as beautiful as Bharatchandra's. But in a few places, especially where he deals with spiritual themes and praises Kali's name, it may be considered better. Also, the person who composed the *Kālīkīrtan* and *Kṛiṣṇakīrtan* is much superior to that of the *Bidyāsundar*, so superior that one can say there are no verses better than these. Formerly Ramprasad's songs were so popular that they provided a livelihood for many people, and even today thousands of people derive their occupation from them. But sadly today, because of the poverty of good singers, the *Kālīkīrtan* and *Kṛiṣṇakīrtan* are beginning to disappear to the extent that there is hardly anyone left who knows their ragas and tunes. If some qualified person was to master these today and sing them he would certainly establish a great reputation for himself.

All the Ramprasadi songs that are so well known in the eastern regions are not produced here. Boatmen in the province of Dacca, Serajgunj and Pabna, are always singing them, and their devotion is so great that they will not sing them unless they have bathed. They say, "May we go to hell if we sing Ramprasad songs in unwashed clothes."

In the Bengali year 1165 [=1759] Maharaja Krishnachandra Ray gave Ramprasad Sen 14 *bighās* of land taxfree, land described in the deed as "uncultivated land for your sons and grandsons in turn to occupy and enjoy." The land is very close to Kumarhatt and the name and seal of the Raja are found on the deed.

When the Raja came to Kumarhatt, he used to bring Ramprasad and Aju Goswami together and watch them engage in singing contests. Ramprasad was a king among poets, and Aju Goswami was half mad, but he had the ability to extemporise humorous verse. So Ramprasad would sing one of his devotional songs, and he would produce a humorous answer to it.

One day before the Raja Ramprasad sang this song:

This world is a screen of delusion,
So, brother, lets enjoy ourselves among its fleshpots.
It is made of earth, fire, wind, water and ether in orderly arrangement,
First *prakṛiti* is gross, then through self-consciousness it differentiates into thousands of forms,
As dishes of water produce different reflections of the sun, but when they disappear its true nature is revealed.
When I was in the womb I was a yogi, but when I was born I ate the earth,
The midwife cut the cord, but how can I cut the cords that bind me?
There is sweetness in a beautiful woman's voice, but really that sweetness is a cup of poison,
Once I drank it eagerly, now I writhe in the poison's pain.
Blissfully Ramprasad says, O Supreme Daughter of the Supreme Being,
O Mother, do whatever you wish, you are the daughter of the Mountain.

After listening to this Aju Goswami replied:

This world is a house of pleasure
Eat, drink and enjoy yourself.
That fellow Sen has no knowledge, that you know.
O brother, friend, wife and son, sit down and have a cup of milk.

The Kabiranjan sang the song:

Come. O mind, let us go wandering
To Kali the wishfulfilling tree
Where you can gather and eat the four fruits.
Of your two wives, enjoyment and renunciation, take only the latter with you.

Her oldest son is called discrimination, question him about the truth.
Send pride and ignorance back to your father and mother.
If illusion drags you into its pit seize hold of the peg of patience for support.
Keep the two goats, vice and virtue, tied to the sacrificial post,
If they don't obey your commands, sacrifice them with the sword of knowledge.
Make your wife's children understand they must keep their distance,
If they don't understand, plunge them into the sea of knowledge.
Prasad says, If you do as I say you can give a good answer to death,
Do all these things, my dear ones, and you will be very dear to me.

The Goswami gave this answer to it:

The poet Ramprasad has said,
'Come, O mind, let us go wandering.'
Don't go anywhere at his say-so,
Does he know the mind of the *sādhaka*?

In his *Kālīkīrtan* Ramprasad Sen has described the incident where Bhagavati tends the cows in a grove of mango trees:

O Gauri, wife of Siva, dressed like a *gopi*
Your youth adorned with the splendour of shining gold.
In Surabhi's family there are inumerable cows
Coming up from *pātāla* you hear the Mother's flute.
O Durga, when the flute sounds, when the flute sounds,
The calf chases the cow, kicking up the dust with its feet,
The dust hides the sun. You pass the night in ecstacy, etc.

The Goswami answered this:

Without knowing God this is impossible,
Can a woman become a cow and wander about?
If that's possible, Yashoda can go,
What will she send to Gopal? . . .

Ramprasad Sen said:

Plunge, O mind, into the ocean of Shyama's existence,
Why float about on the surface any longer.

Goswami answered:

Your pulse is weak,
Don't plunge too deep.
If you catch a fever,
You'll die for sure.

Reading all these verses readers will be able to judge for themselves the disparity between the wisdom and other qualities of Sen and Goswami.

A few days after the Maharaja had given him land he asked, "Well, Senji, are you cultivating the land or not?" Ramprasad answered him with this song:

My body is Tara's field, what more need I fear?
There the Lord of the Gods, like a good farmer, sows as seed the great mantra.
He has surrounded this body with the fence of *dharma* supported by the posts of patience,
Now what can that thief Death do, with Siva guarding it?
Seeing him the six bullocks have come out of the barn,
With the sharp scythe of Kali's name he has cut all the weeds of sin.
The gentle rain of love and devotion falls on it day and night,
From Kali the wishfulfilling tree, O brother, can be obtained the four aims of life.

Ramprasad's verse expresses wonderfully the difference of his condition; he was not able to observe the ritual prescriptions of religion, all this is admirably proved by his songs. He was one who understood the true nature of things, and he worshiped God with thrilling songs totally indifferent to the consequences. Most of his songs are filled with the *rasa* of *prem-bhakti*. He made no distinction between uttering the name of the formless Brahman and the name of Kali, for him there was no difference between *puruṣa* and *prakṛiti*, or *Parameśvara* and *Parameśvarī*, for him the meaning and purpose of *bhāba rasa, bhakti, prem* and *jñāna* were the same.

With regard to his Sakta devotionalism everyone referred to him as Kali's heroic son, they used to say that Annapurna used to come from Kashi every day and inspire his speech and he would compel her to listen to his songs. With respect to this one astonishing miracle is talked about all over the country:

One day, in order to repair the fence round his house, Ramprasad Sen gathered together all the materials and went in search of a builder. When he returned with the builder a few moments later the materials had gone and the fence was all fixed. Immediately there was an uproar among the neighbouring villagers who said, "Annapurna herself has come from Kashi and fixed Ramprasad's fence." So many wonderful happenings like this are reported that if they were to be described they could not be contained in a single book. But Ramprasad never made any such claim himself, lest it detract from reference to his many compositions.

There is also a rumor that the Kabiranjan composed 100,000 songs, but there is no proof of this, the only evidence for it is found in one of his songs:

> I have heard that Mother Shyama's court is very difficult
> The clerk calls for the plaitiff but none appears.
> What defence can I offer in a court where Siva is petitioner,
> O Mother you have appointed yourself as dewan, how can I trust your words?
> I have briefed 100,000 lawyers, what more can I do?
> I call you by your name Tara [the Deliverer], but you don't listen.
> So I abuse you and you become Kali [dark] at the indignity.
> Ramprasad says, You have ruined my life.

It is certainly not impossible that Ramprasad wrote 100,000 songs, and it is in many respects likely, because he never ceased composing them from childhood to the day of his death. Whatever came to his mind he turned to poetry. But the only books we have any record of are the *Kabirañjan, Kālīkīrtan* and *Kṛiṣṇakīrtan.* Other works of his which have been collected together earlier have by now almost disappeared, because in those days people used to guard them carefully like some secret mantra, not showing them to anyone even at the cost of their lives, bringing them out only at *pūjā* time to decorate them with flowers and sandalwood paste, as some people still do today, and though we would have given our all we were not able to obtain any of these songs. Hidden in this way they have become completely lost. Worms and other insects ate them, moisture decomposed them, fire burned them, they were used by the impotent as charms to secure beautiful women or long life, and so people destroyed Ramprasad's reputation.

Twenty-five years have now passed during which I have been engaged in collecting Ramprasad songs, and until now however hard I have tried I have had little success. Some I have even been able to see only with the greatest of difficulty. Some have been eaten by insects, some have been inadvertently copied incorrectly and there is an awful risk in trying to establish the substance of these. Because of this I modestly request those people for whom this is now an important concern not to keep these things to themselves but to allow us to have them printed. Then there will be inexpressible gratitude throughout the country and great joy at their being made available in this way. I have been able with great difficulty to secure a few songs, and I hope that if more are found I will be able by mutual agreement to remove people's doubts about publishing them.

When he was a little over sixty years old Ramprasad abandoned this illusory world and made his journey to his eternal abode. That day of his death was, according to my calculations, not more that seventy-two years ago. The old people say, "When the time came for the immersion of the Shyama image he said to all his family and friends, 'Today I will be immersed with the image of the Mother, so bring the image and come with me, I'm going now.' When he'd said this he departed for the Ganges with a crowd of people, singing songs." During his lifetime he had composed many wonderful farewell songs full of devotion, and on the way they sang some of them, like this:

> Singing Kali's praises and clapping your hands in joy
> Launch out quickly that boat your body.
> Make mind the boatman, for how else can you escape the cares of the world?
> With the south wind at your back helping you,
> You will reach the other shore, while Death can only look on.
> Siva is no liar, supernatural powers will carry out your wishes,
> Prasad says in pleading reply, Death will flee.

Also:

> Tell me, brother, what happens after death,
> Everyone is aguing about it.

Some say I'll become a ghost, others say I'll go to heaven,
Some say I'll be united with God, others that I'll be absorbed in Brahman.
The Vedas say I am a portion of the ether in a pot which will be destroyed at death.
O virtue and vice are nothing, by respecting them you will lose everything.
Prasad says, What you were in the beginning, brother, that you will be at the end,
As bubbles rise up in water and mixing with it become merged in it,
So I sing this song to bring my body to the shore.

And another example:

Surely this day will pass, only the telling of it will remain,
The disgrace of Tara's name will be endless.
I came to the marketplace of the world, and now I sit by the *ghāt*, my marketing over,
O Mother the sun is going down and I need a boatman.
This fellow fills his boat and sends the poor away,
Mother, I need money to sail with him, where can I get it?
Prasad says, O hard-hearted woman, look back and give me a seat,
And I will float away on the ocean of the world, singing your praises.

So the story goes that he died singing the following song:

Tara, do you remember me any more?
O Mother, will I know such happiness as I am experiencing now?
If Siva had been truthful, would I be pleading with you?
O Mother, after deception on deception I tremble in anticipation.
If I had anywhere else to go I would not have pleaded with you,
O Mother, you have given me hope, you have cut my bonds and lifted me to the top of the tree.
Prasad says, My mind is firm, my gift to the priest was a large one,
O Mother, now it's all over, I have done everything I can.

When he'd said "I have done everything I can" he gave up his life. Among the old people it is said that at the time of his death the *brahmarandhra* at the top of his head opened up. Whether or not this in true we are not able to say at all.

I had intended to describe many other events in Ramprasad's life but lack of time and space have prevented this. However in the course of time I will certainly produce an extended account. If there is any mistake in what we have presented here we would be pleased to know so that we can put the matter right in the *Prabhākar*.

Whenever Ramprasad visited Calcutta he stayed with his maternal uncle in Doyehata in the Jorasanko region. He was a great friend of Chiramani Datta, who was a devotee and well spoken of, and used to spend much time with him.

Many people have never had the opportunity of hearing about the different circumstances surrounding the Kabiranjan's songs. For this reason, I have gathered such information and published it here. Most of his songs have up till now not been published, and the beggars and singers in the bazaars do not give such details. The *āgamanī, saptamī, bijayā, Rāmlīlā, Kṛiṣṇalīlā* and *Śivalīlā* songs that he has composed are so beautiful—especially those in the heroic mood, such as the description of Durga in battle—and their like is not found in the *padābalī*, so I have revealed these first of all, in the hope that they might dispell any regrets the learned reader might have.

[Here Gupta includes sixteen songs, all found in Satyanarayan Bhattacharya's collection].

Those who are sincere Tantrikas or who have deep intuitions in the matter will gain a real appreciation of these immortal songs that those without will not have. This is a difficult matter, especially as there are so many deep meanings in Ramprasad's songs, and there are few people left who can understand and explain these meanings.

This song is so captivating in its expression of Ramprasad's former state:

> My time is up and I have lost my job,
> My mind has been won over to the enjoyment of pleasure (*ratiraṅa!*).
> When I used to go about earning my living
> Then I had brothers, friends, wife and children, all of whom I cared for.

Now I'm earning nothing that's all finished,
Now I'm poor they all have turned against me.
Death's messenger comes to sit at my head, waiting to seize my hair (and carry me off).
Then they will make the funeral preparations and bid me farewell.
Calling to Hari a few times they'll throw me into the flames, and return to their homes,
With Ramprasad out of the way they'll stop their weeping and casually return to their eating.

This song comes from the heart of one possessed in a special way by the atmosphere of renunciation and discrimination of those times. Those people not only had deceitful minds, what they said and did was evil too. Hearsay and what is written here both provide abundant proof of that. Ramprasad himself spent much time in religious practice. Ah, what a great man he was.

Because of the many expressions of *Śakta* devotion everyone can reasonably call Ramprasad a *Śakta,* but even though he was a *Śakta* he was no hypocrite, he was a true *bhakta* with respect to the rituals of worship there was no antipathy at all in his mind. There is excellent proof of that in this song:

O Mother, you are in my heart,
Who says you are in my heart, O Shyama?
Mother, you are in my heart.
You are a hard-hearted woman, a terrible delusion—how many different roles you force me to play!
In different kinds of worship you assume five principle forms,
But how can you escape from one who thinks of all five as one!
He who knows and trusts in you, his trust you will bear,
Will he who knows the value of gold be deceived with glass?
Prasad says, My heart is an unblemished lotus,
And you, in that lotus, dance in my mind.

Ramprasad's single-mindedness, the firmness of his faith and the profundity of his love and devotion are obvious from this verse. Now I have completed the writing of this introduction.

Though this account of the life of Ramprasad has come to an end the task is not completed for much more research remains to be done. It is a matter of some regret that I have not been able to write more. I had intended to record the biographies of all the poets of the past who have become famous in this country, but because of the difficulty of collecting material this has not been an easy task to complete. Today practically noone from those times is left alive, and those old people who are are not especially informed. A few of them know a little but regrettably I have not been able to meet any of them. However, in the spirit of 'to do or die' let us see what happens. I will certainly do what I can, whatever the cost and whatever the shortcomings in what I have been able to achieve. This task has taken on the nature of a crusade, so I am appealling to the general public for help in this matter. We will acknowledge a life-long debt of gratitude to any who assist us in this way, and it is not only we who will benefit but the whole country, so we ask you to be generous with such assistance, whether there is any reward in it or not. However that might be, if the task can be completed I will be satisfied.

## *Kabiranjan Ramprasad Sen*[4]

*[Two]*

Many people have written to me expressing pleasure at what I wrote about the life of Kabiranjan Ramprasad Sen in last month's issue of the magazine. Sen, who was a poet without equal, passed on a long time ago, and even though because it is not the custom in this land to record the life stories of great people we cannot know much about him, for this reason I appealed to the public that if they have any of his songs or knowledge of any events of his life I would be pleased to publish it. As a result of this request I have received a letter part of which I will now reveal.

"We were very pleased to read in the Paush edition of your paper what you wrote about the life of Mahatma Ramprasad Sen, because unless the poet's virtues are discussed in this way in some published paper in time the memory of his genuine qualities and uncommon power will probably disappear. Today only a few old people who knew the great man are left, and he is unknown to modern editors, though some of them may be familiar with a few of his songs. But they are certainly ignorant of his inner nature and do not respect him for it. But you have undertaken, with much effort and expenditure of wealth, the glorious achievement of bringing Sen back to life through the collection of his work. Also the Kabiranjan's spirituality and scholarship have never before received the serious attention that you have given them, and we can vouch for the accuracy of your account because Ramprasad Sen was a native of our village and we were well aquainted with him. And when what you had written was read to the wise and knowledgeable old people of the village they unhesitatingly agreed, after having heard it, with what was written, moreover there is no doubt that he composed his *Gītābalī* under the influence of divine power, because how could work of such power and insight be the result of ordinary unaided strength? I have also heard that though the poet did not have a particularly fine voice the people who heard him when he sang thought that it was a beautiful voice, and remained absolutely spellbound as long as he sang. How could that be unless he had divine grace? Once the magnanimous governor of Navadvip, Maharaja Krishnachandra Ray Bahadur went by boat, accompanied by Sen, to Murshidabad where they stayed for a few days in the boat. Ramprasad spent the whole time singing songs to the glory of God. One day the nawab Siraj-ad-daulah passing in his boat as he enjoyed the evening breeze heard Sen singing, and being captivated by it asked whose boat it was and who the singer was. Later when he had established his identity and summoned Sen over to his boat and commanded him to sing, the Kabiranjan sang a *kheyāl* and a *gajal* for the entertainment of the nawab. But the nawab was displeased and said, 'I have no desire to hear your *kheyāl* and such,' and told him to sing the hymns to Kali which he had previously been singing. At the nawab's command he began to sing one of his own songs filled with devotion to Shyama, and even such a hard-hearted man as Siraj-ad-daulah was powerless to prevent tears coming to his eyes. When the song had ended the nawab applauded him and said, 'Ramprasad, you have received divine favour, if you accept my patronage I will give you high rank,' but Ramprasad had no desire for worldly wealth as a result of accepting such patronage. Let the reader judge what kind of man Ramprasad was and what a hard-hearted atheist Siraj-ad-daulah was; so could it have been by other than divine power that he should be so fascinated by those Bengali songs and utter such praise of them? There are inumerable such wonderful stories like this about Sen, that if they were published would fill a book, so many that it is unnecessary to write them here. Moreover, even though Ramprasad mentioned the names of Kali, Durga, Tara, Siva, etc., in all his songs and the names of these deities were on his lips day and night, he was a monotheist; and though he disliked thinking of the Supreme Being as formless, because of the place and time in which he found himself, in the time and dominion of Raja Krishnachandra Ray, he conformed to the customary public worship, drawing near to God with a clear conscience because God knew his inner attitude; and whatever name people used for God, whether Durga or Isvara or Allah or whatever, because all are addressing God then no harm can come of it. A rose by any other name smells just as sweet. And there is proof in this later song that the names he used were a verbal convention only:

> Are you mad, mind, searching about for her in a darkened house?
> You can only know her through ecstatic love (*bhāb*), what can you gain without it?
> First control the moon, making Sakti your only desire.
> There is a secret room in the house where she will hide at dawn,
> You couldn't find her with the six philosophies, nor in the Vedas and Tantras.
> She enjoys the taste of devotion, dwelling always in the house of Nanda,
> To experience that the Great Yogi practiced from age to age.
> When that emotion arises it draws one like a magnet attracting iron,
> Prasad says, She I regard as Mother must I reveal openly?
> You must understand her, mind, through signs and gestures."

# Notes

## Introduction

1. E.J. Thompson and A.M. Spencer, *Bengali Religious Lyrics, Sakta.*

2. See R. Schneiter, *Rāmprasād Sen und Śrī Rāmakrishna Paramahaṃsa (1836–1886).* (Bern, P. Lang, 1986). Note also Sumit Sarkar, "'Kaliyuga,' 'Chakri' and 'Bhakti' Ramakrishna and His Times," 1547, where he speaks about the selective use Ramakrishna makes of Ramprasad. And for a comprehensive study see J.J. Kripal, *Kali's Child.*

3. For example, D.C. Sen, *Baṅabhāṣā ō sāhitya;* Sukumar Sen, *Baṅa sāhitȳer itihās;* Asitkumar Bandopadhyay, *Bāṅlā sāhitȳer itibṛitta; Bhārater śakti-sādhanā ō śākta sāhitya.*

4. Many of the terms used in this paragraph, the "death" of the author, "text", and the "reading" of the text, are technical terms in academic discourse that are explained in chapter 2.

## Chapter 1

1. S.K. De, *Early History of the Vaisnava Faith and Movement in Bengal,* 34. The principal biographies are the *Caitanya-carita* of Murari Gupta, *Caitanya-bhāgavata* of Vrindavan-dasa, and *Caitanya-caritāmṛita* of Krishnadasa Kaviraja (in Bengali). See, however, E.C. Dimock's warning about the unhistorical nature of this material in his "Religious Biography in India: The 'Nectar of the Acts' of Caitanya."

2. E.J. Thompson and A.M. Spencer, *Bengali Religious Lyrics, Sakta*; E.A. Payne, *The Saktas*; R.C. Dutt, *Cultural Heritage of Bengal*; D. Zbavitel, *Bengali Literature*; J. Sinha, *Rama Prasada's Devotional Songs.*

3. For example, Dineshcandra Sen, *Baṅabhāṣā ō sāhitya*; Sukumar Sen, *Baṅa sāhitẏer itihās*; Asitkumar Bandopadhyay, *Bāṅlā sāhitẏer itibṛitta*, vol. 4; and Sashibhusan Dasgupta, *Bhārater śakti-sādhanā ō śākta sāhitya.*

4. L. Nathan and C. Seeley, *Grace and Mercy in Her Wild Hair*, 2 and 13 n1.

5. J.K. Chakrabarti, *Śāktapadābalī ō śaktisādhanā*, 245.

6. S.N. Bhattacharya, *Rāmprasād: jībanī ō racanāsamagra*, 1.

7. First published in *Saṅbādprabhākar*, Thursday 1 Paush 1260 (15 December 1853). The text may be found in Bhabatosh Datta, *Iśvaracandra Gupta racita kabijībanī*, 47–79.

8. Appendix, 152.

9. Appendix, 155f.

10. First published in *Saṅbādprabhākar*, Friday 1 Magh 1260 (13 January 1854). Also in B. Datta, *Isvaracandra Gupta racita kabijībanī.* See Appendix, 156–158.

11. Appendix, 146f.

12. W. Ward, *A View of the History, Literature and Mythology of the Hindoos.*

13. See S.N. Bhattacharya, *Rāmprasād*, 1; Sivaprasad Bhattacharya, *Bhāratcandra ō Rāmprasād*, 43–9; Yogendranath Gupta, *Sādhak kabi Rāmprasād*, 239.

14. See S.N. Bhattacharya, *Rāmprasād*, 2.

15. S.N. Bhattacharya, *Rāmprasād*, 3.

16. Dayalchandra Ghosh, *Prasādprasaṅa*, 11–13. Ghosh also introduces the possibility that there was another Ramprasad, a brahmin, who lived in East Bengal. I will discuss this further in the next chapter.

17. See S.N. Bhattacharya, *Rāmprasād, racanāsamagra*, 107ff. Note that Bhattacharya's book renumbers the pages of the "collected work," the *racanāsamagra.*

18. R.C. Mazumdar, *Baṅīa kulaśāstra*; Sukhamoy Mukhopadhyay has written an appendix, pp 117–35. I am grateful to Professor Ashin Das Gupta, then Director of the Indian National Library, for drawing my attention to this work.

19. R.C. Mazumdar, *Baṅīa kulaśāstra,* 104–7.

20. R.C. Mazumdar, *Baṅīa kulaśāstra,* 127.

21. Mukhopadhyay thinks the *Candraprabhā* and *Ratnaprabha* were first compiled in the seventeenth century. They would have been updated continuously since then, 127.

22. See S.N. Bhattacharya, *Rāmprasād, racanāsamagra,* 36ff.

23. S.N. Battacharya, *Rāmprasād,* 24–7, and Sivaprasad Bhattacharya, *Bhāratcandra ō Rāmprasād,* 36ff.

24. Appendix, 147. A bigha is approximately $^{1}/_{6}$ hectare.

25. Dineshchandra Bhattacharya, *Kabirañjan Rāmprasād Sen,* 21.

26. For the deed see Jyotiprakash Sengupta, *Sādhaka Rāmprasād,* 50ff, and Sivaprasad Bhattacharya, *Bhāratcandra ō Rāmprasād,* 40.

27. See S.N. Bhattacharya, *Rāmprasād,* 14ff.

28. S.N. Bhattacharya, *Rāmprasād,* 23ff, and Sivaprasad Bhattacharya, *Bhāratcandra ō Rāmprasād,* 40–2.

29. Appendix, 151.

30. Appendix, 140f.

31. Appendix, 151.

32. Appendix, 157.

33. E.C. Dimock, "Religious Biography in India," 112.

34. Appendix, 155f.

35. Appendix, 156f.

36. Appendix, 188n2.

37. See A.R. Mallick, "Modern Historical Writing in Bengal," 446–60. Mallick calls the period 1800–1875 "one of imitation, as most of the historians, while of course making some feeble attempts at independent interpretations of their history, followed, on the whole, the beaten paths of the English historians on the subject," 448. Gupta's biography seems to me to be one of the notable attempts at independent interpretation.

## Chapter 2

1. SNB 14, *āmāy deō mā tabildārī.* When referring to songs by Ramprasad I will give the number of the song in S.N. Bhattacharya's collection, and the first line of the song.

2. See Chr. Lindtner, *Nagarjuniana: Studies in the Writings and Philosophy of Nagarjuna.*

3. For Dayalchandra Ghosh see his *Prasādprasaṅa.*

4. Appendix, 147.

5. Ghosh, *Prasādprasaṅa,* 12.

6. Ghosh, *Prasādprasaṅa,* 38.

7. Ghosh, *Prasādprasaṅa,* 15.

8. Ghosh, *Prasādprasaṅa,* 15. He also says, however, on p. 16, that there is little difference between the two in "tune" and "composition" though there is some in "depth of mood."

9. Ghosh, *Prasādprasaṅa,* 17. See also on this question Yogendranath Gupta, *Sādhaka kabi Rāmprasād,* 213, and Satyanarayan Bhattacharya, *Rāmprasād,* 104–9.

10. S.N. Bhattacharya, *Rāmprasād,* 106. See also Ward, *A View of the History, Literature and Mythology of the Hindoos.*

11. Yogendranath Gupta, *Sādhaka kabi Rāmprasād,* 200–17; Amiya Lal Mukhyapadhyay, *Gāne Rāmprasād,* i, ii; Atulchandra Mukhopadhyay, *Rāmprasād,* 251. The works cited here, and in note 14, are the major studies in Bengali on Ramprasad.

12. Yogendranath Gupta, *Sādhaka kabi Rāmprasād,* 214–7; S.N. Bhattacharya, *Rāmprasād,* 110. The issue is further complicated by the fact that a prominent Bengali zamindar, Maharajah Rajballabh (1707–1763) attempted to raise the status of the *boidya* caste: "Rajballah was also a great social reformer. In his days the section of the Vaidya [= *boidya*] community to which he belonged did not wear the sacred thread. At enormous cost he assembled the Brahman Pandits from different parts of India, and after a great deal of discussion they recorded their opinion in writing admitting the right of Vaidyas to use the sacred thread,—a right which they still maintain," R.C. Majumdar, *Maharajah Rajballabh,* Calcutta, University of Calcutta Press, 1947, p. 90. This took place in 1754. I am informed by my colleague David Curley that Rasik Lal Gupta, in his *Maharaj Rajbhallabh Sen,* (1904) gives the text of an inscription confirming this, and the text of the decree itself.

13. S.N. Bhattacharya, *Rāmprasād,* 110; Atulchandra Mukhopadhyay, *Rāmprasād,* 250f. The Bengali caste situation is summarized by Hiteshranjan Sanyal, "The local hierarchy of castes in Bengal is comprised of six successive groups. These are (1) Brahman, (2) Baidya and Kayastha, (3) *Nabasakh,* (4) *Ajalchal,* (5) an intermediary group middling between (3) and (4), and (6) *Antyaj.* Broadly, these groups may be classified into two

viz; the Bahmans and the Sudras, there being no Kshatriya and Vaisya element in the indigenous population of Bengal. Ritually, the rank of the Baidya and the Kayasthas is the same as those of the *Nabasakhs* with whom they constitute the upper strata of the Bengali Sudras known as *satsudra* (*sat* meaning clean). They are also referred to as *jalacharaniya* Sudras because of their right to offer drinking water to the clean Brahmans who can minister to them without defilement. However, in the secular context the Baidyas and Kayasthas, who were mostly landholders and professionals, occupy a much higher rank than the *Nabasakhs,* who are mostly traders, manufacturers, and agriculturalists. It is due to this reason that the Brahmans, Baidyas, and Kayasthas are usually combined together and referred to as *uchchajati,* i.e., higher castes," H. Sanyal, "Temple Promotion and Social Mobility in Bengal," in Debiprasad Chattopadhyaya, *History and Society,* 365.

14. Yogendranath Gupta, *Sādhaka kabi Rāmprasād,* 227–37, sees no difference in style, while Sivaprasad Bhattacharya, *Bhāratcandra ō Rāmprasād,* 213 and 219, thinks it is possible on stylistic grounds to argue for two different Ramprasads.

15. Yogendranath Gupta, *Sādhaka kabi Rāmprasād,* 226f; S.N. Bhattacharya, *Rāmprasād,* 104. For example, the song "*jenechi jenechi tārā*" is found with Ramprasad's name in the *bhaṇitā,* and also Ramdulal Nandi's, see S.N. Bhattacharya 143 and Amarendranath Ray, *Śākta padābalī,* 309.

16. Ghosh, *Prasādprasaṅa,* 14 where he says that the songs he collected were in such a dilapidated state, and written in such "unrefined and rustic" language that, "I have been obliged to the best of my ability to revise them," admitting at the same time some doubts as to whether the poet himself would find this acceptable!

17. S.N. Bhattacharya, *Rāmprasād,* 112.

18. Though Ramprasad is "discovered" writing songs in his account book.

19. Appendix, 151f.

20. Appendix, 151.

21. See T.S. Eliot, *The Waste Land: A Facsimile and Transcript.*

22. Michel Foucault, *The Archaeology of Knowledge,* 23.

23. Foucault, *Archaeology of Knowledge,* 26, 39, 55. He is not alone; on Deconstruction in general; see C. Norris, *Deconstruction, Theory and Practice.*

24. Michel Foucault, "What Is an Author?" 123.

25. Foucault, "What Is an Author?" 123. See also 127f.

26. Roland Barthes, "The Death of the Author," 143. See also 147.

27. Foucault, "What Is an Author?" 127.

28. Foucault, *Archaeology of Knowledge*, 26.

29. Foucault, *Archaeology of Knowledge*, 29.

30. Foucault, *Archaeology of Knowledge*, 28.

31. Foucault, *Archaeology of Knowledge*, 28f.

32. Foucault, "What Is an Author?" 137f.

33. Foucault, "What Is an Author?" 131.

34. Foucault, "What Is an Author?" 138.

35. See *The Cambridge Economic History of India*, vol 1, ed. T. Raychaudhuri and I. Habib; C.A. Bayly, *Indian Society and the Making of the British Empire*; and P.J. Marshall, *Bengal: The British Bridgehead*.

36. We can only speculate as to why this should be. Possibly it was just because of the passing of time, possibly because of the increasing influence of Vaisnava *bhakti* on Saktism. On Kamalakantha, see McDermott, "Evidence for the transformation of the Goddess Kali."

37. In an interesting and similar way the Calcutta University collection *Sakta padābalī* (ed. Amarendranath Ray) has begun to function as a basic, almost authoritative, collection of Sakta songs.

## Chapter 3

1. See Romila Thapar, *Interpreting Early India*, especially chapter 1, Ideology and the Interpretation of Early Indian History.

2. Thus, "form follows function" in these biographies, as Dimock notes of the biographies of Caitanȳa, "Religious Biography in India," 116.

3. J.S. Hawley, *Saints & Virtues*, xii.

4. J.S. Hawley, *Saints & Virtues*, xi.

5. E.C. Dimock, "Religious Biography in India," 112. J. McDaniel, *The Madness of the Saints*, chapter 6, examines a number of saintly characteristics of particular importance for Hinduism and for Ramprasad, such as *guru, siddha*, hero, madman, etc.

6. E.C. Dimock, "Religious Biography in India," 114. Dimock's comments would hardly be acceptable in other traditions, for example New Testament criticism.

7. This is a straightforward narrative account without any critical apparatus whatsoever.

8. See Raychaudhuri and Habib, *Cambridge Economic History of India,* for a good account of the economic conditions of the times.

9. De, *Early History of the Vaisnava Faith and Movement,* 75.

10. *Caitanÿa Bhagavata,* cited by Hitesranjan Sanyal in his excellent account, *Bāṅlā kīrtaner itihās,* 34.

11. Sanyal, *Bāṅlā kīrtaner itihās,* 77.

12. De, *Early History,* 77.

13. De, *Early History,* 79. See also Dimock, "Religious Biography in India," 110.

14. *Sādhaka kabi Rāmprasād,* 192 and cover. The image is of Kali standing on the body of Siva, rather than Durga.

15. Brahmarandhra, "Opening in the centre of the crown of the head through which the Prana in the Yogi escapes at death." J. Woodroffe, *Principles of Tantra,* vol 2, 352. For the song see SNB 156, *tārā! tōmār ār ki mane āche.*

16. See S.K. De, *Early History,* 102; M.T. Kennedy, *The Caitanya Movement,* 51.

17. Dimock, "Religious Biography in India," 109.

18. One is reminded of the legendary physical disappearance of the body of the saint/singer Kabir.

19. We know Ramprasad knew Persian, Hindi, and some English.

20. Appendix, 157.

21. De, *Early History,* 80. For this and similar stories concerning Caitanya, see also Sanyal, *Bāṅlā kīrtaner itihās,* 61f.

22. Which may be found in *śrī-śrī-rāmakṛiṣṇa-kathāmṛita* in several places with minor variations, e.g., 3.9.1.1.

23. J. McDaniel, *The Madness of the Saints,* "Model for Madness: Sri Krsna Caitanÿa," 33. See also D.P. Bhattacharyya, "Madness as Entropy: A Bengali View," in C.B. Seeley, ed. *Women, Politics and Literature in Bengal,* for a discussion of this kind of madness.

24. J. McDaniel, *The Madness of the Saints,* 144.

25. A popular collection of Ramprasadi songs, Pasupati Chattopadhyay, comp. *Rāmprasādī saṅīt,* has as its cover a picture of Ramprasad

mending the fence assisted by a young girl with the Goddess hovering above and behind her in such a way that the young girl is to be identified with the Goddess.

26. P.K. Dasgupta, *Sādhaka kabi Rāmprasād,* prefers to dwell on the supernatural aspects, see 46.

27. " . . . they were used by the impotent as charms to secure beautiful women or long life," Appendix, 152.

28. It may seem strange to find one Goddess sending another to do her work, or one form of the Goddess sending another of her forms. Such a formulation is not uncommon in Hinduism, and has scriptural sanction in the *Devī Māhātmya.* We must bear in mind, of course, that all goddesses are One.

29. Note that this and later accounts of the story all have the Maharaja and his court visiting Ramprasad at his home in Halisahore, not the other way round! A definite case of the mountain coming to Muhammad. Dasgupta, *Sādhaka kabi Rāmprasād,* devotes a chapter to discussing this remarkable state of affairs (pp. 86–91).

30. Sumanta Banerjee, *The Parlour and the Streets: Elite and Popular Culture in Nineteenth Century Calcutta,* 99.

31. Banerjee, *The Parlour and the Streets,* 82.

32. Appendix, 147–150.

33. Kennedy, *The Caitanya Movement,* 40.

34. Note that in both these stories whether or not what happens is "funny" depends on which side you are on!

35. Nagendranath Basu, *Biśvakōṣ,* vol 3, 344.

36. *Biśvakōṣ,* 344.

37. Appendix, 150. On this whole incident, see Asitkumar Bandhyapadhyay, *Bāṅlā sāhitȳer itibṛitta,* vol 3, 1140–43. At the end he comments that Aju gave just the kind of taunting response to Ramprasad's songs that you would expect from someone of his religious faith. This seems to confirm that the whole thing was a set-up, either the debate, or the account of it, or both. Bandhyapadhyay laments that having no reliable facts we have to rely on hearsay in the matter.

38. Appendix, on p. 151 he is the Goddess's "heroic" son, on p. 154 only those who are Tantrikas can really appreciate the songs.

39. See Asutosh Bhattacharya, *Bāṅlā maṅal-kābȳer itihās;* M.T. Kennedy, *Caitanya Movement,* chapter 1; S.K. De, *Early History of the*

*Vaisnava Faith and Movement*, chapter 1, Niharanjan Ray, *Bāṅālīr itihās*, 684ff.

40. D. Zbavitel, *Bengali Literature*, 134.

41. Bhattacharya, *Bāṅlā maṅal-kābyer itihās;* E.C. Dimock, "Goddess of Snakes in Medieval Bengali Literature;" Shashibhusan Dasgupta, *Bhārater śakti-sādhanā ō śākto sāhitya*, chapter 7.

42. S.K. De, *Early History of the Vaisnava Faith and Movement*, 26f.

43. M.T. Kennedy, *The Caitanya Movement*, 2.

44. S.K. De, *Early History of the Vaisnava Faith and Movement*, 29.

45. The main purpose of H.R. Sanyal's *Bāṅlā kīrtaner itihās* is to document in detail these social changes.

46. D.C. Sen, *History of Bengali Language and Literature*, 491. He then gives a translation of "a satirical poem written by a Sakta poet about the followers of Chaitanya Deva," which begins, "What a set of evil-doers has God created in these fools of pretenders who call themselves followers of Chaitanya!" In his *Glimpses of Bengal Life* he says, "Towards the latter end of the 17th century, an animated quarrel between Saktas and Vaisnavas was the most striking feature of the Hindu society," and, "The illustrious poet Ram Prasad Sen, who is known for his piety and spiritual devotion to Kali, has several pungent verses against Vaisnavas, that were no doubt relished by the orthodox Saktas of his time," 229, 231. M.A. Rahim, *Social and Cultural History of Bengal*, also refers to the hostility between Saktas and Vaisnavas, "The Saktas hated the Vaisnavas and openly criticised their faith. The Vaisnavas also abhored the rites and practices of Saktas. They shuddered if the name of Kali was uttered in their presence. They declared that the Sakta shrine of Vadrikasrama was not worth a straw," 378.

This rivalry with Vaisnavas thus replaced the earlier rivalry with Saivites recorded in the *maṅal-kābyas*. By the eighteenth century Saivism has virtually been eclipsed. Rahim says, "From the sixteenth century the cult of Siva began receeding into the background . . . [T]here appeared new religious beliefs, such as the cults of . . . female goddesses in the Hindu society," 369.

47. H.R. Sanyal, *Bāṅlā kīrtaner itihās*, passim.

48. Janhabikumar Cakraborti, *Śāktopadābalī ō śaktisādhanā*, 236.

49. See, for example, the book of the same name, Sukumar Ranjan Datta, *Śākto Boiṣṇaba milan*, S.N. Bhattacharya, *Rāmprasād*, also takes this position, 63–80.

50. For example, "Kali, Krishna, Siva, Rama, they are all my Wild-haired One," SNB 209, *man kara nā dveṣā dveṣi*. This might be acceptable

to a Sakta, but hardly to a Vaisnava, who would rightly see it as a subordination of Krishna as he is absorbed into the Goddess.

51. S.K. De, *History of Bengali Literature,* 417. But De also represents this puzzling tendency to see in Ramprasad an attempt to bring the two sects together. On p 418 he sees, " . . . a general desire with these poets of the 18th century to afford a common ground of reconciliation and good feeling between the two antagonistic sects." In his *Baṅabhāṣā ō sāhitȳa*, 594f, D.C. Sen says, "Ramprasad was full of animosity against Vaisnavism," and gives some examples of the "power of his sarcasm in his vilification" of it from his *Bidȳāsundar*. And he sees Aju Goswami's ridiculing of Ramprasad as some kind of retaliation for this, p. 595. As does Jadunath Sinha, who says Aju was a "devout unmarried Vaisnava." At the court of Maharaja Krishnachandra, "[Aju] composed songs condemning the cult of Sakti. [Ramprasad] composed songs refuting his charge." J. Sinha, *Rama Prasada's Devotional Songs,* iii. Sanjukta Gupta, *Hindu Tantric and Sakta Literature,* 200, thinks that the custom of worshipping Kali in public pūjās, which began in the mid-eighteenth century, caused "serious sectarian conflict" between Vaisnavas and Saktas.

## Chapter 4

1. SNB 195, *bāmā ōke elōkeśe.*

2. SNB 196, *bājbe gō maheśer hride.*

3. The characteristics listed here are found in a group of more than forty-five songs.

4. On this theme see Wendy O'Flaherty, *Women, Androgynes and Other Mythical Beasts,* passim.

5. SNB 319, *her kār ramaṇī nāce re bhayankarā beśe.* I have rather freely translated some of the more culturally-based images of beauty—thighs like banana palm trunks, for example.

6. These terms are used by Ramprasad himself in respect of the Mother's actions in song SNB 137, *jay kālī jay kālī bala.*

7. I have translated *māgī* as "bitch." There are nine references to the Goddess as *māgī*, and in four of these songs she in a mad *māgī. Māgī* is a word used without too much of a pejorative sense amongst the lower classes, but which would convey an insult among the higher classes. One writer wants to translate *māgī* as "whore" (N.P. Sil, *Rāmakṛṣṇa Paramahaṁsa*, 8) and certainly this meaning is given in the dictionary of colloquial Bengali, *Byabohāric śabdakōṣ.* McDermott, "Evidence for the Transformation of the Goddess," translates it as "slut," 214n. And I seem to remember once seeing *kṣepā māgī* translated as "mad old hag." Kripal, *Kali's Child,* agrees with my "bitch."

8. SNB 178, *nyāṅṭā meye kālī.*

9. SNB 250, *mā āmāy ghurābe kata.*

10. SNB 3, *anna de gō anna de gō.*

11. SNB 103, *kālī nām japa kara.*

12. SNB 35, *ār kāj ki āmār kāśī.*

13. SNB 210, *man kālī kālī bala.*

14. SNB 4, *aparā janmaharā jananī.*

15. SNB 48, *ei nibedan kari kālī.*

16. SNB 205, *bhūter begār khāṭibo kata,* and see also 119, *kebol āsār āśā. Nim* is a tree whose products, twigs and leaves, are very bitter.

17. SNB 130, *cintāmōyī tārā tumi.* There is a double pun here, stony-hearted woman, daughter of the mountain, and then she turns to stone/stony woman. The wish-giving jewel is the Goddess, also the philosopher's stone.

18. SNB 248, *mari gō ei man duḥkhe.*

19. SNB 285, *ýe hay pāṣāṇer meye.*

20. SNB 296, *śib saṅe sadā raṅe ānande maganā (mā).*

21. SNB 57, *ebār bhebe halem sārā.*

22. SNB 157, *tārā nāme sakali ghucāy.*

23. SNB 7, *abhay caraṇ sab luṭāle.*

24. SNB 250, *mā āmāy ghurābe kata.* 249, *mā āmāy ghurābi kata* is similar.

25. SNB 262, *mā mā bale ār ḍākbanā.*

26. SNB 114, *ke jāne śyāmā tumi keman.*

27. I have also dealt with this theme in my "At the Whim of the Goddess."

28. SNB 65, *e sab kṣepā māyer khelā.*

29. SNB 301, *śyāmā mā uṛācche ghuṛi.*

30. *śrī-śrī-rāmakṛiṣṇa-kathāmṛita,* 1.2.5.1. Ramakrishna lived from 1836 to 1886. "Wilful" is my translation of *icchāmōy,* one whose will is law, intent on having one's own way.

31. SNB 315, *se ki sudhu śiber satī.*

32. SNB 108, *kālī hali mā rāsbihārī.*

33. SNB 119, *kebal āsār āśā.*

34. SNB 262, *mā mā bale ār ḍākbanā.*

35. SNB 57, *ebār bhebe halem sārā.*

36. SNB 73, *ōmā tōr māyā ke bujhte pāre.*

37. SNB 160, *tumi e bhālo karecho mā.*

38. SNB 182, *pūrlanākō maner āśā.*

39. For the importance of this text, the way it gathers previous goddesses together as the one Goddess, and makes her the predominant power in the universe, see T.B. Coburn, *Devī-Māhātmya,* and *Encountering the Goddess;* and J.N. Tiwari, *Goddess Cults in Ancient India.* Here, when quoting from the text, I am using Coburn's translation.

40. In the Mahisa episode in the *Devī Māhātmya,* the erotic element is not present, but Mahisa does first see the Goddess "filling the triple world with her radiance" (2.36) before she assumes her terrible form to fight him, and in the hymn which follows the gods say, "Slightly smiling, spotless, like the orb of the full moon, as pleasing as the lustre of the finest gold (is your face)./ Wondrous is it that when the Asura Mahisa saw (this) face, he suddenly struck it, his anger aroused." (4:11) These cryptic references are interpreted as erotic/sexual in the *Devī-Bhāgavata Purāṇa;* one of Mahisa's ministers says that her body is delicate, that she is a girl in full youth (V.X. 17–28). He says, "The saying of that lady, 'I will lay your lord in the death-bed in the battle-field' is to be taken in the light of inverted sexual intercourse, where woman is above the man," and promises to make her submissive to Mahisa "like a slave girl." (V.XI. 17–30) So the battle is again a sexual battle. Mahisa says to the Goddess, "My heart is enchanted very much with your beauty. . . . O One having beautiful thighs! I am very much struck with the arrows of Cupid . . . " The Goddess makes it clear that it is lust rather than love that is involved, and says he is stupid for wanting sexual union with her ("You now want to serve the source of urine . . . ") (V.XVI) When battle is about to commence, Mahisa says, "O Beautiful One . . . why have you desired to fight instead of to enjoy sexual pleasures." V.XIV.5–23. Toward the end of the battle, Mahisa is still at it. Besotted with lust for the Goddess, he assumes a beautiful human form himself in a final attempt to possess her sexually. V, XVI. And so it goes on.

41. SNB 314, *se ki emni meyer meye.*

42. SNB 307, *samare kere kālkāminī.*

43. SNB 282, *ýāō gō jananī, jāni tōre.*

44. SNB 62, *elō cikur bhāro, e bāmā.*

45. SNB 42, *āre ei āilo kere ghanabaraṇī.*

46. SNB 297, *śib nay māyer padtale.*

47. The arguments and conclusions are fully covered in T.B. Coburn, *Devī-Māhātmya*, and J.N. Tiwari, *Goddess Cults in Ancient India.*

48. SNB 122, *ke mōhinī bhāle bhāl śaśī param pupasī.*

49. See, for example, Banerjee, *The Parlour and The Street.*

50. *maṅal-kābya*, or "eulogistic poetry" tells a story the purpose of which is to eulogise a particular god or goddess, such as Chandi, Siva, Manasa, Sitala, whose name usually appears in the title of the poem, for example, as *Manasā-maṅal.* They "tell of the power and magnificence of a particular divinity, how man [*sic*] prospers by the worship of that divinity and suffers by denying it," E.C. Dimock, "The Goddess of Snakes in Medieval Bengali Literature," 307.

51. A. Bhattacharya, *Bāṅlā maṅal-kābyer itihās*, 239–45.

52. D.C. Sen, *Bāṅābhāṣā ō sāhitya*, 184. For another similar song see his *History of the Bengali Language and Literature*, 489. Bhang, datura and siddhi are all forms of drugs.

53. S.B. Dasgupta, *Bhārater śakti sādhanā ō śākta sāhitya*, 201. In his *Glimpses of Bengal Life* D.C. Sen says, "The Saiva songs are characterised by much witty writing and many humorous sketches. They are mostly of an indecent nature. Shiva's agricultural operations in the field, his marriage, his drug-eating and quarrels with his wife, her jealousy and his trouble, have formed an inexhaustible source of mirth to our country-folk for centuries," 219f. He then gives a number of examples. This sort of humour features in Ramprasad's *Bidyāsundar.*

54. *Sivapurāṇa*, eleventh century, see D.C. Sen, *Baṅabhāṣā ō sāhitya*, 464.

55. See *Bāṅlā maṅal-kābyer itihās*, 205; O'Flaherty, *Siva.*

56. See O'Flaherty, *Siva*, 30–32 for a summary of the Puranic version of the story.

57. A woman from a lowly Hindu caste.

58. Bengali girls and women love wearing conch shell bangles, and they form part of marriage rituals, where the reason for wearing them is linked to this myth, see L. Fruzzetti, *The Gift of a Virgin*, 69f, 74f. Conch bangles appear again in chapter 6 below. On Siva as an unsuccessful beggar see also the story of Annapurna in chapter 6.

59. A. Bhattacharya, *Bāṅlā maṅal-kābyer itihās,* 205f.

60. A. Bhattacharya, *Bāṅlā maṅal-kābyer itihās,* 62f.

61. S.B. Dasgupta, *Bhārater śakti sādhanā,* 179. On women's *bratas,* see D.C. Sen, *The Folk-Literature of Bengal,* 246–260.

62. S.B. Dasgupta, *Bhārater śakti-sādhanā,* 179.

63. For the story of Manasa see Dimock, "The Goddess of Snakes" Zbavitel, *Bengali Literature,* 156–8; P.K. Maity, *Historical Studies in the Cult of the Goddess Manasa;* and W.L. Smith, *The One-Eyed Goddess.*

64. The lotus flower, because of its shape, is a symbol of the yoni/vagina, and hence of fertility.

65. SNB 99, *kālī gō kena leṅṭā phera.*

66. S.B. Dasgupta, *Bhārater śakti sādhanā ō śākta sāhitya,* 201f.

## Chapter 5

1. SNB 71, *ō man, tōr bhram gela nā.*

2. SNB 91, *kāj ki āmār mukti pade.*

3. SNB 171, *dukha koi gō pāṣāṇer māyyā;* 101, *kālī brahmamoyī gō;* 113, *kulakuṇḍalinī brahmamoyī;* 150, *tāi kālōrup bhālōbāsi,* etc.

4. SNB 314, *se ki emni meyer meye.*

5. SNB 186, *bạcite sādh ār nāi mā tārā.*

6. SNB 78, *ōre man bali bhaj kālī.*

7. SNB 122, *ke mōhinī bhāle bhāl śaśī param rupasī.*

8. SNB 298, *śyāmā bāmā ke birāje bhabe.*

9. SNB 52, *ebār āmi sār bhebechi,* and see also 115, *kena miche mā mā kara.*

10. SNB 56, *ebār bhāla bhāb peyechi.*

11. SNB 93, *kār bā cākarī kara.*

12. SNB 180, *patitapābanī tārā.*

13. SNB 21, *āmār man ẏadi hō maner mata.*

14. SNB 63, *eman din ki habe tārā.*

15. SNB 316, *hayechi (mā) jōr phariyādī.*

16. SNB 23, *āmi eta dōṣī kise.*

17. SNB 27, *āmi ki duḥkher daṛāi.*

18. SNB 306, *sakali jānis tārā āgāgōṛā āmār joto.* Goudriaan reminds us in, *Hindu Tantrism,* that "The chief difference of Tantric Advaita with that expounded by Sankara is the reality of the world as against Sankara's doctrine of pseudo-evolution," 51f, because it is "usually considered to be an aspect of the God(dess)'s eternal Sakti. . . . " 53.

19. SNB 278, *mahākāler manōmōhinī sadānanandamoyī kālī.*

20. SNB 136, *jananī pad paṅkajaṅ dehi śaraṇāgata jane.*

21. SNB 310, *sābās mā dakṣiṇā kālī.*

22. SNB 257, *mā gō tārā ō śaṅkarī.* See also 45, *ei saṅsār dhọkār ṭāṭi.*

23. *Śaktihīn śib śaba,* "without śakti Siva is a corpse," see also Upendrakumar Das, *Śāstramūlak bhāratīya śaktisādhanā,* 345f, and also "If Siva is united with Sakti, he is able to exert his powers as lord; if not, the god is not able to stir," opening lines of *Saundaryalaharī,* trans. W.N. Brown, *The Saundaryalaharī,* 48.

24. SNB 72, *ō mā śyāmā nebe dāṛā.*

25. SNB 72, *ō mā śyāmā nebe dāṛā.*

26. SNB 317, *hō re man kāśībāsī.* Varanasi proper lies between the Varuna and Asi rivers, see D. Eck, *Banaras, City of Light,* 26f. Manikarni is a well, now the site of Manikarni Devi's worship. The nearby ghat with the same name is the site of the most famous burning ghat, Eck 247f. The word translated here as 'Siva', *visvesvara,* is also the name of Kashi's Siva lingam, see Jnanendramohan Das, *Bāṅālā bhāṣār abhidhān,* 2/1603. (See also J.P. Parry, "Death and Cosmogony in Kashi.")

27. SNB 180, *patitapābanī tārā.*

28. Parry, J.P., "Death and Cosmogony in Kashi," 337, 347.

29. See Goudrian, T., *Hindu Tantrism,* 57–60, and chapter 6 below.

30. D.C. Sircar, *The Sakta Pithas*; Kinsley, *Hindu Goddesses,* 37–41.

31. SNB 245, *man tōmār eki bāsanā.*

32. SNB 115, *kena miche mā mā kara.* This song is discussed in chapter 7.

33. W. Beane, *Myth, Cult and Symbols,* 204f. In the song cited here it is Ramprasad's effigy that is burned, but in song SNB 261, *mā boleḍākis*

*nāre man,* it is the Mother who is dead and whose effigy is burned. In song SNB 13, *āmāy chụ̄yō nā re,* Ramprasad refers to the fact that Death can now not approach him because he has become a sannȳāsī and lost his caste.

34. A. Mookerjee and M. Khanna, *The Tantric Way,* 143–63.

35. SNB 37, *ār bāṇijȳe ki bāsanā.*

36. See p. 88 below.

37. SNB 113, *kulakuṇḍalinī brahmamoyī, tārā āche gō antare.*

38. SNB 286, *roili nā man āmār baśe.*

39. SNB 320, *hrit kamal-mañce dōle karālabadanī śyāmā.*

40. SNB 240, *manre tōr buddhi eki.*

41. SNB 4, *aparā janmaharā jananī.*

42. SNB 19, *āmār mane bāsanā jananī.*

43. SNB 97, *kālī kālī bala rasanā re.*

44. SNB 298, *śyāmā bāmā ke birāje bhabe.*

45. SNB 159, *tui ȳāre ki karbi śaman.*

46. SNB 113, *kulakuṇḍalinī brahmamoyī.*

47. Sarasvati as the Goddess, but also as the central river at Prayag, where the three rivers flow together.

48. SNB 19, *āmār mane bāsanā jananī.*

49. SNB 166, *dibāniśi bhāber man.*

50. SNB 35, *ār kāj ki āmār kāśī.*

51. SNB 67, *ō kār ramaṇī samare nāciche.*

52. SNB 200, *bhāb ki bhebe parāṇ gela.*

53. SNB 252, *mā āmār antare āche.*

54. See *śrī-śrī-rāmakṛiṣṇa-kathāmṛita,* 4.16.1.1, "Then there's the seventh plane of the *sahasrāra* lotus, when the Kundalini reaches that you go into samadhi. Saccidananda Siva is in the *sahasrāra* and he unites with Sakti. It's the union of Siva-Sakti! . . . If you stay in this state for twenty-one days you die, just as a ship which goes into the black waters never returns."

55. SNB 80, *ōre surā pān karine āmi.* See also 233, *man bhūlanā kathār chale.* Note here the triple pun—being drunk, Tantric wine-

drinking, the bliss induced by consuming nectar. Note also that the Goddess is drunk on nectar in her guise as the erotic warrior.

56. SNB 17, *āmār antare ānandamoyī*. See also 187, *bala man male kōthāy ẏābi.*

57. The word *man* refers to the inner being of the individual. Just how it is to be understood will become clear as we proceed.

58. SNB 236, *maner āmār ei minati.* I will have more to say about the meaning of the song below.

59. Upendranath Bhattacharya, *Bāṅlār bāul ō bāul gān,* 27, *man tōr āpan balte ke āche.* Siraj Sai was Lalan's guru, see Sudhir Chakraborty, *Brātẏa lōkāyat Lālan,* 31.

60. See E.C. Dimock, *The Place of the Hidden Moon,* and M.M. Bose, *The Post-Caitanya Sahajiā Cult.*

61. U. Bhattacharya, *Bāṅlār bāul ō bāul gān,* 291–368. See also S.B. Dasgupta, *Obscure Religious Cults.*

62. *Obscure Religions Cults,* 166.

63. *Obscure Religious Cults,* 84.

64. *Obscure Religions Cults,* 166.

65. *Obscure Religious Cults,* 181, *tomār maner madhye ār ek man āche go.*

66. *Obscure Religious Cults,* 182.

67. *Obscure Religious Cults,* 182f.

68. *Obscure Religious Cults,* 183f. The attribution here is uncertain, the song is by either Phakir-chand or his disciple Praphulla Bandopadhyaya. The translation is Dasgupta's.

69. *Kulārnava Tantra* 2.24. This translation cited in H. Zimmer, *Philosophies of India,* 576.

70. *Obscure Religious Cults,* xxxiv and xxxv.

71. T. Goudriaan, *Hindu Tantrism,* 8.

72. U.N. Bhattacharya, *Bāṅlār bāul ō bāul gān,* 369–481.

73. Cited in H. Zimmer, *Philosophies of India,* 586.

74. Perhaps I should add at this point that I did not look for a Baul whose work shows particular similarity to that of Ramprasad. In this respect the choice of Lalan was arbitrary. See also Sudhir Chakrabarti, *Bāṅlā dehatattver gān,* for similar songs by other singers.

75. As boat, SNB 41, *āy man byāpāre ýābi*, 163, *tōmār sāthe kere, ō man.* As house, SNB 55, *ebār bāji bhōr hala*, 138, *jay kālī jay kālī bale*, 211, *man kara ki tattva tāre*, 218, *man jāna nā ki ghaṭbe leṭha*, 268, *māyer e param kautuke.*

76. As in SNB 214, *man kena re peyeche ēta bhay.*

77. SNB 41, *āy man byāpāre ýābi.*

78. SNB 268, *māyer e param kautuke.* Note the word for "blowing out" the lamp is *nirbbāṇ kore* which also means to attain Nirvana, or realize *mokṣa.*

79. *Bāṅlār bāul ō bāul gān*, 50, *ei mānuṣ sei mānuṣ āche.* See also *Bāṅlār bāul ō bāul gān*, 27, 39, 87, 94, 165, 193, and 1 for the body as a boat.

80. *Bāṅlār bāul ō bāul gān*, 87. The "mind-fetter" is *man-beṛī.*

81. p. 77f.

82. See *Bāṅlār bāul ō bāul gān*, 375, for the interpretation of "moon" in Baul songs.

83. C.H. Capwell, "The Esoteric Belief of the Bauls of Bengal," 259.

84. *Obscure Religious Cults*, 161f.

85. *Obscure Religious Cults*, 181f. The song quoted here is by Kangal Harinath.

86. SNB 218, *man jāna nā ki ghaṭbe leṭhā.* The bird might escape through one of the "nine doors," the nine orifices of the body. The six self-willed friends are the six passions.

87. SNB 161, *tumi kār kathāy bhuleche re man.* Here the "enemies" are probably the passions.

88. See C.H. Capwell, "The Esoteric Belief of the Bauls of Bengal," 255–64, and J.J. Kripal, "Kali's Tongue and Ramakrishna."

89. *Bāṅlār bāul ō bāul gān*, 204, *mānuṣ bhajle*, and 50, *ei mānuṣ sei mānuṣ.*

90. p. 77.

91. SNB 286, *raili nā man āmār baśe.* We may also note that in the wider corpus of both poets the Tantric elements are even more prominent.

92. SNB 235, *man jadi mōr auṣadh khābā.* Ramprasad refers to "Srinath" in eight songs. R.F. McDermott, "Evidence for the transformation of the Goddess," wants to take "Srinath" as "Siva." I think, with

S. Gupta, *Hindu Tantric and Sakta Literature,* 199, and S.N. Bhattacharya, footnote to song 9, that this refers to his guru—though ultimately perhaps the guru is to be identified with Siva, as he is in the *Kulārnava Tantra,* and a guru might then take the name of Siva, "Srinath Datta," as his religious name. In the *Kulārnava Tantra* (17.17) "Srinath" is one of the epithets of the guru—"Because he imparts the knowledge of prosperity and liberation, because he instructs on the *Nāda Brahman* and Ātman, and because he is an emblem of the blocking of Ignorance, he is, O My Beloved, called *Śrīnātha,*" There are many other mentions of the "gift of the guru" *gurudatta,* usually meaning mantras, in Ramprasad's songs.

93. See SNB note to 78, *ōre man bali bhaj kālī.*

94. SNB 225, *man tōre tāi bali bali.* See also 33, *āy dekhi man,* 41, *āy man byāpāre ýābi.*

95. SNB 33, *āy dekhi man.*

96. The version of the song in Isvarachandra Gupta's biography has different word order, which changes the meaning of this line, see Appendix, 158.

97. SNB 211, *man kara ki tattva tāre.*

98. *Hindu Tantrism,* 121–63.

99. *Hindu Tantrism,* 124.

100. *Hindu Tantrism,* 127.

101. *Hindu Tantrism,* 127f.

102. *Hindu Tantrism,* 128.

103. *Hindu Tantrism,* 130.

104. SNB 35, *ār kāj ki āmār kāśī.*

105. *śrī-śrī-rāmkṛiṣṇa-kathāmṛita,* 3.1.6.2.

106. M. Eliade, *Yoga: Immortality and Freedom,* 207. The *Tantrasār* has almost endless lists of deities, with descriptions of them (as aids to visualisation) and their mantras.

107. *Yoga: Immortality and Freedom,* 208. A. Bharati, *The Tantric Tradition,* 219, says "The correct notion . . . is simply that there is a dualism on the level of mystical practice, on the level of a heuristic polarity, and there is monism on the ontological level."

108. *History of the Tantric Religion,* 356. See also song 19 above p. 74.

109. *Bāṅlā kīrtaner itihās,* 152.

110. *Bāṅlā kīrtaner itihās,* 28f.

111. *Bāṅlā kīrtaner itihās,* 120. On *siddha*-yoga see M. Eliade, *Yoga and Immortality,* 283.

112. *Bāṅlā kīrtaner itihās,* 125f.

113. *Bāṅlā kīrtaner itihās,* 128–30.

114. See M.M. Bose, *Post-Caitanya Sahajiyā Cult,* 137, and E.C. Dimock, "The Bauls and the Islamic Tradition."

115. SNB 217, *man gariber ki dōṣ āche.*

116. SNB 136, *jananī pad paṅkajaṅ dehi śaraṇāgata jane.*

117. J.K. Chakraborti, *Śāktapadābalī ō śaktisādhanā,* 9.

118. See S.B. Dasgupta, *Bhārater śakti-sādhanā,* 76.

119. "Krishnananda Agamabagis's *Tantrasār,* Brahmananda Swami's *Śaktānanda Taraṅiṇī,* and Purnananda's *Śrītattva Cintāmaṇi,* were famous Tantric treatises. But they were written in Sanskrit for particular sects," J.K. Chakraborti, *Śāktapadābalī ō śaktisādhanā,* 8.

120. Ramprasad refers to it by name in song SNB 211, *man kara ki tattva tāre.* "The *Tantrasāra* of Krsnananda Agamavagisa is the most comprehensive and popular of the numerous digests known in India," says Bhattacharyya, *History of the Tantric Religion,* 70. See also Goudriaan and Gupta, *Hindu Tantric and Sakta Literature,* 139f. and R.C. Mazumdar, *History of Mediaeval Bengal,* 267. This *Tantrasār* should not be confused with the earlier *Tantrasār* of Abhinava Gupta.

121. Banerji, *Tantra in Bengal,* 87.

122. Banerji, *Tantra in Bengal,* 78f.

123. Banerji, *Tantra in Bengal,* 79.

124. Chintaharan Chakravarti, *Tantras: Studies on their Religion and Literature,* 92.

125. See E.A. Morinis, *Pilgrimage in the Hindu Tradition,* on Tarakeswar, 77–121, and Tarapith, 165–201.

126. See J. McDaniel, *Madness of the Saints,* 127–33.

127. On Tantric elements in Ramakrishna see Kripal, *Kali's Child,* and Schneiter, *Rāmprasād Sen und Śrī Rāmakrishna.* It is the thesis of R.F. McDermott however that at the same time there was also a trend to sweeten this Tantrism, or at least some aspects of it, "Evidence for the Transformation of the Goddess."

128. See H.H. Urban, "The Strategic uses of an esoteric text," 75.

129. See Goudriaan and Gupta, *Hindu Tantric and Sakta Literature,* 192–4, S.C. Banerji, *Tantra in Bengal.* 153f, and S.N. Bhattacharya, *Rāmprasād,* 129–38.

130. Goudriaan and Gupta, *Hindu Tantric & Sakta Literature,* 176.

## Chapter 6

1. For the making of the images, see J.D. Robinson, "The Worship of Clay Images in Bengal," 74–101, and A. Ostor, *The Play of the Gods,* 38–41.

2. For details of the ritual see D. Kinsley, *Hindu Goddesses,* 106–15 and A. Ostor, *The Play of the Gods,* 33–97.

3. Chintaharan Chakravarti, *Tantras: Studies on their Religion and Literature,* 101ff says that this form of the image as worshiped today has no scriptural sanction. He sees its origins in local Bengali social customs ("Whatever be the date of origin, the conception is quite in keeping with the ideal of life of the people of India, especially of Bengal, who are usually accompanied by members of the family wherever they go. A mother would not usually part company with her children if she has to go to any place, particularly to the house of her father"), and possibly in the person of Raja Krishnachandra (" . . . it is not possible to determine the actual date when the images of these deities came to be added to the image of Durga proper. It may be that this was done at the instance of Maharaja Krsnacandra of Nadia (eighteenth century). According to a local tradition, it was he who introduced *Durgā-pūjā* in Bengal. The tradition, if it has any value, may be partially true in that he might have introduced the *pūjā* in its present form.").

4. D. Kinsley, *Hindu Goddesses,* 113f.

5. C. Chakravarti, *Tantras,* 100.

6. The lotus flower, because of its vaginal shape, has long been considered a symbol of sexuality and fertility in India.

7. See Dimock, "The Goddess of Snakes in Medieval Bengali Literature, Part II," P.K. Maity, *Historical Studies in the Cult of the Goddess Manasa,* 77–130, A. Bhattacharya, *Bāṅlār maṅal-kābyer itihās,* 282–430.

8. For the story of Chandi see D. Zbavitel, *Bengali Literature,* 164–69, and A. Bhattacharya, *Bāṅlār maṅal-kābyer itihās,* 459–72; on their similarities see Dimock, "The Goddess of Snakes," 320–22.

9. I am grateful to Gautam Bhadra for drawing my attention to the importance of this goddess in the context of the recognition of the Devi as daughter.

10. Sashibhushan Dasgupta, *Bhārater śakti-sādhanā ō śākta sāhitya,* 6, 201.

11. This is a close paraphrase of the story as given by Dasgupta, *Bhārater śakti-sādhanā*, 202.

12. The darker side of her past is indicated in one story in which an image of the goddess was established by a raja who ordered that every day a man be sacrificed to her. A certain brahmin, learning of this, fled the village, but on the way was accosted by the goddess disguised as a brahmin woman. She asked him why he had fled the village, and he replied that he was fleeing in fear beacause the raja had introduced "a rakshasa named Jogadya" who ate a man every day. The goddess then revealed herself and told the brahmin he could return home because she did not eat brahmin blood. The brahmin could still not quite believe this, so Jogadya then assumed a ten-armed form (i.e., as Durga). See G. K. Basu, *Bāṅlār laukik debatā*, 89f.

13. Hamsanarayan Bhattacharya, *Hinduder debdebī,* vol 3, 339f.

14. G.K. Basu, *Bāṅlār laukik debatā*, 88. Tantric forms of her worship are also found.

15. S.B. Dasgupta, *Bhārater śakti-sādhanā,* 202.

16. "Annada" is another name by which Annapurna is known. Bharatchandra's *Annadāmaṅal* is in three parts, only the first of which is given to the glorification of the goddess. Part two recounts the story of Bidya and Sundar, and part three glorifies the Raja. The worship of Annapurna had been associated with the Krishnanagore raj since the sixteenth century, see J.D. Robinson, "The worship of clay images in Bengal," 178.

17. *Bhāratcandrer Annadāmaṅal,* ed. Kartik Bhadra, 72. The story is based on the account in the *Mātsya Purāṇa.*

18. We know Raja Krishnachandra was supposed to have been responsible for introducing the worship of Annapurna to Bengal, and this no doubt accounts for it. See H.N. Bhattacharya, *Hinduder debdebī,* vol 3: 334.

19. For an account of how high society and low society grew further apart in later years, see Sumanta Banerjee, *The Parlour and The Streets.*

20. S.B. Dasgupta, *Bhārater śakti-sādhanā,* 202.

21. Cakes of dried cowdung were, and are, used as fuel in cooking stoves by village people.

22. Outbursts such as "My pride is hurt, Mother/ At what you have done to me/ You've made me poor and needy by saddling me with a family like this" (SNB 29, *āmi tāi abhimān kari*), and *kāj hārālām kāler baśe* SNB 89 and Appendix 154f, where Ramprasad says that his death will mean nothing to his family, arouse suspicion. Gupta links domestic problems to poverty, "Ramprasad went home and passed his time quite happily on his new stipend, but with a wife and family he was not able to prosper domestically on so small an income, and his dependents began to nag him constantly. . . . When his wife or son or daughter became very annoyed at him he would call God to mind . . . " Appendix 141f. See Manashi Dasgupta, "Adhyatmik akuti o jagatik udbeg," *Citta*, 2, BS 1380, 23–36, for further speculation on Ramprasad's domestic problems.

23. See *Tantrasār*, 173.

24. See G.K. Basu, *Bāṅlār laukik debatā*, 87f.

25. See *Tantrasār*, 365.

26. In the *Devī Māhātmya* 11.44f, the Goddess says, "Then I shall support the entire world with life sustaining vegetation, produced from my own body, until the rains come. . . . In this way, I will attain fame on earth under the name "She-who-supports-with-vegetation'." (Coburn's translation, *Encountering the Goddess*, 78, with one alteration.)

27. S.B. Dasgupta, *Bhārater śakti-sādhanā*, 25. See also D. Kinsley, *Hindu Goddesses*, 143.

28. *Tantrasār*, 367.

29. SNB 213, *man kena māyer caraṇ chāṛā.*

30. SNB 112, *ki guṇe mā balba tōre.*

31. SNB agamani 2, *ōgō rāṇī, nagare kōlāhal.*

32. SNB 194, *basan para mā basan para tumi.* In a similar song, SNB 99, *kālī gō kena leṅṭā phera*, Ramprasad adds the line "You stand there naked, Ma, yet you pride yourself in being a king's daughter," thus underlining the daughter conceit.

33. SNB 255, *mā kata nāc gō raṇe.*

34. SNB 266, *mā dāṛāye śiber buke.*

35. See SNB 85, *kai tārā tōr bibecanā*, 130, *cintāmoyī tārā tumi*, 136, *jananī pad paṅkajaṅ dehi śaraṇāgata jane*, 305, *samar kare ō ke ramaṇī*, and the *agamanī* songs.

36. Goudriaan and Gupta, *Hindu Tantric and Sakta Literature*, 180.

37. SNB 267, *mā birāje ghare ghare.*

38. SNB *bijayā* song. The "mountain lord" is Uma's father; Mahakala is Siva: the *cakōrī* bird feeds only on nectar which drips from the moon.

39. Manashi Dasgupta, "The Living Goddess," 134.

40. See, for example, Tapan Raychaudhuri, *Bengal Under Akbar and Jahangir*, 146, and S.K. De, *History of Bengali Literature*, 417.

41. *Kulārnava Tantra*, 10.20–33. I have used Ram Kumar Rai's translation. See Goudriaan and Gupta, *Hindu Tantric and Śākta Literature*, for references to the ritual in many other Tantras.

## Chapter 7

1. See Appendix.

2. See S.B. Dasgupta *Obscure Religious Cults*, 14–34; D.S. Ruegg, *Buddha-Nature, Mind and the Problem of Gradualism*.

3. S.K. De, *Early History of the Vaisnava Faith and Movement in Bengal*, 408–541.

4. E.C. Dimock, *The Place of the Hidden Moon*.

5. On Bama Ksepa, see J. McDaniel, *The Madness of the Saints*, 127–33; on Ramakrishna see N.P. Sil, *Rāmakṛṣṇa Paramahaṁsa*, J.J. Kripal, *Kali's Child*. On the ambivalence towards Tantrism in Bengali society see J.J. Kripal, "Kali's Tongue . . . "

6. Appendix, 151f.

7. P.J. Marshall, *Bengal: The British Bridgehead*, 17ff, 96; Nikhil Sur, *Chiyāttarer manvantar ō sannȳāsī-phakir bidrōha*.

8. SNB 117, *ke jāne gō kālī keman*.

9. SNB 217, *man gariber ki dōṣ āche*.

10. SNB 278, *māhākaler manōmōhinī sadānandamoyī kālī*.

11. SNB 136, *jananī pad paṅkajaṅ dehi śaraṇāgata jane*.

12. SNB 217, *man gariber ki dōṣ āche*.

13. SNB 301, *śyāmā mā uṛācche ghuṛi*.

14. SNB 81, *kaō śaman ki mane kare*.

15. SNB 92, *kāminī ȳāminī-baraṇe raṇe elō ke*.

16. SNB 115, *kena miche mā mā kara*.

17. " . . . Śakta-pīthas, where some portion of the dismembered corpse of the goddess Sati fell—thus immediately establishing the connection with death. The power of death is continually unleashed by the animal sacrifices which are characteristic of these centres; while (at least in the case of three Śakta-pīthas in West Bengal) a large cremation ground adjoins the temple of the goddess," J.P. Parry, "Death and cosmogony in Kashi," 362. On the pīṭhasthāns in Bengal see also E.A Morinis, *Pilgrimage in the Hindu Tradition.*

18. On this self-shraddh, see also Kane, *History of Dharmasastra*, IV, 542–45. Notice also that in this song Ramprasad is "Dvija Ramprasad" as if the priest who performs his own ritual. On the use of a grass effigy in the funeral rites of Tantrics, see Gupta, Hoens and Goudriaan, *Hindu Tantrism,* 158f.

19. J.P. Parry, "Death and Cosmogony in Kashi," 339. Parry notes, 345, "The real Kashi is in the heart, and [the] external one is merely an aid to its realisation. If this realisation is achieved, then there is no need to go to the physical tirtha, for it will came to the worshipper." Kashi also has a particular association with the goddess as Annapurna. In SNB 13, *āmāy chũyō nā re,* Ramprasad defies Death, saying that death cannot approach him because he has become a *sannyāsī* and lost caste, i.e., he has already "died" to the world. See also SNB 79, *ōre śaman ki bhay dekhāō miche,* on this theme. But in SNB 261, *mā bale ḍākis nāre man,* Ramprasad wants to burn a kusa-grass effigy of the Mother, because she is obviously dead, so little does she care for him!

20. SNB 156, *tārā! tōmār ār ki mane āche,* see Appendix, 152–4.

21. P. Bandyopadhyay, *Mother Goddess Durga,* 96. Brooks says, "Developing a relationship of identification with the divine involves two stages of practice. In the first stage, the Tantric affirms a distinction between the spiritual and the material forms of reality. . . . The basic Tantric pattern imitates the classical Sankhya-Yoga division of reality into spirit (*puruṣa*) and matter (*prakṛti*). However, after assuming Sankhyan dualism for practical purposes, the Tantric attempts to reunite dichotomous spirit and matter," *The Secret of the Three Cities*, 58.

22. See T. Goudriaan, *Hindu Tantrism*, 48, 51. He says, "The chief difference of Tantric Advaita with that expounded by Sankara is the reality of the world as against Sankara's doctrine of pseudo-evolution." 51f. He also sounds a salutory warning to the interpreter—"In many epithets, the terminology is Vedantic, but the Tantras often use well-known expressions in deviating meanings," 50.

23. SNB 166, *dibaniśi bhābre man.*

24. SNB 301, *śyāmā mā uṛācche ghuṛi.*

25. SNB 65, *e sab kṣepā māyer khelā.*

26. SNB 273, *mukta kara mā muktakeśī.* I have translated *mukta* here as "Loose" in an attempt to convey something of the pun on *muktakeśī,* loose hair. Ramprasad's stepmother is the goddess Ganga.

27. SNB 306, *sakali jānis tārā āgāgōṛā āmār ỳata.*

28. SNB 309, *sādhe ki karuṇāmoyī kari mā tōr upāsanā.*

29. D. Kinsley, *The Sword and the Flute,* 144. In my interpretation of Ramprasad I am very much in agreement with that of Kinsley, *The Sword and the Flute,* 133–49. I would place much greater stress than he does on the Tantric basis of this interpretation, as does C. Mackenzie Brown, see his "Kali, the Mad Mother."

30. SNB 63, *eman din ki habe tārā.*

31. SNB 201, *bhāb nā kālī bhābanā kibā.* The allusions to lotuses, which may be taken as referring to the fact that lotuses only open when the dawn sun strikes them and also to the awakening of the lotuses of the Kundalini yoga, and the specific reference to the hero-devotee, make this a very Tantric song. The market place signifies life in the world, and likening it to a stage play refers back to the idea of *māyā.* This market place is also the place where bliss is realized.

32. SNB 211, *man kara ki tattva tāre.*

33. SNB 87, *kāj kire man.*

34. SNB 2, *annapūrṇār dhanỳa kāśī.*

35. SNB 87, *kāj kire man.*

36. M. Biardeau, *Hinduism,* 157. A similar trend may be seen in sects like the Bauls: "The poets of these sects have produced an enormous number of lyric songs which are mystic in nature and devotional in tone. Many of these poems contain Tantric postulates even though the Goddess does not occur in them," T. Goudriaan & S. Gupta, *Hindu Tantric and Śākta Literature,* 177f.

37. Personal communication, Gautam Bhadra.

38. *Tantrasār,* 489f.

39. The ritual use of five forbidden things, meat, fish, parched grain, wine, sex.

40. On possible domestic problems, see chapter 6, note 22.

41. This can be seen as a device for the self-protection of the followers of an esoteric cult. In similar vein one of the Tantras says that "one

should be a Kaula in one's heart, a Saiva by external behaviour and a Vaisnava among the people." See T. Goudriaan and S. Gupta, *Hindu Tantric and Śākta Literature*, 96.

42. SNB 21, *āmār man ẏadi hō maner mata.*

43. SNB 277, *māyer mūrti gaṛāte cāi.*

44. SNB 46, *ekbār ḍākre kālītārā bale.*

45. SNB 282, *ẏāō gō jananī.*

46. As people do today with Baul songs. See also J.J. Kripal, "Kali's Tongue" also on the way "unacceptable" Tantric elements in Ramakrishna are glossed over or reinterpreted.

47. SNB 223, *man tōmār bhram gela nā.*

48. Krishna Sharma, *Bhakti and the Bhakti Movement: a New Perspective,* New Delhi, Munshiram Manoharlal, 1987.

49. *Bhakti and the Bhakti Movement,* ix.

50. Ibid.

51. Ibid, 5. "Bhakti is a general and relative term which can be used in a wide range of contexts, secular as well as religious . . . it can mean devotion to God only in a general sense, with no implication of any particularised image or conceptualisation of God," 40f.

52. *Bhakti and the Bhakti Movement,* 124–29.

53. Sharma deals at length with the *nirguṇā bhakti* of Kabir in chapter VII. This line on *nirguṇā bhakti* is also taken by some of the contributors to *The Sants; Studies in a Devotional Tradition of India*, ed. Katherine Schomer and W.H. McLeod.

54. *Bhakti and the Bhakti Movement,* 5.

55. Appendix, 141 and 155. On 139 he is "devotee and *jñānī,*" and on 150 "for him the meaning and purpose of *bhāb, rasa, bhakti* and *jñāna* were the same."

56. Thus the Goddess here functions somewhat like a character in a novel, or a film, which we can discuss "as if" they were real, though they are part of a fiction. And such a fictional character might actually contribute to a transformation in our lives.

57. On these and many other epithets used in the *Devī Māhātmya,* see Coburn, *Devī-Māhātmya,* 89–208.

58. This is also the situation in the Sakta Puranas, according to Pushpendra Sharma, who says,"A *Śākta* has to identify himself in

meditation with the *Śākti,* he worships and places before himself the fully blossomed condition represented by the deity as the ideal to be realised. . . . The *Śākta Purāṇas* on this point differ from the usual *Bhakti Marga,* where dualism is an established step. We find the complete identification of the devotee with the deity, a stage higher than the . . . surrender to the deity, preached by the *Bhagavatas,"* *Sakti Cult in Ancient India,* 209.

59. SNB 115, *keno miche mā mā koro.*

60. SNB 52, *ebār āmi sār bhebechi.*

61. SNB 166, *dibāniśi bhāber man.*

62. From the *Nīla Tantra,* cited from Woodroffe, *Hymns to the Goddess,* 58, with one slight change.

63. Ram Kumar Rai's translation. We also read, "Because by his adoration (*bhajnāt*), with supreme devotion, with his mind, speech, body and action he crosses all miseries, [the guru] is called *bhakta."* (17.29).

64. "In sectarian Sakta traditions, ritual *nyāsa* is a process by which the pantheon of subdeities is systematically identified with aspects of the Supreme Sakti and with the individual's various physical, verbal, and mental components. . . . *Nyāsa* as a ritual process of identifying deities as physical, verbal, and mental aspects of the adept's personality has both worldly and soteriological implications. As the adept gradually dissolves the notion of a distinction between the divine source and its physical, mental, or verbal manifestations, he or she gains a complete mastery over that faculty or form." Brooks, *The Secret of the Three Cities,* 59.

65. *Bhakti and the Bhakti Movement,* 164.

66. Like most commentators I am using the second edition, translated into English by George Eliot and published in London in 1854 (Buffalo, New York, Prometheus Books, 1989).

67. *Essence of Christianity,* xvi.

68. Feuerbach not un-naturally concerns himself with Christianity, though his theory would apply to all religions, and his later *Lectures on the Essence of Religion* (published in 1851) is an attempt to extend the theory in this way.

69. *Essence of Christianity,* 14.

70. *Essence of Christianity,* 3.

71. *Essence of Christianity,* 13.

72. *Essence of Christianity,* 23.

73. *Essence of Christianity,* xv.

74. *Essence of Christianity,* 26.

75. *Essence of Christianity,* 27f.

76. *Essence of Christianity,* xx.

77. *Essence of Christianity,* 13.

78. *Essence of Christianity,* xix.

79. *Essence of Christianity,* 31.

80. *Essence of Christianity,* 15.

81. It is the thesis of R.F. McDermott, "Evidence for the Transformation of the Goddess," that this trend gained in strength through the nineteenth century.

82. Appendix, 141, 142.

83. Appendix, 150. *Rasa* and *prem-bhakti* are terms taken directly from Gauriya Vaisnavism.

84. Appendix, 154. *Vīrarasa* is adapted from the *vīra* stage in Tantrism.

85. T. Goudriann and S. Gupta, *Hindu Tantric and Śākta Literature,* 177.

86. For a brief discussion of three more recent uses of the goddess symbol in literature and film, see Manashi Dasgupta, "The Living Goddess."

87. U. Eco, *The Limits of Interpretation,* 24

88. *The Limits of Interpretation,* 40.

89. See R. Barthes, *The Pleasure of the Text.* The French word *jouissance* which is here translated as "pleasure" has, as we are frequently reminded by writers on the subject, strong overtones of sexual bliss, and is thus a particularly appropriate consequence of reading Tantric texts. For the reader of Bengali it perhaps yields the experience of *ānanda.*

## Conclusion

1. *śrī-śrī-rāmkṛiṣṇa-kathāmṛita,* 3.4.3.1. It is interesting to note that even during his lifetime claims were being made that Ramakrishna was an avatar of Caitanya, see *kathāmṛita* 3.19.3.1, 3.24.2.3, 5.16.4.3. Also Jogindra Nath Chatterji says that Caitanya was reborn as Ramprasad, who was reborn as Ramakrishna! See his *Rāmprasād,* Calcutta, Kisori Mohan Bagchi, 1917, p. 281. (I am grateful to Rachel McDermott for pointing this out to me.)

2. An attempt at such an understanding has been made by McDermott, in her "Popular Attitudes towards Kali."

## Appendix

1. *Saṅbādprabhākar,* Thursday 1 Paush 1260, 15 December 1853.

2. Here there are two traditions, some say Ramprasad used to work as a clerk for Gokulchandra Ghosal, dewan of Kidderpur, others say he worked in Calcutta for Durgachandra Mitra's family [Gupta's note].

3. *Sahaj,* the *paramātmā* or the individual's *sahaj* [Gupta's note].

4. *Saṅbādprabhākar,* Friday, 1 Magh 1260, 13 January 1854.

# *Bibliography*

## *Bengali*

Bandhyapadhyay, Asitkumar, *Bāṅlā sāhitẏer itibṛitta,* Calcutta, Modern Book Agency, 1966.

Basu, Gopendrakrishna, *Bāṅlār laukik debatā,* Calcutta, De's Publishing, 1966.

Basu, Nagendranath, *Biśvakōṣ,* vol 3, Calcutta, Nagendranath Basu, 1893.

*Bhāratcandrer Annadāmaṅal,* ed. Kartik Basu, Calcutta, S. Banarji & Co., 1985.

Bhattacharya, Asutosh, *Bāṅlār lōk-sāhitẏa,* Calcutta, Calcutta Book House, second edition 1959.

———, *Bāṅlā maṅal-kābẏer itihās,* Calcutta, E. Mukharji and Co, 1939.

Bhattacharya, Dineshchandra, *Kabirañjan Rāmprasād Sen,* in *Sāhitẏa Sādhak Caritamālā* series, Calcutta, 1952.

Bhattacharya, Hamsanarayan, *Hinduder debdebī; udbhab ō kramabikāś,* vol 3, Calcutta, Firma KLM, 1980.

Bhattacharya, Satyanarayan, *Rāmprasād: jībanī ō racanāsamagra,* Calcutta, Granthamela, 1975.

Bhattacharya, Sivaprasad, *Bhāratcandra ō Rāmprasād,* Calcutta, Modern Book Agency, n.d.

Bhattacharya, Upendranath, *Bāṅlār bāul ō bāul gān*, Calcutta, Oriental Book Company, 1957.

Cakraborti, Janhabikumar, *Śāktopadābalī ō śaktisādhanā*, Calcutta, D.M. Library, n.d.

Chakraborty, Sudhir, *Brātya lōkāyat Lālan*, Calcutta, Pustak Bipani, 1992.

———, *Bāṅlā dehatattver gān*, Calcutta, Pustak Bipani, 1990.

Chattopadhyay, Pasupati, comp., *Rāmprasādī saṅit*, Calcutta, General Library & Press, n.d.

Das, Jnanendramohan, *Bāṅlā bhāṣār abhidān*, Calcutta, Sahitya Sangsad, 1979.

Das, Upendrakumar, *Śāstramūlak bhāratīya śaktisādhanā*, vol 1, Birbhum, Santiniketan Press, BS 1373.

Dasgupta, Manashi, *"Adhyatmik akuti o jagatik utbeg," Citta*, BS 1380, 23–36.

Dasgupta, Pranabkumar, *Sādhaka kabi Rāmprasād*, Calcutta, Purnaprakashan, 1980.

Dasgupta, Sashibhusan, *Bhārater śakti-sādhanā ō śākta sāhitya*, Calcutta, Sahitya Sangsad, BS 1367.

Datta, Bhabatosh, *Iśvaracandra Gupta racita kabijībanī*, Calcutta, Calcutta Book House, 1958.

Datta, Sukumar Ranjan, *Śākto Boisnaba milan*, Calcutta, Basu Bhavan, 1974.

Ghosh, Dayalchandra, *Prasādprasaṅa*, ed. Pramathnath Chaudhuri, Calcutta, Kalikanath Chaudhuri, 1966.

Gupta, Yogendranath, *Sādhaka kabi Rāmprasād: sampūrṇa granthābalī samanvita*, Calcutta, 1954.

'M' (= Mahendranath Gupta), *śrī-śrī rāmakṛiṣṇa-kathāmṛita*, Calcutta, Kathamrita Bhavan, 1949, 1951.

Mazumdar, R.C., *Baṅīa kulaśāstra*, Calcutta, Bharati Book Stall, 1973.

Mukhopadhyay, Atulchandra, *Rāmprasād*, Calcutta, Bhattacharya & Son, 1923.

Mukhyapadhyay, Amiya Lal, *Gāne Rāmprasād*, Calcutta, Gurudas Chatterji & Sons, 1952.

Odud, Abdul, and Ghosh, Anilchandra, *Byābahārik śabdakōṣ; bāṅlā bhāṣār abhinab abhidhān*, Calcutta, Presidency Library, n.d.

Ray, Amarendranath ed., *Śākta padābalī,* Calcutta, University of Calcutta, 1963.

Ray, Niharanjan, *Bāṅalir itihās,* Calcutta, Book Emporium, 1971.

Sanyal, Hiteshranjan, *Bāṅlā kīrtaner itihās,* Calcutta, P.K. Bagchi, 1989.

Sen, D.C., *Baṅabhāṣā ō sāhitȳa,* Calcutta, Pascimbanga Rajya Pustak Parsad, 1986.

Sen, Sukumar, *Baṅa sāhitȳer itihās,* Calcutta, 1965.

Sengupta, Jyotiprakash, *Sādhaka Rāmprasād,* Calcutta, 1968.

Sur, Nikhil, *Chiyāttarer manvantar ō sannȳāsī-phakir bidrōha,* Calcutta, Subarnarekha, 1982.

## *English*

Bandyopadhyay, P., *Mother Goddess Durga,* Calcutta, United Writers, 1993.

Banerjee, Sumanta, *The Parlour and the Streets: Elite and Popular Culture in Nineteenth Century Calcutta,* Calcutta, Seagull Books, 1989.

Banerji, S.C., *Tantra in Bengal; A Study in Its Origin, Development and Influence,* Calcutta, Naya Prokash, 1978.

Barthes, R., "The Death of the Author," in his *Image-Music-Text,* London, Fontana/Collins, 1977.

———, *The Pleasure of the Text,* ET New York, Hill & Wang, 1975.

Bayly, C.A., *Indian Society and the Making of the British Empire, (The New Cambridge History of India, II/1),* Cambridge, Cambridge University Press, 1988.

Beane, W.C., *Myth, Cult and Symbols in Sakta Hinduism; A Study of the Indian Mother Goddess,* Leiden, E.J. Brill, 1977.

Bharati, A., *The Tantric Tradition,* London, Rider, 1965.

Bhattacharya, A., "The Cult of the Village Gods of West Bengal," *Man in India,* 35/1 (1955) 19–30.

Bhattacharyya, D.P., "Madness as Entropy: A Bengali View," in C.B. Seeley, ed. *Women, Politics and Literature in Bengal,* East Lancing, Michigan, Asian Studies Centre Michigan State University, 1981, 31–40.

Bhattacharya, N.N., *History of the Tantric Religion,* Delhi, Manohar, 1982.

Biardeau, M., *Hinduism: The Anthropology of a Civilization,* Delhi, Oxford University Press, ET 1989.

Bose, M.M., *The Post-Caitanya Sahajiyā Cult of Bengal,* Delhi, Gian Publishing House, 1986 reprint.

Brooks, D.R., *The Secret of the Three Cities: An Introduction to Hindu Śākta Tantrism*, Chicago, University of Chicago Press, 1990.

Brown, C.M., "Kali, the Mad Mother," in *The Book of the Goddess Past and Present,* ed. C. Olsen, New York, Crossroad, 1983.

Capwell, C.H., "The Esoteric Belief of the Bauls of Bengal," *Journal of Asian Studies,* XXXIII/2 (February 1974) 255–264.

Chakravarti, C., *Tantras: Studies on Their Religion and Literature,* Calcutta, Punthi Pustak, 1963.

Coburn, T.B., *Devī-Māhātmya: The Crystallization of the Goddess Tradition,* Delhi, Motilal Banarsidass, 1984.

———, *Encountering the Goddess: A Translation of the Devī-Māhātmya and a Study of Its Interpretation*, Albany, SUNY Press, 1991.

Dasgupta, S.B., *Obscure Religious Cults,* Calcutta, Firma KLM, 1976.

Dasgupta, M., "The Living Goddess," in *The Calcutta Psyche,* ed. Geeti Sen, Calcutta, India International Centre/Rupa, 1990–1.

De, S.K., *Early History of the Vaisnava Faith and Movement in Bengal,* Calcutta, Firma K.L. Mukhopadhyay, 2d ed., 1961.

Dev, U., *The Concept of Sakti in the Puranas*, Delhi, Nag Publishers, 1987.

Dimock, E.C., "The Bauls in the Islamic Tradition," in *The Sants; Studies in a Devotional Tradition of India,* ed. K. Schomer and W.H. McLeod, Berkeley, Religious Studies Series and Delhi, Motilal Banarsidass, 1987, 375–83.

———, "The Goddess of Snakes in Medieval Bengali Literature," *History of Religions,* I (1962) 307–21.

———, *The Place of the Hidden Moon: Erotic Mysticism in the Vaiṣṇava-Sahajiyā Cult of Bengal,* Chicago, University of Chicago Press, 1966.

———, "Religious Biography in India: The 'Nectar of the Acts' of Caitanya," in F.E. Reynolds and D. Capps eds, *The Biographical Process: Studies in the History and Psychology of Religion,* The Hague, Mouton, 1975, pp 109–117.

Dutt, R.C., *The Cultural Heritage of Bengal,* Calcutta, 1962.

Eck, D., *Banaras, City of Light,* New York, Knopf, 1982.

Eliade, M., Yoga, *Immortality and Freedom*, New York, Princeton University Press, 2d ed 1969

Eliot, T.S., *The Waste Land: A Facsimile and Transcript of the Original Drafts Including the Annotations of Ezra Pound*, Valerie Eliot ed., London, Faber and Faber, 1971.

Erndl, K.M., *Victory to the Mother: The Hindu Goddess of Northwest India in Myth, Ritual, and Symbol*, New York, Oxford University Press, 1993.

Feuerbach, L., *The Essence of Christianity*, tr. George Eliot, Buffalo, NY, Prometheus Books, 1989.

Foucault, M., *The Archaeology of Knowledge*, London, Tavistock, ET 1972.

———, "What Is an Author?" in *Language, Counter-Memory, Practice*, D.F. Bouchard ed., Ithaca, Cornell State University Press, 1977.

Fruzzetti, L., *The Gift of a Virgin; Women, Marriage, and Ritual in a Bengali Society*, New Brunswick, Rutgers University Press, 1982.

Goudriaan, T., ed. *Ritual and Speculation in Early Tantrism; Studies in Honor of Andre Padoux*, Delhi, Sri Satguru Publications, 1992.

———, in S. Gupta, D.J. Hoens and T. Goudriaan, *Hindu Tantrism*, Leiden, E.J. Brill, 1979.

Goudriaan, T., and Gupta, S., *Hindu Tantric and Śākta Literature*, Wiesbaden, Otto Harrassowitz, 1981.

Gupta, S., in Goudriaan, T., and Gupta, S., *Hindu Tantric and Śākta Literature*, Wiesbaden, Otto Harrassowitz, 1981.

Hawley, J.S., *Saints and Virtues*, Berkeley, University of California Press, 1987.

Inden, R.B., and Nicholas, R.W., *Kinship in Bengali Culture*, Chicago, University of Chicago Press, 1977.

Kamenka E., *The Philosophy of Ludwig Feuerbach*, London, R & K Paul, 1970.

Kane, P.V., *History of Dharmasastra*, Poona, Bhandarkar Oriental Research Institute, 1930–75.

Kennedy, M.T., *The Chaitanya Movement*, New York, Garland Publishing, 1981.

Kinsley, D., "Freedom from Death in the Worship of Kali," *Numen*, XXII/3 (December 1975) 183–207.

———, *Hindu Goddesses: Visions of the Divine Feminine in the Hindu Religious Tradition,* Berkeley, University of California Press, 1986.

———, *The Sword and the Flute; Kālī and Kṛṣṇa, Dark Visions of the Terrible and the Sublime in Hindu Mythology,* Berkeley, University of California Press, 1975.

Kripal, J.J., *Kālī's Child: The Mystical and the Erotic in the Life and Teachings of Ramakrishna,* Chicago, University of Chicago Press, 1995.

———, "Kali's Tongue and Ramakrishna: 'Biting the Tongue' of the Tantric Tradition," *History of Religions,* 34/2 (November 1994) 152–89.

Lindtner, Chr., *Nagarjuniana: Studies in the Writings and Philosophy of Nagarjuna,* Copenhagen, Akedamisk Forlag, 1982.

McDaniel, J., *The Madness of the Saints: Ecstatic Religion in Bengal,* Chicago, University of Chicago Press, 1989.

McDermott, R.F., "Evidence for the Transformation of the Goddess Kali: Kamalākāntha Bhaṭṭācarya and the Bengali Śākta *Padāvalī* tradition," PhD dissertation, Harvard University, 1993.

———, "Popular Attitudes toward Kali and Her Poetry Tradition: Interviewing Saktas in Bengal," in *Wild Goddesses in India and Nepal,* eds. Axel Michaels, Cornelia Vogelsanger, and Annette Wilke, Bern, Peter Lang, 1997, 383–415.

McLean, M.D., "At the Whim of the Goddess: The *līlā* of the Goddess in Bengal Saktism," in *The Gods at Play: Līlā in South Asia,* ed. W. Sax, New York, Oxford University Press, 1995, pp 87–96.

———, "Ramakrishna: The Greatest of the Saktas of Bengal?" in P. Bilamoria and P. Fenner eds, *Religious and Comparative Thought; Essays in Honour of the Late Dr. Ian Kesarcodi-Watson,* Delhi, Indian Books Centre, 1988, pp 151–72.

Maity, P.K., *Historical Studies in the Cult of the Goddess Manasa,* Calcutta, Punthi Pustak, 1966.

Mallick, A.R., "Modern Historical Writing in Bengal," in C.H. Philips ed., *Historians of India, Pakistan and Ceylon,* London, Oxford University Press, 1961, pp 446–60.

Marshall, P.J., *Bengal: The British Bridgehead, Eastern India 1740–1828 (The New Cambridge History of India II/2),* Cambridge, Cambridge University Press, 1987.

Mazumdar, R.C., *History of Medieval Bengal,* Calcutta, G. Bharadwaj & Co., 1973.

Mookerjee, A., and Khanna, M., *The Tantric Way: Art, Science, Ritual,* London, Thames & Hudson, 1977.

Morinis, E.A., *Pilgrimage in the Hindu Tradition: A Case Study of West Bengal,* Delhi, Oxford University Press, 1984.

Nathan, L., and Seeley, C., *Grace and Mercy in Her Wild Hair: Selected Poems to the Mother,* Boulder, Great Eastern, 1982.

Nicholas, R.W., "The Village Mother in Bengal," James J. Preston (ed), *Mother Worship; Theme and Variations,* Chapel Hill, University of North Carolina Press, 1982, pp. 192–209.

Norris, C., *Deconstruction, Theory and Practice,* London, Methuen, 1982.

O'Flaherty, W.D., *Siva, the Erotic Ascetic,* London, Oxford University Press, 1981.

———, *Women, Androgynes and Other Mythical Beasts,* Chicago, University of Chicago Press, 1980.

Ostor, A., *The Play of the Gods: Locality, Ideology, Structure, and Time in the Festivals of a Bengali Town,* Chicago, University of Chicago Press, 1980.

Parry, J.P., "Death and Cosmogony in Kashi," in *Way of Life: King, Householder, Renouncer (Essays in honour of Louis Dumont),* ed. T.N. Madan, Delhi, Vikas, 1982.

Payne, E.A., *The Saktas,* New York, Garland, 1979.

Rahim, M.A., *Social and Cultural History of Bengal,* vol II, Karachi, Pakistan Publishing House, 1967.

Raychaudhuri, T., *Bengal under Akbar and Jahangir: An Introductory Study in Social History,* Delhi, Munshiram Manoharlal, 1969.

Raychaudhuri, T. and Habib, I., eds, *The Cambridge Economic History of India,* vol 1, Hyderabad, Orient Longmans, 1982.

Robinson, J.D., "The Worship of Clay Images in Bengal," D.Phil dissertation, Oxford University, 1983.

Ruegg, D.S., *Buddha-Nature, Mind and the Problem of Gradualism in Comparative Perspective: On the Transmission of Buddhism in India and Tibet,* London, School of Oriental and African Studies, 1989.

Sarkar, Sumit, "'Kaliyuga,' 'Chakri,' and 'Bhakti' Ramakrishna and His Times," in *Economic and Political Weekly,* July 18, 1992.

Sax, W., Gender and Politics in Garhwal, Nita Kumar (ed), *Women As Subjects; South Asian Histories,* Calcutta, Stree, 1994, pp. 172–210.

Schomer, K., and McLeod, W.H., eds, *The Sants: Studies in a Devotional Tradition of India*, Berkeley, Berkeley Religious Studies Series, & Delhi, Motilal Banarsidass, 1987.

Sen, D.C., *The Folk-Literature of Bengal*, Calcutta, University of Calcutta, 1920.

———, *Glimpses of Bengal Life*, Calcutta, University of Calcutta Press, 1925.

———, *History of Bengali Language and Literature*, Calcutta, University of Calcutta Press, 1954.

———, *History of Bengali Literature*, New Delhi, Sahitya Academy, third edition 1979.

Sharma, K., *Bhakti and the Bhakti Movement: A New Perspective*, Delhi, Munshiram Manoharlal, 1987.

Sil, N.P., *Rāmakṛṣṇa Paramahaṁsa, a Psychological Profile*, New York, E.J. Brill, 1991.

Sinha, J., *Rama Prasada's Devotional Songs: The Cult of Sakti*, Calcutta, J. Sinha, 1966.

Sircar, D.C., *The Śākta Pīṭhas*, Delhi, Motilal Banarsidass, 1973.

Smith, W.L., *The One-Eyed Goddess: A Study of the Manasā Maṅgal*, Stockholm, Almqvist & Wiksell International, 1980.

Thapar, R., *Interpreting Early India*, Delhi, Oxford University Press, 1992.

Thompson, E.J., and Spencer, A.M., *Bengali Religious Lyrics, Sakta*, Calcutta, Association Press/London, Oxford University Press, 1923.

Tiwari, J.N., *Goddess Cults in Ancient India: With Special Reference to the First Seven Centuries A.D.*, Delhi, Sundeep Prakashan, 1985.

Urban, Hugh H., "The Strategic Uses of an Esoteric Text: The *Mahānirvāna Tantra*," *South Asia*, XVIII/1 (1995), 55–81.

Van Kooij, K.R., *Worship of the Goddess According to the Kālīkapurāṇa*, Part I, a translation with an introduction and notes of chapters 54–69, Leiden, E.J Brill, 1972.

Wartofsky, M.W., *Feuerbach*, Cambridge, Cambridge University Press, 1977.

Woodroffe, J., *Hymns to the Goddess and Hymn to Kali*, Wilmot WI, Lotus Light Publications, 1981.

———, *Principles of Tantra*, vol 2, Madras, Ganesh & Co, 1970.

———. *The Serpent Power*, Madras, Ganesh & Co, tenth edition 1974.

Zbavitel, D., *Bengali Literature*, Wiesbaden, Otto Harrassowitz, 1976.

Zimmer, H., *Philosophies of India*, London, Routledge & Kegan Paul, 1953.

## *Other*

Agamabagis, Krisnananda, *Brihat Tantrasār*, tr. Rasikmohan Cattopadhyay, Calcutta, Nababharat Publishers, 1982.

*Kulārnava Tantra*, text with English translation by Ram Kumar Rai, Varanasi, Prachya Prakashan, 1983.

*The Saundaryalaharī or Flood of Beauty*, tr. and ed. W.N. Brown, Cambridge, Harvard University Press, 1958.

Schneiter, R., *Rāmprasād Sen und Śrī Rāmakrishna Paramahaṃsa (1836–1886)*, Bern, P. Lang, 1986.

# Index

## R



## S

## T



## U



## V



## W



## Y



## Z